Lost shores,
forgotten peoples

DEC 2 9 2000

D0219876

A Book in the Series

Latin America in Translation/En Traducción/Em Tradução

Sponsored by the Duke—University of North Carolina

Joint Program in Latin American Studies

LOST SHORES, FORGOTTEN PEOPLES

Spanish Explorations of the South East

Mayan Lowlands

Edited and translated by

Lawrence H. Feldman

Chronicles of the New World Order

DUKE UNIVERSITY PRESS   DURHAM / LONDON   2000

© 2000 Duke University Press
All rights reserved
Printed in the United States of America on acid-free paper ∞
Typeset in Plantin by Keystone Typesetting, Inc.
Library of Congress Cataloging-in-Publication Data appear
on the last printed page of this book.
The preparation of this work was made possible by a grant from the
National Endowment for the Humanities, an independent federal agency.
Latin America in Translation / En Traducción / Joint Em Tradução
is a collaboration between the Duke—University of North Carolina
Program in Latin American Studies and the university presses of
Duke and the University of North Carolina. The series is supported
by a grant from the Andrew W. Mellon Foundation.

*To John Jay TePaske
and the National Endowment for the Humanities
translation program for providing the funding
that made this work possible.*

*To Norman Hammond,
Mareike Sattler, Robert Trisco, and all the others
whose expertise helped in this book's preparation.*

*To the memory of
Frances Scholes and Ralph Roys,
who explored the unknown lands.*

*To Carol and Norman Albert,
with best wishes that their voyage
will also be a happy one.*

*And to Judith Lelchook and
Francine Albert for help in
completing the final pages.*

CONTENTS

ILLUSTRATIONS

☩

Figures

Maps

NOTE TO THE READER

There are several ways to organize a book of writings by different authors. The least confusing is the one chosen here—that is, to start at the beginning and go to the end. In other words, a chronological sequence. But many readers might want another way. So to help them, I suggest the following:

Readers attracted by the title, and looking for stories of adventure in new lands and places, should begin with Tovilla (chapter 3). Tovilla is a newly appointed governor of a frontier province and has never visited the New World. It is all new to him, and he tells, as it happened, his own story of exploration, adventure, and conquest in the distant lands.

Anthropologists, and especially Mayanists, looking for new accounts of life and times in these Mayan lowlands by someone who participated in their conquest should begin with Salazar. Language, geography, social organization, Indian clothing, stone tools as agricultural implements, even the famous "horse idol" of the Itza, all that and much more Salazar discusses in 1620 (chapter 2). Yes, Salazar was a missionary, but one willing to speak about the faults of other missionaries and the virtues of the inhabitants. This is the type of letter, not written for public consumption, that has rarely survived the perils of time.

Finally, I do recommend reading the preface first. Whether a teacher, reader of adventure stories, or Mayanist, whoever you are, it will provide the historical background and identify the major players in this seventeenth-century Mayan world.

PREFACE

⊕

Who Were the Maya?

Everyone knows the names of the three famous American Indian civilizations: the Aztecs, Incas, and Maya. What most people don't realize is that long after the Aztecs and Incas were half-forgotten memories, the Mayan culture was still flourishing in the interior of Central America. The first to be discovered yet the last to be conquered, independent Mayan states continued to exist more than a century after the Europeans landed in Mexico in 1517.

The northern lowlands—that portion of the Yucatan Peninsula containing Campeche, Mérida, and Cozumel—took more than a quarter century (1517–1546) to subdue. Bamboozled and starved with the aid of a Spanish turncoat, the first Spanish army went elsewhere. The second Spanish army lost its soldiers to desertion with the discovery of Peru. Since South America promised an easy gold-filled conquest, why die in Yucatan? It was the third campaign of the Montejo family that finally vanquished the north, and even then it was a hard-fought, blood-soaked conquest. Robert Chamberlain (1948) provides details of that conquest.

A series of campaigns by Pedro Alvarado and his captains during the 1520s and 1530s smashed the Mayan kingdoms of the Guatemalan highlands. These southern Maya, who in many ways had a culture closer to the Aztecs than their neighbors to the north, wrote their own histories of this conquest. *The Annals of the Cakchiquels* (Recinos and Goetz 1953) offers a good description of that conquest; long ago translated into English, this account was penned by upper-class nobles of one of these former kingdoms.

By the 1550s, only the central Mayan lowlands remained free from Spanish control. It held one kingdom, that of the Ah Itza centered on

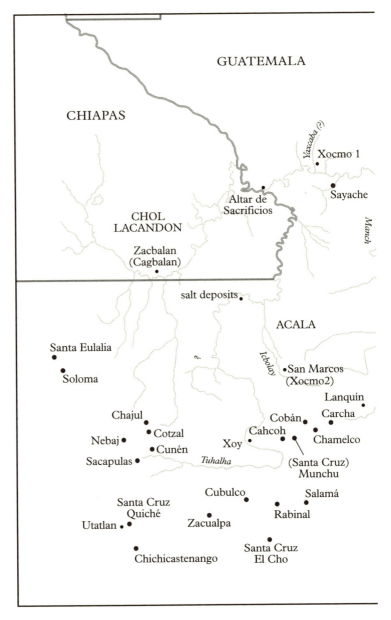

GUATEMALA

CHIAPAS

Yaxcaba (?)

Xocmo 1

Sayache

Altar de
Sacrificios

Manch

CHOL
LACANDON

Zacbalan
(Cagbalan)

salt deposits

ACALA

Santa Eulalia

Icbolay

San Marcos
(Xocmo2)

Soloma

e

Lanquín

Chajul

Cobán

Carcha

Cotzal

Cahcoh

Chamelco

Nebaj

Cunén

Xoy

Sacapulas

Tuhalha

(Santa Cruz)
Munchu

Cubulco

Salamá

Santa Cruz
Quiché

Rabinal

Utatlan

Zacualpa

Chichicastenango

Santa Cruz
El Cho

Map 1. Southern Mayan Lowlands (in Three Parts)

Lake Petén Itza

ITZA

BRITISH
HONDURAS

Dolores

MOPAN   San Luis

Punta Gorda
*Yaxal
(Moho)*

Gulf of
Honduras

*only canoes
beyond here
a*
Yol *Amatzin*   *Cancuén*   Pusilha   *Timax*
   Manché
Tuij   Chocahau

Cape Higueras

Yaxha

San Lucas Tzalac

Maxtol   (Sarstun)

Amatique (Nito)

Munguía

Santo Tomás
de Castilla

Castle San Felipe
and Xocoloc

Cahabón

TOQUEGUA

*Lake Izabal
(Munguia)*

Polochic   *Polochic*

Motagua

Bodegas (?)

HONDURAS

Gualan

Zacapa

0   50
Kilometers

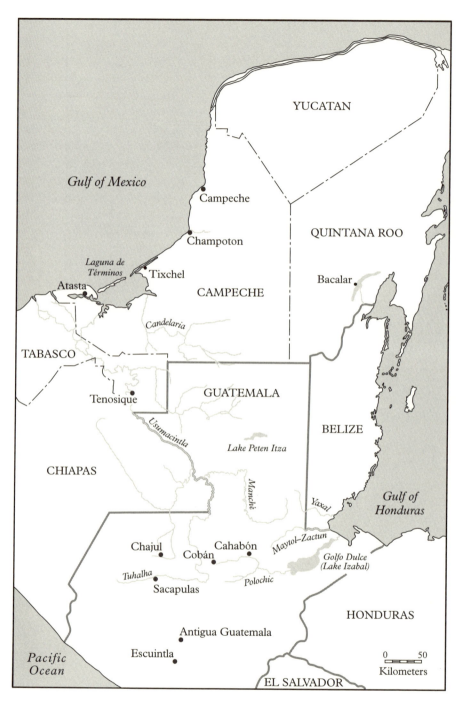

Map 2. Usumacintla Drainage and Adjacent Areas

what is today Lake Peten Itza Guatemala, and many independent towns to the south and east in lands that the early documents call Lacandon, Manché, and Mopan. Although I will discuss them all, the focus of this book is on Manché. It was also the focus of Spanish attention.

Who Were the Spaniards?

Spain was divided into four kingdoms in 1492: Castile and León, Aragon, Navarre, and Portugal. By 1580, they all had the same king. But, as the old chronicles made clear, it was for Castile and León alone that Christopher Columbus discovered the New World. By treaty and papal dispensation, Portugal would get what is today Brazil. The remainder was for the Castilians to explore and subjugate. In the early years, this involved a private enterprise system of conquest. People would contract with the Crown to conquer a land, in return for which they got the tax revenues and power to rule that land. These privileges were not permanent. Supposedly, they were only for three generations, and the Crown quickly sent over a horde of lawyers and administrators to turn the conquistadores' holdings into an empire for itself.

The head of the colonial government was called the viceroy, or in the Mayan-speaking lands, the captain general. In Guatemala, the same man usually served as president of the audiencia, the supreme court of the colony. Below him were the provincial governors, the appointed heads of the various provinces. And below the governors were the mayors and city councils that ran the Spanish cities. On the Manché frontier, however, things were a little different.

The Dominican order had its own contract for conquest. It was to be a peaceful takeover: no armies, just Dominican missionaries who would persuade the natives to submit to both Christian teachings and Spanish governance. This strategy worked in the Verapaz, the land of "True Peace" in the northern highlands of Guatemala, although having Spanish armies stationed on the frontier may have ensured the missionaries' success. The lowlands proved another matter. There, the Indians could easily vanish into the rain forest, leaving the priests and soldiers with no one to conquer.

This book is the story of these Spanish efforts to subdue the Manché lowlands. The words are those of the intruders since no indigenous accounts survive. Nevertheless, because even the most bitter enemies of the Maya mention indigenous beliefs and values, it does present both sides of this long-lasting conflict.

Map 3. Guatemala, Belize, and Honduras

Forgotten Lands

The Manche Chol—and their northeast neighbors, the Mopan—represent the last major lowland Mayan group without a systematic study of their colonial history. The Tamactun Chontal of Acalan-Tixchel (Scholes and Roys 1948), Maya of northern Yucatan, Chol Lacandon of Chiapas (Vos 1988), Yucatec speakers of northern Belize (Jones 1989), and others have all been the subjects of monographs, yet the Manche who sat astride a major river system, along whose shores are many of the most famous sites of classical Mayan antiquity, have all but been forgotten. The reason lies in the accidents of historical research and colonial political boundaries.

When the staff of the Carnegie Institution of Washington initiated modern studies of the Mayan past, their investigators concentrated on the northern Yucatán Peninsula. Given colonial jurisdictions, this meant working with papers of the Audiencia of Mexico. But the Manché were always under the jurisdiction of the Audiencia of Guatemala. Thus, the Carnegie investigators, and those who followed in their footsteps, spent much less time with the manuscripts of the southern lowlands.

Likewise, those whose field of study was Guatemala tended to ignore what in colonial times was the farthermost Guatemalan frontier in favor of peoples closer to the administrative centers of the highlands. The few exceptions were André Saint-Lu (1968) with his pioneering study of the Dominicans of Verapaz; Nicholas Hellmuth (1970), whose work first drew my attention to these people; and before all the others, Frances V. Scholes and Eleanor Adams (1960), who edited the first (Spanish) edition of the Tovilla manuscript.

Dominican Enterprise

During the colonial era, mostly it was the Dominican friars who penetrated this frontier into unconquered Guatemala. This took place in four phases. Beginning in the sixteenth century and ending early in the seventeenth, the first generation of friars in the Verapaz learned the Chol language from Indians under Spanish control. It was in this initial phase that the Dominicans compiled the Chol dictionary wrongly attributed to Friar Francisco Moran.

The second period, that of Friar Gabriel Salazar, lasted until 1628. Here, the Manché Chol were under Dominican influence but not under the royal government. The land was, in effect, a Dominican protectorate, and the Spanish military or administration was absent.

In 1628, the administration of the Manché towns came under the rule of the Spanish governor of Verapaz, and Moran replaced Salazar as the ecclesiastical head of the Manché. What followed were raids by the unconquered Itza from the north, a Manche revolt, the abandonment of the Indian settlements, and the arrival of Spanish soldiers in a futile attempt to reconquer the province. In the end, for forty years, the Spanish government would make no moves to regain control of this land and its people.

Who, or what, was responsible for this debacle? Did the arrival of the Spanish tax collectors spark the revolt? The Guatemalan archives give their assessments, but the documents speak of Itza raids as the cause of the troubles. Certainly, the heavy-handed attempt to deal with these troubles by bringing in soldiers, until this point kept out of the Manché, aggravated grievances. With the arrival of the soldiers, one can trace the role of Friar Moran, who unlike previous Dominicans, felt that the sword would be a more potent weapon than the word. It was, but the Indians were wielding it, and the Spanish lost.

The fourth phase, the return to the Manché in the 1670s, could be called the reconquest. It began with the arrival of Francisco Gallego and his disciple, Joseph Delgado, in the lowlands. They came without any other Spaniards. Both Gallego and Delgado, who literally lost his shirt (and most of his clothes) in an encounter with an English pirate, got along well with the Chols. But soon, the missionary effort came under the control of Agustin Cano, a friar trained by Moran, and the soldiers returned to the Manché.

This fourth period ended at the beginning of the eighteenth century in the removal of the Indians from the lowlands. In the interior, the missionaries instituted and the soldiers enforced the resettlement of the Indians within Spanish-controlled lands. On the coast, with the Mosquito Zambos carrying off everyone they could catch as slaves for the British plantations, and the remainder of the population fleeing into the highlands, the process was just as effective. The abandoned lowlands eventually received new settlers, and the former inhabitants survived only on paper in distant Spanish archives.

A Bloody Frontier

Given this history of Spanish penetration, conquest, and displacement, it is easy to view the Indian lowlanders as passive creatures whose only recourse was to flee from their oppressors. This is not the whole story.

The Manche were indeed more passive than most of the Chol lowlanders—although Friar Moran, with his church burned, possessions lost, and hiding in a tree from Mayan headhunters, might disagree about that—yet other Indians carried warfare to their enemies. Friar Vico lost his head in Acala, and in the process, became a Catholic martyr. The Chol Lacandon raided, and kept on raiding for decades, towns on the Chiapas and Guatemalan frontiers. Towns like Chajul or even the outskirts of Coban would receive a visit and human hearts would be yanked from living bodies and left scattered in the fields or the aisles of the local church. For the Dominicans, it was always a religious war against the demons that they felt ruled these lands. The Lacandon raiders, with their sacrifices of captives, would have agreed with them on the nature of the warfare if not whose gods were demons.

Ultimately, the Spanish government agreed it really was a war, and a major effort was launched at the end of the seventeenth century, south from Yucatan and north from Guatemala, to conquer the lowlands. It was this military effort, not the words of the friars, that defeated the Itza, Manche, Mopan, and most of the lowlanders, forever ending the Indian raids on the settlements in Spanish territories.

The Xocmo: An Answer to a Puzzle

One pagan lowland group survived into the twentieth century. These are the Yucatec-speaking people today known as the Lacandon. Who were their ancestors? The documents of this volume may provide an answer.

Salazar speaks of the Xocmo, a Yucatec-speaking people who had moved into the abandoned lands of the Acala, and as late as the eighteenth century, Spanish expeditions went looking for these supposedly lost people. What happened to them?

The lands of Acala are not far from what was the border between the colonial provinces of Chiapas and Verapaz. It is in the Chiapas lowlands that the Yucatec Lacandon suddenly appear in the eighteenth century. The suggestion I'm putting forth here is that the Xocmo, whom the Spaniards couldn't find in the Verapaz lowlands, had moved again, but this time into the Chiapas lowlands where they appear in the historical record as the Yucatec Lacandon. In this manner, by retreating beyond the jurisdiction of the authorities of Verapaz, they preserved their culture and identity into the twentieth century as the last of the pagan lowlanders.

A Translation, Not an Analysis

This volume is not an analytical study of the Manche people and culture. That work has yet to be written. Instead, it is a systematic compilation and translation of the most useful documents on these forgotten peoples. Many of these works have never been published in any language. My hope is that they will take readers on a happy voyage across the great Ocean Sea of centuries past to a time when exploring unknown worlds meant traveling to an unknown shore, whose forgotten kingdoms offered both exotic delights and a sacrificial knife to strangers from afar.[1]

LOST SHORES,
FORGOTTEN PEOPLES

1

BEGINNINGS, 1574–1606

The pacification and colonization of the lands of the Manche Chol Maya began in the sixteenth century. Spanish landings on the coast of Belize as well as the expeditions of Hernán Cortés and other early conquistadores throughout this region provide the first descriptions. In the 1560s, when the Guatemalan Verapaz highlands obtained a bishopric and secular governor, several of the communities that shared a common language with the Manche were already under Spanish control. These were Campin, Bolantin, and Yaxal in southern Belize, and the various settlements of the lower Polochic River valley and region around Lake Izabal (Cahaboncillo, San Pablo, Polochic, and Xocolo).

Francisco Viana, Lucas Gallego, and Guillermo Cadena describe the earliest years of the penetration into the country of the Manche. Their comments speak of the then-new Manche settlement of Zulben. They provide a cultural and geographic background for the lands that would serve as a springboard for incursions into the more distant lowlands.

More than twenty years of indifference since the Viana, Gallego, and Cadena report and a lack of resources by the friars ended with the arrival of a new captain general. Friar Juan Ezquerra explains how the Manche begged for iron, while the new captain general went about buying souls with machetes, hats, and axes. Antonio Nunez relates how the ongoing spread of that influence affected hairstyles.

*Report of the Province of the Verapaz Made By the
Monks of Saint Dominic of Cobán, Friar Francisco
Prior of Viana, Friar Lucas Gallego, and Friar
Guillermo Cadena on the 7th of December 1574*

Report of the province and land of the Verapaz, and of the things contained in it, such as forests, springs, animals, birds, plants, and plantations. Of the number of the towns, churches, and their foundation and what each has, and finally, of the number of people, their languages, their government and Christianity from the year of 1544 until this of 1574.

The province and land of the Verapaz are north of Guatemala and thirty leagues from it.[1] In longitude from east to west, it contains sixty leagues counting in a straight line from the Ocean Sea, the mouth of the Nito River, until the great river called Sacapulas and Chixoy, where it ends in the west. Its latitude from north to south would be fifty leagues. In the mountains of Salama and Rabinal, whose waters run toward the north, lays the origin of two great rivers that flow through the province, the one called Tucuru and the other Cahabón.[2] These go by different mountain ranges, whose water they take, until they join twelve leagues before entering Lake Izabal and taking the name Polochic River.[3] As the Nito River, it flows for twelve leagues and is five leagues wide before entering the Ocean Sea [Gulf of Honduras] near the Cabo de Higueras.[4]

The river beginning in the east, going to the north, and then returning to the west and the mountains of Sacapulas, borders great forests and pagan people who live on the edge of the sea beginning behind Yucatan and [Laguna de] Términos until one comes to Tabasco. On all this northern coast, the winds come from the northeast. From the town of Cahabón in this land and bordering its lands, there is no road nor does one know of one for Yucatan. It is all forests, rivers, and swamps. One must go on the road more than six or seven days before arriving in the settled part of Yucatan. In this desert are those who have fled from Yucatan. On a fortified islet in the north are the Ah Itza Indians.[5] They are more than 2,000, and in the interior there are towns. They [the Ah Itza] went to the lands of San Pedro [Carcha] of this province and killed two Indians of San Pedro two days travel from it. Therefore, in fear, they stopped cultivating these lands. Beyond them, downstream, is the pagan Acala and Lacandon.[6]

All of this land is forest-covered hills with slopes so steep nowhere can one find a half league of flat land fit for the site of a town. Its climate is mostly hot, and in the remaining temperate zone are the towns and most or perhaps all the people in them. Their fields, forests, and valleys are always green and flowery, and this verdure, which we see in Spain in the month of May, continues without ending or loss throughout the year. It rains each day and night, and the waters never cease throughout the year. In the months of March and April there is less, although even then there is no day without some. The sky is always dark and drab from the clouds and mists that cover it. Never, neither in the morning nor evening, have I seen them leave the sun clearly visible.

The winds are soft and temperate, although wonderfully rapid. The wind from the northeast lasts the longest, continuing four months from May until September, and the north wind from September onward is distressing and less healthy in this region. The wind from the southwest, which is rare, is the best and most healthy. It blows away the clouds and mists.

Earthquakes normally come from the South Sea and Guatemala, and pass quickly and mildly.[7] Thunder and lightning are rare, and found when traveling on the water. In this, and in being free of storms and strong winds, it is better than the other lands of the Indies. We are speaking of the highlands and temperate region, because in this hot land, storms and winds are strong and continuous.

The water of the rivers and canyons is clear, sweet, somewhat thick, and a little cold and hard. Yet, until one reaches the hot lands so very distant from the large towns and inaccessible to the people of the province, neither rivers nor canyons have fish. Thus there is a lack of fish, and those who want it must have it brought from Lake Izabal, Sonsonate, or Guatemala.[8]

The forests and valleys are high and rough, and are filled with trees, undergrowth, and impenetrable vegetation. One can neither walk in them nor break through them. The Indians walk naked on their own paths, and if some have a shirt or mantle, they take it off. They put it under their armpit so it won't tear. Spaniards travel only on the royal highway.

Of the woods and trees that they have, pine is common and very good; there are also liquidambar, cedars, oaks, evergreen oaks, blackberries, thorns, dwarf palms, palms, wild pears, and an infinite number of others in this land neither known nor named in our Spain.[9] Unless planted, there are no fruit trees like those of Spain. The fruit trees in the hot lands and lowlands are better than those in the cold highlands, where there are few. The oranges, citrons, lemons, peaches, and quinces give very well, but only in the gardens of the monks because the Indians neither esteem nor eat them if they are not quinces. Peaches don't ripen well, and so are considered dangerous and naturally bad. The grapes and figs give badly because the grapevines don't give fruit and the figs only ripen partially. Although sown many times, the yield of wheat is poor since it rots because of the continuous rains. Sown only in San Cristóbal and Santa María de Tactic, the yield is so poor that they can't make bread out from it, and thus no longer cultivate it.

Cabbages, radishes, lettuce, parsley, coriander, mint, borage, marjoram, fennel, thistles, and onions give very well and not less so because of being irrigated. The Indians don't use these vegetables nor care for them. There are also irises, white lilies, carnations, and basil. All these things are mostly in the high and temperate towns.

In some towns and in their forests there is sarsaparilla.[10] Although it is far and distant from them, [being] one, two or three days away, it is very good and of such a quality that even in Seville, some merchants slander it so that it doesn't go farther. Those here esteem it and hold it to be good. It comes from five towns.[11] Also there are, but only in San Miguel Tucuru, copal, mechuacán, and quinine; however, except for copal, the Indians value none of them.[12]

In these forests, and in all the land, there are many jaguars, lions, monkeys, foxes, mountain goats, various deer, some rabbits (but no hares), swine, and wild dogs that destroy the fields. There are great apes like horrible and ugly mastiffs whose distressing and fearful howls one can hear for more than a league.[13] One finds some tapir in the hot lands. There are also some horses and pigs in Castile. There are many snakes and vipers; in the hot land, many Indians that they bit die within twenty-four hours.

Also in these forests and lands are many and different kinds of birds; some, like eagles, herons, seagulls, cormorants, kites, goshawks, lanners, owls, and many varieties of parrots in the hot land, destroy the fields and cultivated lands. There are some pheasant and a few partridge. There are turtledoves, wood pigeons, black martins, window swallows, goldfinches, some auras, and ravens. Birds like magpies and other thrushes do great damage in the cornfields. There is a green bird that is the size of a pigeon, whose feathers the Indians value. They hunt it in two ways. One is with birdlime, the other with a hook.[14] This bird makes its nest in the highest trees, where the Indians climb to the shy bird, tie its feet, and remove its feathers. Previously, in the time of their heathendom, there was a penalty of death for killing the bird, and even now, many are hurt or killed falling [from trees while harvesting the feathers]. Some towns or private persons hunt in forests for these birds that they own. Earlier, many used to hunt these birds. Now only the oldsters go to them, but only a few, for these forests are distant from the towns. Turkeys and chickens do well in all the towns.

There are no, nor can there be, ranches in a land so mountainous and lacking savannas. There is a severe lack of cattle, goats, and sheep. People suffer because of it. Only at the abandoned settlement of Monguja [Monguia], on Lake Izabal, are there some Spanish-owned cattle. They can't supply the towns for they are very distant from them and lack a road. The cattle of the town of San Pedro are abandoned. There is wild livestock everywhere, but people can't capture them because of the rough and mountainous nature of the land.

What is lacking everywhere is gold, silver, and other metals. Some Spaniards have searched with great diligence, expense, and life for it. The greatest amount was in canyons below San Estéban Tamahú, but one couldn't mine this gold.[15] Juan Correa and Juan González, the Spaniards who discovered yet gained nothing from it, told Father Friar Domingo de Azcona that they removed more than 20,000 pesos of gold from the broken ground of Monoa next to Lake Izabal. On a hill that is above San Cristóbal and next to it there is lead or tin. In Tamahú [there is] iron. In the lands of Cuculin that are near Yaxal, they say there is [a] good [deposit of] gold.[16]

All this province needs salt, and there is a great lack. The Sacapulas highlands, four days distant, provide it. On Lake Izabal, it comes from Yucatan. Similarly, there is a lack of cacao, being brought from Sonsonate, Chiquimula, Soconusco, and the coast.[17] In the hot lands, they grow some cacao with patastle, but so little that it is not enough for normal demand, and thus neither sold nor sent elsewhere.[18] The Indians themselves consume it. They lack cotton for it is only harvested in the hot land towns of San Agustin [Lanquin] and Cahabón. Fish, game, and meat are scarce. Although common in the lowland towns and hot lands around Lake Izabal, they are extremely rare in the highlands.

The harvests of maize are large. They are sown twice a year. First, in April for harvesting in October. This, the most important planting they make, is done where they cut down and burn [the vegetation] in the large forests. This is within the twenty days they call summer, because if for lack of sun they don't burn it, although they sow it there are no seedlings, since many rats appear who destroy them. This clearing or felling of new forests is every second year because the maize will not give more than twice in them, and it takes more than ten or fifteen years until they return to sow. Because of this preparing, the field takes considerable effort since they have to cut many thick trees.

They make another field in November in the lowlands and on the

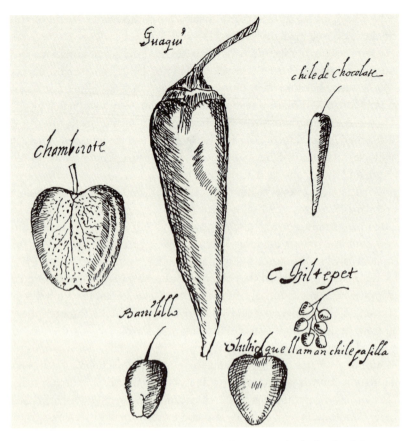

Figure 1. "Also there are abundant chile peppers in the hot lands"
(Fuentes y Guzman 1933)

banks of rivers, the harvest being in May. It is small and produces little because of a lack of sufficient humid lands to be of use. But it provides a good harvest of beans and sweet potatoes. Also there are abundant chile peppers in the hot lands. In the cold towns, the harvest isn't good, and people go to sow in the hot land two or three days away. Smoking maize conserves it, so they place it above some barbecue and leave it there for ten or fifteen days. When not smoked, it is dangerous to make bread from it, being infested within two or three months by the weevil. To conserve it all year, they place it below the land in some pits or silos. In the hot land, they can't keep it more than four months. In the highland towns, perhaps a half year but no more goes without damage.

For lack of natural or artificial riches, the entire province is very poor, and many understand nothing more than this. Of fields, harvests, and fruits, now we have said and counted the things that there are and that are produced, noting the sterility that is common in the highland cold towns. The most fertile of all is in the hot [land] towns where the people of the cold land can't go because then they sicken and die in them. Thus they forbid them to go below Tucuru toward Lake Izabal. Also because the adjacent lands are of infidels and deserts, the Indians must go outside their province for eight, ten, or twelve days on the road to Sonsonate, Soconusco, Chiquimula, and the Zapotitlán coast to hire themselves out and gain a livelihood. There they sicken and die, or many times remain, leaving their children and wives alone and needy, often without maize or firewood. This travel is necessary because, in the land, they don't have places where nor people with whom they can earn a daily wage, and if someone hires himself, the salary is forty cacaos (or ten maravedis) each day, and they value the Sonsonate over the other because for equivalent work the salary is two reals each day.[19] They all go there, without any way of stopping them, because they insist it is necessary for paying the head tax, and to obtain their shirt and pants.

In many of the towns, there are Indian merchants who take away feathers, copal, chile peppers, beans, boxes, shawls, and pieces of cotton. They bring cacao, red woolen thread that they call *Jochomit,* and woolen blankets or jackets from Oaxaca for which they go to and come from the above-mentioned towns.[20] Their wealth is very little, and there are [only] six in the land whom they call great merchants, who bring in trade up to 100 or 150 tostons.[21] The others with 10 or 15 tostons come and go with merchandise. Others hire themselves in Sacapulas at the saltworks and are paid in salt, which they retail. All come and go loaded with these things. There are no Spaniards in this land. Once every six months one sees a Spaniard, but since there is no work here for him, he doesn't return again.

The monks of Lord Saint Dominic of the Order of Preachers entered this land in 1544 on the 19th of May. Through their holy doctrine and laudable preaching, the Indians abandoned their arms and received the holy gospel and true peace that Christ our Lord through his compassion had sent them. Received under certain conditions and given the royal word of good treatment by the Crown, the Indians came to diminish on counting. With the increase of the tribute, and the great decrease in the number of Indians, they say His Majesty did not keep his word.[22] We ask for pardon, saying that His Majesty didn't know what would happen. What we do know is that he will remedy it because his word is impossible to doubt.

The Fathers found in this land seven languages. Two all understand,

and in these they preach.[23] There is another language in the three tiny towns of Lake Izabal.[24] It is quite different from these two. None of these towns understand it for it is very distant and they don't communicate with those upstream.

Then, on entering [the land], the monks began to gather the people in the towns, building the churches and giving charity for the ornaments and cult of the temples with which—along with the good diligence and work of the monks (even being masons and carpenters for lack of specialists and the money to pay them, and donating from their salary to help the temples and provide for ordinary expenses)—they have come to the state, little by little over a period of thirty years, they have at the present. This was without His Majesty's charity for any of them, although with abundant hope and his royal permission. To sustain them this is very necessary since there is no dowry or endowed position, neither a maravedi of rent nor hopes of any for lack of those who can and have something to give. They have made do with the work, charity, and sweat of the Indians, whom the monks, with very good and devout intentions, exhort them to do so. To better understand each town, we provide a report on each of them. The first of these is on the provincial capital, the town of Cobán.

Saint Dominic of Cobán

The town of Saint Dominic of Cobán has, by the count of three years ago, 525 tributaries, of which 120 who came from Acala don't pay tribute for they are very new and have infidel relatives at the door, and so that they don't flee as some have by being cowardly and being very new plants.[25] This town is in a valley, and close to it on the south is a river that passes under three often rebuilt wooden bridges. The [river] frequently carries away these bridges. In the town are situated the monastery and convent of Lord Saint Dominic, with a capacity of twelve monks. Along with his church, these buildings are of roughly worked stone. The monks built the church with some help from the adjacent towns, and the people of Cobán, with their quickness and great desire, have greatly helped with it. The doorway of the church is not yet finished. The vestry is half done because since the Indians of the town are so poor, there is very little they could give. What exists of a convent had to be acquired through the industry of the monks. The support of the monks comes principally by the gift of 300 pesos and maize from this town that His Majesty makes to them each year, and charity and other good works, but little charity given by the Indians. As is well known, it is not enough, but thanks to the help of the Lord Bishop, with all this we withstand need. We have asked for charity and support from His Majesty and again so request that it be so conceded. There are in this convent ten monks for four dependencies, but we need more for this very spread-out province.[26]

San Juan Chamelco

This town of San Juan is a league and a half from Cobán. It has, by the past count made three years ago, 555 tributaries. There was here, afterward, a pestilence that killed more than 600 souls and left all the people so ill that they couldn't sow or produce anything to eat in the time of harvest, and thus, there was great hunger after this pestilence had ended. There is a church of rough stone with three naves and some pillars of wood. The chapel has an altarpiece, and on the sides are a large crucifix and a large image of our Lady. It has in the vestry ornaments for celebrating High Mass of a cloth similar to bright red velvet with their vestments, cloak, and cords with which the monks tie up the vestments and gown. There are five other common habits; four ornaments and mantles for the altars. There are two silver chalices, linen, and cloth for altar services. There is a silver cross, the silk case that hangs on it, some silver candlesticks and others of gilt wood, silver censers, and vessels for serving wine and water after mass, some for holidays and other small ones for weekdays. There is a silver jar for baptism, a small silver pot for holy water, a small silver casket for the Holy Sacrament, and a wooden cross with a black silk case for the dead. There is a small organ, flutes, trumpets for divine service, four bells, and garments of the type used locally for children at the altar. There is a stone house for the ministers and five wooden bridges. Although with some difficulty, one can use the roads all year round. It is intemperate and unhealthy, and the town is poorer than the others for the adjacent land belongs to someone else. Its own [land] is rough, cold, and receives much water. Above all, there is sicknesses in their houses from which they die. They came to this valley twenty years ago, and not having lands for sowing, they of necessity continue to suffer.

San Pedro and Santiago [Carcha]

The town of San Pedro is a league from Cobán and another from San Juan. This is the largest [town] of the province, assessed in the past count for 622 tributaries. It has a church of rough stone, and in the chapel an altarpiece, and on the sides are a crucifix and a large image of our Lady. It has three small bells, one of 101.5 pounds or more in weight, a circle of bells, some old flutes, trumpets, four altar ornaments, a chalice, mantles for the sides, and altar linen and cloth to cover the altar.[27] There are four habits of bright red velvet with vestments of damask and their gowns, a censer, vessels for serving wine and water after mass, a jar and holy water stoup of silver, a cross and silver candlesticks, an old silk case, some candlesticks of gilt wood, a wooden cross and black silk case for the dead, an old cape of satin, and garments used by children at the altar. There is a house of stone for the ministers. Four large bridges of wood are cleaned and repaired twice each year. The town has ten leagues of bad roads broken by many hills and forests, which if not cleaned twice each year would be impassable either by horse or on foot. This town has forests bordering those infidels that they call Ah Itza who are on the edge of the North Sea and the lakes of Términos. In past years, the infidels killed two Indians of this town of San Pedro. There is no road nor communication between them [Términos and Carcha] because of the forests and rough mountains. The distance between Carcha and the [North] Sea would be sixty leagues. These three towns are in the temperate highlands.

San Agustin [Lanquin]

The town of San Agustin is ten leagues distant from San Pedro and lies in the hot land; when assessed three years ago, there were 127 tributaries. It lacks a church, but had one until it and half the town burned with all that was there. It has a little tile-covered house for the ministers, a church with reed and clay walls, a half quintal [fifty pound] bell, and a large image of our Lady. It has two vestments, two altar ornaments, some tablecloths, and altar linen and cloth for use with the altar. It has a cross, censer, chalice, vessels for serving wine and water at mass, a silver jar, wooden candlesticks, and garments for the children. At the foot of this town rises a large river, passing by a large bridge of reeds, which with others of wood and the bad roads are cleaned twice [a year]. This town has very poor land and [little] maize for there is always hunger. One obtains cotton in it.

Santa Maria Cahabón

The town of Santa Maria Cahabón is six leagues below San Agustin and in the hot land. The last count assessed it as having 537 tributaries. The church is of rough stone, with a roof being built. It has a large crucifix and a large image of our Lady with a silver crown. It has flutes and trumpets for its services, four bells, a cope, an altar ornament, a strip of cloth hanging from the shoulder of clerical cloaks, bookstand cloth, and a vestment with simple red velvet embroidery. It has four vestments with their gowns, cross, vessels for serving wine and water at mass, a pitcher, censer, two chalices, two candlesticks, and a silver holy water container. It has five altar ornaments, three tables of tablecloths, altar linen and cloth for the altar, bells to repeal a decree of excommunication, and a thatched house for the ministers.

This town and San Agustin are the only source of cotton in the province. It is seventeen leagues from Cobán and, at present, is very needy because of the pestilence of this year in which 400 souls died within three months and the whole town was ill. For this reason, they couldn't clean and guard their fields, and thus had no harvest this year. Their lands are barren of maize, and because there isn't a district that can help them, they have much work. Doctor Sedeño was counting the town for its assessment when it was struck by disease. It was clear that there were not even forty healthy Indians on their feet in the entire town, and he saw them burying eight, nine, and ten Indians each day. Throughout the town there was not a grain of healthy maize nor any for their beasts. They asked him in the name of His Majesty to give some charity to these people who were dying of hunger. He responded that he lacked permission. Desirous for an order from the tribunal to provide something, they spent fifty tostons on the petition, notaries, scribes, and agents with the response, after two months, that the investigation was over. In this manner they were helped, or better to say, they remained without help. Being vassals of His Majesty, it is unnecessary that their horses need pampering. Rather cure and pamper these poor Indians, and that in their illnesses be helped with charity, for the Indian lacks any resources other than his health—without which he doesn't have the resources to live. The towns of the *encomenderos* are in this better off because they help them more with their persons and gifts.[28] His Majesty's towns consume themselves, their lives, and their resources with petitions.

This town is responsible for two bridges of vines, bad roads, canyons, ravines, and hills.

San Lucas Zulben

San Lucas is the last town of this province toward the north. It is three leagues below Cahabón and twenty from the convent. It is being settled with Indians coming from the infidel forests and bordering the lands of

Yucatan. It has sixty houses, and being very new doesn't pay tribute. It has a church of reeds and equipment for saying mass. On the altar is an old painted linen and there is a small quarter quintal [twenty-five pound] bell. From this town to Lake Izabal it is twenty leagues of bad road going through many hills, canyons, and swamps. There is a path the Indian uses to go far downstream, four or five days from this town. They say four years [ago] the Ah Yol [Ahiol] and Ah Manche [Ali-maché] settled it. They are Indians on the borders and limits [of the land] behind Yucatan. On this side, there is no road nor path that one knows of between these towns for there are many forests and rivers between them. It is all hot land.

We teach these six towns—San Diego, San Juan, San Pedro, San Agustin, Santa Maria Cahabón, and San Lucas Zulben—in the Kekchi language.

Santa Cruz

The town of Santa Cruz is three leagues from Cobán. This with the others that follow is taught in a language called Pocomchí. It has sixty inhabitants and a church of adobe covered with tile. It has an altarpiece and equipment for saying mass, a broken one quintal [101.5 pound] bell, and a little adobe house. It is responsible for five roads and two bridges of wood.

San Cristóbal Cacoh

The town of San Cristóbal is a league from Santa Cruz. It has 300 houses. The church is of adobe and covered with tile. It has an altar-piece, and an image of the crucifix and another of our Lady on the sides. There are three vestments, a chalice, three altar ornaments, three little quarter quintal [twenty-five pound] bells, a cope, a bookstand cloth, a censer, a silver cross with its silk case, three tables of altar cloth, and a silver jar for baptism. It has an adobe and tile house. Next to the town there is a lake a quarter league in size without [any] fish. It takes care of two wooden bridges and six leagues of very bad road toward Sacapulas as well as a canoe [ferry] in the great river of Chixoy.

Santa María Tactic

The town of Santa María Tactic is four leagues from San Cristóbal. It has eighty inhabitants. The church is of adobe and tile. It has three vestments, three altar ornaments, a chalice and cross of silver with its silk case, and a little quarter quintal [twenty-five pound] bell. It has an altarpiece, an image of the crucifix and another of our Lady at the sides, a silver jar for baptism, altar linen, a tablecloth and cloth for the altar, and tin vessels for serving wine and water at mass. There is a little adobe and tile house for the ministers. It takes care of four bridges and cleans four roads, one going four leagues toward Salama.

San Estéban Tamahú

The town of San Estéban Tamahú is three leagues from Tactic on a bad clay road with many canyons. It has seventy houses. The church is of adobe and tile. It has an altarpiece, and an image of the crucifix and another of our Lady at the collateral. It has two sets of equipment for saying mass, three altar ornaments, some candlesticks set on poles, an altar cloth with napkins, a chalice, vessels for serving wine and water at mass, and a silver jar. Their half quintal [fifty pound] bell, being broken, is useless. There is a little house of adobe and tile with two cells. The town takes care of two bridges and [is responsible for] repairing its bad roads.

San Miguel Tucuru

The town of San Miguel Tucuru is three leagues from Tamahú. On the road to Lake Izabal, it is the first in the hot land. There are ninety houses. The church is of adobe and tile. There is an altarpiece, and an image of the crucifix and of our Lady on the sides. It has three altar ornaments and a chalice of silver, three vestments and equipment for saying mass. It has silver vessels for serving wine and water at mass, a cross, a censer, a silver jar for baptism, a silk case, and a small bell. It has a thatched hut as a house for the ministers. It has two cacao fields near one of the old towns going toward Lake Izabal; one is seven leagues and the other fourteen leagues away. They are hardly worth the cost of exploiting because, in most years, the river carries away half of the cacao and what's left the animals eat since, thanks to the distance from the town, it is neither guarded nor looked after. They take care of six leagues of road, with many often impassable rivers, going to Lake Izabal.

Santa Cruz Cahaboncillo

It has seven inhabitants. It is seven leagues from Tucuru. This town, with the three that follow, is in the hot and humid land. Mosquitoes swarm day and night, and the people are very ill. If the Indians of the highlands go down to them, it only takes but three days for them to become ill or die. The church is of reeds. It has equipment for saying mass, a quarter quintal [twenty-five pound] bell, and an old painted board on the altar for an image.

San Pablo

San Pablo has twenty-six inhabitants. It is five leagues below Cahaboncillo. The church is of reeds. It has equipment for saying mass, a quarter quintal [twenty-five pound] bell, two images—a crucifix and an image of our Lady—a small silver jar for baptizing, and a little reed house for the ministers. From San Pablo, one can go by canoe to Lake Izabal. They take care of two canoe river crossings for going to Polochic. From this town to Xocolo there are twenty-two leagues, ten by river and the others through Lake Izabal. Because of the rapid current, going upstream on this river is very difficult, it taking eight days to go up to San Pablo.

San Andrés Polochic

This has forty houses, four leagues from San Pablo by way of three very large rivers, two of which one crosses in canoes. It has a church of reeds and a house for the ministers. It has equipment for saying mass, an image of our Lady, a large crucifix, and a small quarter quintal [twenty-five pound] bell. Four leagues from this town one embarks on canoes on a river that goes to Lake Izabal. Leaving from the south side of the lake, they cross its expanse to go to San Mateo Xocolo, the port where they unload for transport to Guatemala the merchandise coming from Puerto de Caballos [today's Puerto Cortés]. These three towns swarm with bad vermin—like toads, snakes that kill people, and many mosquitoes—so that the natives can't work, nor can the women spin or sew. They look like lepers because of the mosquitoes that eat them.

San Mateo Xocolo

The town of Xocolo is twenty leagues from Polochic and forty-four from the convent. It is on the eastern bank of Lake Izabal and across from the port. The crossing is five leagues long. It has a church with clay and reed walls, an old vestment of a thin silk, and equipment for saying mass—an altar ornament of the same silk, a small cross of silver, two small quarter quintal [twenty-five pound] bells, and a large crucifix. It has thirty-six inhabitants including those of Yaxal and Campin. Here, the ships that come from Puerto de Caballos stop and get provisions. For this reason, it is very necessary to preserve this town and provide good treatment of the natives since, in provisioning and maintaining the ships and passengers, it greatly serves the republic. For this reason, and since the inhabitants are few, they can not be used in personal service and for constructing houses at the port. This lack of people also prevents sowing, keeping of poultry, and having supplies for the passengers.

Settled here were the fifty houses of Yaxal and Campin, but because of bad treatment, they [the Indian inhabitants] returned to the forests. They say that, at the present, some have come back.[29]

Seven leagues farther upstream to the north is the site of Munguía that Captain-General (1559–1563) Landecho settled in the year 1561. He intended to use it for unloading the merchandise coming from Puerto de Caballos. For it the Indians made—by building bridges, breaking rock, and opening forests and rugged mountains—a road of forty leagues. For ten hard months they worked on it, 600 and 700 Indians walking on this road each week, going twenty and thirty leagues on it, many becoming ill or even dying on it. They were promised pay, and it was given to them the first week. The nine months and three weeks left they owed it to them. It was brought before the council of His Majesty and I don't know the conclusion. Although they waited, they never received their daily wages.

All the above-cited towns have the names of the saints of their churches. In all of them, the Indians confess each year, at the day of the rosary and of communion. Of the other [Indians] they are few, in part because of the lack of ministers, and many because they are still unfit for this sacrament. Others, who are very few among those that came to the faith, still don't have an understanding of this sacrament. Commonly, they know four prayers, and many the ten commandments and articles of the faith and the sacraments. They show a liking for the things of our holy religion without [having] any trace of the old one. From what we can understand, there are some not baptized, which we believe can come with flattery and good works.

There are in this province fifteen churches and fifteen large and small towns. The description and picture that goes with the report clearly show their location.[30] It indicates their distance from each other, and the site they have in the major sphere and by themselves. Their latitude is fifteen and a half degrees. The space that contains them is sixty leagues, the longitude of forty-four going from the town of Cobán to Xocolo. The diameter is twenty. By the circumference or said half-moon there is only a single road to come and go from them. There are no roads in the diameter or traverse because of the great forests and canyons that are there. The number of people contained in these towns, according to the count and assessment made three years ago, is 3,135 tributaries, and has diminished in these three years by more than 500 tributaries, as noted by the count that was completed by Doctor Sedeño.

The province is in notable diminution and unexpectedly ending. In the year 1561, when the tribute began, they had assessed 7,000 and some more tributaries, and in the thirteen [years] since had decreased until the above-stated number. What is the cause of this diminution only God knows, although one can say that this land lacks the good conditions needed for inhabiting or populating it as well as other special causes, among which one is having brought them [the Indians] together in towns.

While it is natural and necessary for the government and teaching, because of the sterility of the fields near them, their distance from the forests and canyons preventing them from providing help, there is great suffering for them and their children and wives even when there is ordinary and sufficient sustenance. Thus, in keeping with the rejection of nature and lacking sustenance, they become thin and diminish in natural health and force. Given the lack of doctors, medicines, and relief, we see that the Indians become ill and die. Lacking not only comfort in their illnesses, most times they continue with meals of salt, chile peppers, beans, and cooked herbs. In this province have died recently many women and more men. The lack is so great everywhere in the province that they leave it in search of sustenance and, lacking gardens or property to cause them to return, easily remain elsewhere.

The province of the Verapaz, according to the declaration of His Majesty, is 60 leagues long, 50 wide, and perhaps 200 in circuit. There are two means of entering it; one from Términos behind Yucatan, and the other from the west by the land of Acala.

There is no settlement of Spaniard in it nor can one be placed close to it without permission of His Majesty.

There is neither, nor can there be in it, wheat nor [grape]vines. There is a lack of cacao and little cotton, and that only in two towns.

There is not nor can there be a ranch for cattle, goats, mares, and sheep for lack of pastures, but near Lake Izabal are four good ranches.

No church has a chaplaincy, dowry nor income, nor any hope of one for lack of someone to give it and to have it to give.

They use roads in all seasons, although in all there is much mud and clay because of the many rains that don't cease all year.

There is a notable lack of salt, meat, and fish, for these only exist in the hot land and Lake Izabal.

There are many and very good pines and liquidambar, sarsaparilla, mechuacán, and quinine. Although carefully looked for, there is a lack of metals.

The people are ending and in notable diminution, and very quickly.

All the above is certain and true. In testimony of which we sign here our names.

Letter of Friar Juan Ezquerra, March 17, 1605

From the more than two other accounts that I have made about the conversion of the Indians of Manché, which was my duty from its beginning, I will give briefly how the others define the duty, first describing what I heard and then what I saw.

I heard what the fathers who have lived a very long time, and had been old residents in Cobán, told me. These Indians had for more than thirty years been known and come to the attention of the towns of the Christians, among which Cahabón is the closest to their lands. Some of their leaders, three or four Indians, came to Cobán when Friar Tomás de Cárdenas was bishop [1575–1580]. There, they made gifts to all of them. The Manche liked it when the monks showed them all possible courtesy. But they fled when the monks attempted to persuade them to receive the faith.

Little by little, due to want, they acted in this manner for some years, coming and going obscurely to the Christian Indians, saying that they would receive the gospel, given the same treatment and always leaving on seeing a monk. This coldness in them, and for the other part the danger of upsetting the faith of those in Cahabón with whom they commonly had contacts, resulted in orders that they should not come again to the town, and those of the town should not go anymore to the lands of the infidels. This continued for more than twenty years, so that now there no longer was any memory of who had so ordered this. So said Friar Diego Lázaro, referring me to Father Friar Francisco de Viana, who had been fifty years there in the Verapaz, and Father Friar Lucas Gallego, who had come there twenty or more years ago.

Again in the past year of 1596, I have seen come to Cahabón, Father

Friar Marcos Martinez being there, eleven of these Indians and [Martinez] provided them what they wanted. Having asked that God lead them to the faith, they responded that they would consider it and, having given us this reply, departed from us very content. They had come many other times, and once I had seen twenty-two in Cahabón on the day of the town festival when, contrary to fleeing from Our Lady, all of those that came preached to always give the same response, agreeing to receive the gospel. They often sent messengers crying that salt was scarce in their land, and that they would value greatly some knives and machetes. These requests and responses continued until 1597, when President Doctor Alonso Criado de Castilla came to this city of Guatemala. On learning of these people, he wrote to the priors of the convent of Cobán who were in charge [of their conversion] many letters; always carefully helping and sending for the Indians hats, machetes, and axes that they desire so much because of their lack of iron. I divided them among ten of the Indians, giving each an ax, machete, and hat, and sending more into their land for their rulers and principal lords.

Another time, forty of the most important men came to Cahabón [asking for] assistance. In order not to keep them waiting, for lack of a bishop, Father Friar Alejo de Montes—who was then prior of Cobán and now is the head of the convent of Saint Dominic in Guatemala—on their accepting the gospel, ordered the appointment of fiscals for all the towns, this now being the title of [town] secretary [and teacher]. After this, since many Indians were unenthusiastic and the duty burdensome for some, the monks spoke of themselves assuming this duty, that to effect change they themselves should enter these lands. The chapter meeting at Sacapulas agreed to this in 1603. So on the 1st of May in that year, we arrived at their town of Cucul. It being the day of the apostles San Felipe y Santiago, and in respect of the King our Lord, we called this town San Felipe and the headman of it Don Diego.

Here we placed a large cross, and spent six days contacting the caciques of the other towns and offering to go to their land. After long conversations with them, and many conferences, thanks to the charity of God, they resolved to become Christians. Happy with these results, they went to their towns and we returned to Cahabón, sending them masters who taught them the doctrine and catechized them. Then, in the following year in the month of February, we returned—that is, the same father friar Salvador and myself—and beginning with this first town baptized all.[31] The Indians had been first catechized and well taught the mysteries of our holy Catholic faith. We left here and went to all the other towns, seven in total, being received well in all. Until taught we would not baptize them, so we did not baptize more than two sick children and one who went to heaven on being baptized. These towns, the two largest each having 100 houses and the others being smaller, were: the first, Cucul; the second and largest of them, Manché; the third, Chocahau; the fourth, [Ah]lxil; the fifth, Matzin; the sixth, Chixbox; and the seventh, Yaxha.

In the past year of 1603, I being in this city on business pertaining to the Indians of the Verapaz, Father Friar Salvador twice brought these Indians here so that the lord president might see them, one time bringing three and another time six. The reception of his lordship pleased them greatly, and under my care [they] received gifts and all they desired and they were very content and happy, and all the city took pleasure in these beginning agreements. In past year of 1604, they discovered the port of Santo Tomás, and the lord president requested that I go there and teach and catechize other infidels called Toqueguas who were there on the coast of Puerto de Caballos.[32] Thus, we established a small town of Christian Indians four leagues upstream from the new port and town called Amatique.

Because of these activities I stopped going to Manché, but Father Friar Salvador and Father Friar Alejo de Montes were there more than three months, during which they undertook much work and labor because of the contradictions that they found there, and served God by clearing up the many lies that the demon adopts to impede the conversion of these people. They baptized about 500 persons, and among those newly baptized were many Christian fugitives from Cahabón and other places that had fled and were with the infidels sharing their idolatry.[33] Counting these among those newly baptized, it seemed to me that the number exceeded 500, and there are perhaps two times this number awaiting baptism in five other towns awaiting discovery, of which I have much information, and among the many other people scattered throughout these forests, with which divine favor I hope I can quickly subject to the gospel and the royal crown of Castile as has been done with others within these boundaries on conversion.

All thanks to the Divine Charity for the fervor that He instilled in Lord Doctor Alonso Criado de Castilla, since assuming the office of president of this audiencia, to give and send to the Indians many things to inspire them. Also to us alms and help in the cost for the expenses of these expeditions, for the convent was very poor and those in the lands very poor, and the Indians being very needy could not nor can assist. In letters that I have written to the Lord President, and in two other reports that I have made, I have provided a report on organization and location of their towns and ranches, and their climate.[34] It is all as I have certified and provided to give service. Signed in Guatemala on the 17th day of the month of March of 1605.

"Hair Usually Worn Long and
Braided Like the Women," January 25, 1606

I [Antonio Nunez] have seen in the province of the Verapaz some pagan Indians of the new settlements that have cut their uncombed hair usually worn long and braided like the women braid their hair. This is because, as I have heard through an interpreter, they say that they are now Christians. They [have] settled in towns, and I heard [are] learning the Christian doctrine by means of the monks and the fiscal teachers whom they placed there for them. At the present, the monks swear to continue the reduction [to Christianize them], there being in the province of Manché Friar Salvador Cipriano and Friar Bartolomé de Plaza. I have noticed from testimony that there are more than 6,000 Indians that they help with much care. They have many expenses and put their life in risk as can be sworn to by others. I have seen that as a result of the expeditions, infidel Indians have come to the land of the Christians for their commerce and profits from cacao and any other thing brought to sell, and the Christian Indians of the province of the Verapaz also go to their lands, entering and leaving without any risk.

2

GEOGRAPHY OF THE LOWLANDS:

GABRIEL SALAZAR, 1620

Friar Gabriel Salazar presents a vivid picture of a land undergoing "peaceful" conquest in the first quarter of the seventeenth century. We follow Salazar on trip to an unknown land where we learn that the ancient name for Lake Izabal was Munguía and that the indigenous name for the entire Usumacintla was the Icbolay, a word that translates into English as the "Black Killer." The Rio Pasion, along whose shores are the classic period cities of Altar de Sacrificios and Seibal, was the river of the Manche.

Southwest, the river of Acala (today still known as the Icbolay), where the Chol once beheaded a Spanish friar, was close to the famous salt deposits of the Usumacintla. The people of Xocmo, fleeing south (from Xocmo 1) under pressure from Lacandon raids, occupied some of the abandoned Acala lands (see Xocmo 2, map 1). North of them, but west of the Itza lands, was a series of pagan Yucatec-speaking towns: the Çequichan, Noquichan, and Achacan. Salazar's travels on the coast of what is now Belize locate the major Chol centers and define their boundaries with the Yucatec speakers. He also describes how coastal villages fled inland, and bride-seeking men from the interior came to settle on the coast.

More than depicting places and locations, however, Salazer's accounts reveal how people lived in those times. We learn that mashed and badly cut vines denote stone ax users, and how one made maps with cacao beans. Salazar bemoans the infidel trading networks centered in Xocmo and Tayasal that brought trade goods to heathen towns, and curses the Chol of Xocolo who, in his words, would "cast a spell for a cup of chocolate and from the moment of birth begin to do evil." His story of the "cracked pots"—what his pilot-informant called the Itza—is less than complimentary to the Franciscan missionaries chased out of

Tayasal. They were "new in the language," Salazar explains, and imagined nonexistent "wicked" things. Again, in his travels to the Yucatán Peninsula, he shows contempt for the Franciscan fathers who "go fearfully among the natives" and "don't care for the others" living in unconverted villages beyond their boundaries.

Salazar was a careful chronicler, recording not only his own experiences—his abortive expedition to San Marcos and how he found gold in copper axes—but also those of others. He interviewed an old Acala informant who remembered the death of Friar Vico, and young Mayan adventurers from Yol who searched for Yucatan in the empty lands north of them. Indian elders told him how a single Spaniard, not wanting to hide in the woods during a raid, repelled an invasion of leaping and howling Lacandons. Ship pilots told him, and written documents confirmed, "how many came but few returned" from the Caribbean port at Amatique.

This manuscript is neither finished nor polished. Rather, it is composed of overlapping documents with inconsistent dates, showing additions spread over more than a year and comments that, for all their insight, were most likely never intended for publication. It is precisely this freshness, uncorrupted by the need to please official censors, that lends special value to these somewhat disorganized yet candid writings from the early seventeenth century.

Brief Description of the Manché: The Roads, Towns, Lands, and Inhabitants

Treatise of Friar Gabriel de Salazar to our very Reverend Prior Father Friar Alonso Quinao offering, with his humble description, an account of what had happened and was seen in the travel made in this year of 1620 in the lands of the Manche and Chol Indians.

We left impatiently from the last town of the Verapaz, known as Cahabón, and after three days of very bad road we arrived at the town called San Lucas Tzalac. In this town there are six or eight old Christians of Cahabón living on the site of Tzulben, and with them are twenty of the most subservient new Christians of the Manché, who because they live with the old Christians, are somewhat good.[1] This town of San Lucas is four leagues and days of road from the inlet of the Gulf [of Honduras], and here there are Indians who know and go to the beach. More than twenty Indians from this town fled from Father Friar Alejo

Montes. They went behind Xocolo and left by the river that they call Niha, meaning "water nose."[2] These [Indians] are those who, having fled from this town of San Lucas less than a year earlier, contacted those of Amatique in this year of 1619 and told the Spanish governor of the port that they wanted to be Christians.

The three trips made from Cahabón to San Lucas were quite similar. On each trip, we spent two nights in the forest, and we spent them in two hamlets often used by the Indians of Cahabón and San Agustin [Lanquin]. In opening these rough roads, we always kept to the paths of the Indians and [thus] it was necessary to travel on foot. Being mainly on level land, one could turn most of them into very good roads because there are no swamps or cliffs, and one could eliminate most of the passes. Over the rivers, one could make bridges like those in the Verapaz. There only lacks someone to supervise the work and make the Indians do it.

On these trips, we walked toward the east; and on the first day, we took the road going toward Xocolo, above the lake they call Munguía [Lake Izabal]. This road to Xocolo is in very bad condition and endangers many Indians. This past year when I went to the gulf, three Indians died, and two of them died on this road. They died on returning to Cahabón, and the other, the one with me, died in Polochic. I say this to warn against this road from Cahabón to the gulf. I mention this because it seems that many Indians come from these lands [and become] very ill due to the different foods, and they are our responsibility.

From San Lucas to the second town of the Manché, called San Pablo Yaxha, it takes a day in the dry season; but in the rainy season, one will spend a night in the forest. Here, there is a wide river difficult to cross, where the beasts run a risk entering it because of the stones, boulders, and strong current. It is so deep that one can't wade it in any season. To pass, God provided us with large trees that, when cut, reached to the other bank and served us as a bridge. This river, called the Chiyu, runs toward the east and joins on the coast those coming from the sea of the gulf, this being the coast toward Tzoite.[3] In the mouth of this river, which those of Xocolo call Hechonoche, they [Manche of the interior] found traces of people, burned pieces of wood, and some cut vines trimmed not with axes of iron but with axes of stone, as in the manner of ancient times that left the vine mashed and badly cut. Thus, they infer that there are forest people and do not dare settle near the mouth of this river.

Çactun, meaning "the egg" in the Chol language, indicates a smooth-sided and sharp-pointed peak that rises high above the ground resembling [in shape] an egg. During these two trips, we used it for a peak well known among them and full of boulders called Xeuluchan, meaning "seats of snakes." This peak is extremely rough, and a beast of burden could hardly pass single file through the stone passageway. It is certain that here the demons spoke and they advised those that passed to the other side of the peak. They were not about when the fathers walked this bad road since God would not permit their plans and, thus, opened the road. We walked it, although below it is another small one where Father Friar Gonzalo Ximeno died when returning, in the company of Father Friar Juan Ezquerra, from his holy conquest, working until leaving life as ordered for a good soldier of Christ. This father died under a cliff where perhaps our Lord gave him the reward of his work. He died saying some pious Latin verses that he had composed in honor of the Virgin Mary. I stop here to consider this event and decide how to reply. [I] know not [whether] to cry or be pleased to see such work at his death, and on the other hand, [I am] happy for his soul and thus say, "*Pium est flexe martinum et pium est gaudere Martino.*"[4] They did not bury him here but in the first town, and now his bones are in the convent of Cobán.

Also this year we had the death of Father Friar Alejo, who also died in this manner, and they buried him by Lake Izabal, saying that he died of a poison given in Xocolo; one can't deny that it is made there. Although they live in sin, and they'd cast a spell for a cup of chocolate and from the moment of birth begin to do evil, I don't know how one could investigate it since they are Chol Indians. It is enough to understand that many speak with demons. They have then this village, a place of fifteen Indian inhabitants and not very large; indeed there are hardly enough to fulfill their duties. Certainly, it is a shame they call it a town. They don't have a headman nor anyone in charge, and there are no more than three houses and all live there. Above all, they hide the infidel Indians of Xocmo who come here to buy what is necessary from merchants.[5]

After the town of Yaxha, there are no more disagreeable peaks nor bad roads such as those past as the lands are very beautiful and flat. Nor are the towns far from one another—only three to four leagues—and thus from the second town to the third there are [only] three leagues. They call the third town San Jacinto Amatzin.[6] It is on the banks of the very beautiful Cancuén River.

Rio Cancuén

This river, near whose banks are these three towns, after first flowing toward the west, ultimately enters the Laguna de Términos. It never ceases [to flow]. In these towns the friars receive fish as a gift. This town has from twenty-five to thirty inhabitants, although they live somewhat apart.

The river below Cancuén turns to the west above the mountains of Cahabón. On these beautiful flat lands is the town of Santo Domingo Yol. Because of its good lands, the fathers wanted it to be the capital of the province. The idea was to open a road to Cahabón, it not being far and the land between the two being burned over. This is a town of 100 Indian tributaries although there are more than 400 souls, but very rebellious. It is divided among two headmen. Here, we took up the burden of paying those who brought children to baptize, and after discovering they were in want, with gifts. There was very little profit in these people because they could always easily leave by boat. They worried about nothing beforehand. All the other towns feared them.

There were four Indians of another language different from Cholchi that they called Ahitzachi.[7] They were natives of a town of infidels they called Xocmo, a two-day journey below by the same river. These four were baptized and lived there in Yol. I asked them for the number of inhabitants of Xocmo, and they swore that there were 200 families and that there were even more in another larger town. Now that I have sent my messengers to the headmen, and know their names and some words of the language, God willing, I will do well in this town.

While eating a large fish similar to their mojarras, an old Christian of Cahabón who lives here told me that we are near the sea because one finds all kinds of fish.[8] From this one can deduce that downstream, the river is calm and without any breaks. This Indian said that the river joined with the Tuhalha, the river of Sacapulas that they call the Icbolay, and that this is what fills the Laguna de Términos.[9] This Indian is the most experienced traveler in this province and knows all the land belonging to the people of San Marcos as far as the salt hill, and knows the land of the Lacandon that borders with the Tzendales, and beyond this all the Manché.[10] Beyond the Manché he has gone to the Ahitza, this being the town visited by the Franciscans from Yucatan. He also knows all the lands that border Yucatan near the district above Champoton. It is this Indian who has given me the satisfaction of telling me many of them and corrected much of what I thought I knew about the Ahitza.

I spent four days with them and learned of four towns beyond the Manché. It is certain that he, by himself, would lovingly guide us toward Yucatan as easy by land as by water. He is one of the old Christians, born in Cahabón, and wants the Spaniards to enter the land the Franciscans call Σa.[11] He has been brave and clever in coming and going, with many kinds of merchandise, from the lands of Xocmo.

I learned that from the fourth town there was no road to the fifth, and thus had to return to the third and from there take the road for San Pedro Noxoy, which is four leagues from Amatzin. Always following the banks of the Cancuén River there, between two other towns and at a good site for uniting these towns, is Noxoy, [a town] of forty inhabitants. This year many came to their fair, and during the following holy week came all the headmen of the nine towns. Because it is in the middle of the land, it only takes a day to reach Noxoy from the town of San Lucas. I made it enough of a festival, and those who enjoyed it most were the headmen for they very much wanted to meet their people, and they said that when the people are together they are lords and that it would please them if their towns were like those of the Christians. All the other towns of the Manché are, in the order given, northeast of these.

The town of San Vicente Ahixil is an additional four leagues and more from Noxoy. It is the same size and has as head a good Indian, Don Alonso Ahixil, who removes from the forest those who have fled. They made a very good church and house at his request. This is the one who asked that we bring a teacher so that his children could learn the things of the church and who contributed his share of the salary [for that teacher]. Since the people of Cahabón don't come as previously, he accompanied me in person when I entered the town of Manché. He challenged the views of those who had not spoken well of me and came with me when I spoke with them.

Between this town of Ahixil and [that] of Xicupin, called Santa María de La Asuncion, there is another called Chocahau, and on the death of the ruler they moved all the inhabitants to Xicupin, although some didn't want to, and made a beautiful settlement in Xicupin. It is certain that the rulers made a good impression on me and introduced me to enough youth. There were many people, and the roads were in very good condition. It seemed to me that there was fifty families and all appeared at the church with impressive solemnity, receiving me at the door of the church in two lines, all the men and all the women of the town. Afterward, the Indians did not leave me during the entire day, showing special pleasure in having me see that the church is large enough for all who live within six leagues of it. They told me of the many problems of the seventh town of the Manché, and I advised them that it wasn't their fault. I did summon the two headmen. On their arrival, I requested that they, with the completion of the church, assume their duties just as those had in the other towns.

The eighth town, San Miguel del Manché, was no more than two leagues or a little more from Xicupin. It is the capital of their lineages and from where came the people of the other towns they call Manché. The principal headman is Don Martin Cu, and another headman of a subdivision is Don Cristóbal Yaxax. Although formally united, in reality they are very dispersed. They didn't come at the same time, and those that came seemed different from those of yesterday; thus I infer, following what all the Indians say, that there are many people in this town. There appear to be ninety inhabitants, but as they are on the border and live close to the infidels, this is an estimate without actually having visited them. In truth, they presented me with 100 ears of corn and sweet potatoes in abundance. Thus, I had no problems with them although I baptized few. What is a pity is that the total number of baptized on this trip was 118 infants, and these after six years.

The Indians of the other town who came with me accused the others of hiding them, and after telling me of this lack, I asked about [the] settlement of Don Juan Coatzun and I sent my messengers to its location, a league and a half from here. Agustin Coatzun, his older brother, came and said that they were in their towns and their lands with their women, oldsters, and children, and could not come to another town to hear mass because of the discomfort; they could not do it and could not welcome me because I was here. They had come to receive their orders and provide me with bread. They gave me some kernels of corn. Because enough rich people presented themselves here it was possible for me to estimate the number of adult males, not counting the oldsters or the children. I counted thirty-one [individuals] and, being pleased, granted them what they asked, and they stayed to prepare the church and houses and open the roads. With this they remained very content that I would postpone for another time my trip to their town.

One of the reasons that motivated me to name this town now called Santa Cruz Yaxcoc of the Manché was because of where it was and that I could go to its lands. I would know that there were other large towns beyond this cross [that is, Holy Cross of Yaxcoc]. According to what the Indians told me, the road that goes to the right extends toward the north and below Yucatan like my belt [in other words, across the base of the Yucatan Peninsula]. The elder of Yol, who says he knows all this land, says one town is Çequichan, another Noquichan, another Achacan, [and another] Ah Mopan.[12] Here, next to this Ah Mopan, is the water of Tzibistun that they call the pier of the Ahitza.[13] In two days, the Indians [of Yol] can arrive at the islet of those of Ahitza.[14] The rest stop between these two journeys is Chacchilan, so that it takes no more than four days to come to the Ahitza: two by water and two by land. Of the five towns here, although they are of different languages, the four called Ahitzachi have a lengthy border with [those who speak] Yucatec, and I believe that they are in Yucatan.[15] The fathers say that the language is somewhat different from Yucatec. I acquired some knowledge of these towns when I had an encounter with someone whom those Franciscans of Yucatan who went to this town of the Ahitza had asked for help.

The past year when I was in the gulf, I asked two pilots of Bacalar what they call the infidel Indians, and the oldest said sarcastically that they call them "cracked pots."[16]

Town of the Itza

"His excellency, the lord bishop and head of their order in this province, sent two friars to explore this town of the Ahitzas. It is on an islet between two arms of rivers and one goes there by canoe. They welcomed them and made a kind of church. Although they didn't know the language very well, they began their work of conversion.

"The fathers found a large ceramic horse in a stable. Every day, hay and grass were brought to it. The fathers had a bad feeling about this and inquired if this was a kind of superstitious idolatry. They went to a headman to ask what it meant, and he told them that long ago a great captain and lord came from above these lands.[17] He fought with them as they all gathered here on the crag and island. They did not want to provide him with a canoe to come here, but he made a road with sticks over the water and entered with his people. He came on horse and the others came on foot, and defeated them and forced them to surrender. Afterward, he treated them very well and offered presents. He said that the site of the island seemed very good, and that he would return and establish here a great city. Therefore, in token of his intentions, he left us his horse and we promised to feed it every day. The aged horse did not lack maintenance but died of old age. The headman stated that we greatly regretted and worried over the death of the horse, and decided in counsel to make this horse of ceramic in memory of the other who died. We provided hay each day as before. Not because we believe he will eat, but to show that we are not negligent in the duties given us by the captain. The horse didn't die because of lack of food. In this way, if the captain comes and asks for his horse, we will have appeased him.

"The ruler explained it to the fathers, but as they were new in the language, they did not understand very well and imagined that it was some wicked thing. With religious fervor to end idolatry and similar superstition, with sticks, they broke it [the horse] into pieces. The ruler and the headmen were very annoyed with how they treated their relic.

They ordered such people killed or expelled from their lands. The Christian Indians advised the fathers of the disturbance and that they were coming for them. Therefore, they seized some canoes and fled, leaving the Indians indignant and saying that they would not allow them to return."

All this the pilot at Xocolo, in front of the entrance to Lake Izabal, told me and the captain of the merchant ship and other Spaniards, and confirmed it in total. The others from Bacalar said that it [the capital of the Itza] was a very large town with many Indians, and that they [the Itza] know well the houses of the Manché and recounted what had happened and what they knew to the Dominican fathers. This is certain since all the Indians of Manché, especially those advanced in years, know the language and town of the Ahitza and that of Xocolo. They prepare all the merchandise behind Santo Domingo [Yol], going to the river below and the town of Santa Cruz de Yaxcoc. There is a powerful Indian merchant, a relative of the ruler called Coatzun, and he takes all the cargoes and never sells to the Christians but to those of these five infidel towns.

Afterward, Father Friar Salvador de Molo advised me that an Indian told him of going east to another large town called Yaxal.[18] It was in the channels of the coast of Bacalar and had 400 Indians and beautiful cacao orchards near the lands of Tzoite, where there is much cacao.

Another large, secluded town is much spoken of in Cahabón. It is in the water called Cuculem, near Yaxal.[19] An elder of San Marcos told me all this. The Lacandons captured him when he was fleeing, from the revenge of the glorious martyr Friar Domingo de Vico, toward this island of the Ahitza. This helped me make the map that God hid until these times—because the Lacandon had been so powerful—[and] that others without doubt ought to revise like another Saint Stephen. Father Friar Domingo de Vico prayed to God for those who killed him, and in this year of 1620, died two elders of more than 100 years in age who, after having been administered the sacraments more than forty years ago, had not done so again because they said that since they had confessed with Father Friar Guillermo Cadena, they did not need to do it again.

This elder spoke of another town on a peak between those, calling the site Σqueach, and these next to another that was also a town called Chacvelen. It surprised me to learn that this name meant "red pitch." All these towns are in the hills between Bacalar and the recently converted towns that are above Champoton.[20] These lands are usually considered to be in Yucatan along with the towns of the priests of Bacalar that they call Campin, Tzoite, Xibun, Maiha, Chinamit, Çactam, and Guatibal, until one reaches the ranch of Pedro Hernández that borders with those of Manché.[21] I have seen in the town of Tzoite three married Indians who were now Christians. One, a teacher, came from Manché and wore the same clothes.[22] They had the same language and pierced ears, and had come here in search of women to marry.[23] They had been converted inside the Manché. It happened one time that Indian merchants of the Manché came to the town of Santa Cruz.[24] The ruler, seeing an Indian with a kerchief and white doublet through the wall of his lavatory, jumped from his hammock to speak with these Indians for it was the first time anyone saw clothing like this in all the land.

Besides, for two years the entire town of Campin hadn't wanted to obey the father priest of Bacalar and left for the Manché. The people of a town called Ahixil said that they spoke with Don Alonso, pleading that they be protected, given lands to sow, and allowed to live in his town. The Indian ruler did not wish to tell them that they were now subject to the Spaniards. When a Spaniard came in search of them, he didn't want the Spaniard to take them, but he also knew that if they didn't go it would bring war to his town, and thus, he sent them away even though one boy was the nephew of Don Pablo de Xocolo. He had many relatives in the Manché, who they feared, and in speaking with him they used his language, it being the same as here.

Although I can't provide all the details on these lands and their borders, I can say in brief that these lands are well populated, making it necessary to conquer them since they are filled with souls. Up to now, you should know that I have yet to speak of the lands of the true Lacandons as defined by the bank of the river of Sacapulas and the lands of San Marcos down to the Laguna de Tĕrminos. There is another crag like that of the Ahitzas on an island. Its water runs from the land of the Tzendales to the Laguna de Tĕrminos, but first it joins the river of Sacapulas that we call Tuhalha.[25] This river of the Lacandon is the Çacacha, about which, if there is need to speak of it and its lands, I can prepare another report.[26]

Beyond these towns, Santiago the Old of San Marcos said that when they fled downstream, on that portion of the Sacapulas River known as the Icbolay, he and a Lacandon and another of San Marcos were looking for the mouth of Cancuén River.[27] It is in the Manché, and they followed that river until reaching a stream on the left-hand side that comes from Ahitza. It took three days from its mouth to arrive in Ahitza. This site, where there are houses, is Ihebec. I was told that the ruler is Pophitza, and another is called Tuxu ΣalelaΣu and another Yax Ahau AΣequicance—

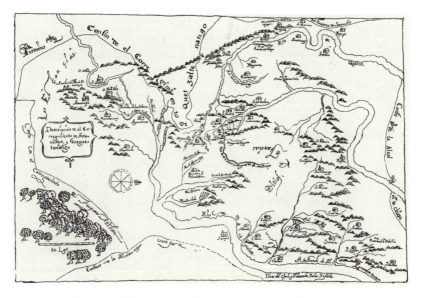

Figure 2. "The river of Sacapulas that we call Tuhalha"
(Fuentes y Guzman 1933)

all these being, not counting those who live on the left-hand side [of the river], lords and warlike people.

Going northeast between the land on the lake and the towns of Tixchel, there are two or three settlements (both towns) and many Indians, known as Buchiquin and Vayha.[28] These are Chol names. The first signifies "fenced ears" and the second "zapoyol water."[29] These lands extend from Bacalar to Champoton, they being as a girdle [across the base of the Yucatan Peninsula] without going completely from one to another and whose bottom reaches the Ahitzas, who have the most people, certainly above all others in needing conquest. There is no doubt. It is to these towns that they go hiding from the voice of the gospel in order not to place the yoke of the law on their necks, which for them seems so heavy.

All these lands are no more than twenty to thirty leagues from the Manché and surrounded by those of the Christians, thus restricting the spread of their hamlets. Doubtless there are more, because some have not come to my attention. The towns that I have noticed are twelve or thirteen. Perhaps even more if you add the other two towns said to be near the mouth of the Cancuén to those thirteen, and all this without discussing those of the Lacandon. All thirteen are of one language, that is Ahitzachi [Yucatec Maya], and those of Manché speak another, that is

Cholchi [the language of the Chol].[30] In this manner, there are thirteen towns of infidels and nine of Christians, making a total of twenty-two towns that up to now have come to my attention, and they are administered in the two languages for they are all together. The names of these towns are:

New Christian Towns	Number of Inhabitants
San Lucas Calac	26
San Pablo Yaxcha	15
San Jacinto Amatzin	30
Santo Domingo Yol	100
San Pedro Noxoy	40
San Vicente Ahixil	40
Santa María Xicupin	50
San Miguel Manché	50
Santa Cruz Yaxcoc	31
	382

Known towns that are infidels but not Lacandons are these thirteen towns:

Xocmo.	Squeach	Ah Mopan
Çequichan	Vayha	Cuculem
Achacan	Chiquiz	Chacvelen
Ahitza	Noquichan	Bucchiquin[31]
Yaxal		

The number of inhabitants cannot yet be certain. Enough to say that many hide and that they are always timid. Regarding the Christians, I have heard from an oldster that there are even more here. Of this I can't be certain. In another town said to be beyond them, called Caccolon [and] Caclam, it is not certain if they have sixty houses there on the edge of the ocean. It is Christian now and known as Cactan, a town where the Spaniards change canoes when they go from Tzoite to Bacalar (to which it is closer).

I will now put all this in order. You know and understand that we could not do our duties without much work. Neither could we gather together these people without the help and support of His Majesty for the buildings as well as the expenses of the friars since, until now, there is nothing established to assist us with sufficient bread and for ornaments, images, bells, and other necessary things. We also lack the support of [Indian] officials to go with us in the service of the church. They are all tributaries and they lack help; they can't accompany us and leave harvests and fields neglected, and their women and children alone all this time without support. What consoles me is that this year, you have seen and examined what was necessary for this conquest.

On other activities with the aid of local inhabitants, we have been observing these lands from nearby highways and hills. Indeed, Brother Friar Juan Pardo and I have entered the lands of those of San Marcos, which border on those of the Lacandons, looking for information and in search of the Laguna de Términos. Therefore, I am most willing to begin this discovery when Your Reverend wants it done, and having been ordered to write an account of the ceremonies and bad rites that the demon has taught all in pain and contradiction of the sacraments, I have now so written to Your Reverend.

I pledge to our Lord all will be prepared for your holy service and good of these souls who for *twenty-one* years have received the faith, and I will continue to sit at your feet.[32] Your Reverend entrusts such a holy enterprise to our Lord and order it placed in the hands of the fathers, for which I thank Your Reverend, for it is as you see necessary. I also offer thanks for your prudent help and aid. In Cobán, the 2nd of December of the year 1620.

Second Essay on the Description of the Lands of the Manché, and Drainage of the Rivers and Lands of the Lacandon

To our Father Prior Friar Alonso Guirao and, as Your Reverence has requested, our Father who has seen and pleaded before the President of the Royal Tribunal, the Lord Count of Gomera.[33] I have provided a notebook giving a description and number of towns of the Manché and lands with inhabitants, and you have ordered me to continue with the same material, and to give an account with my advice and judgment of what I know and would seem convenient for the execution of this conquest and its completion. In obedience to Your Reverence, I write again emphasizing the crossing of these lands to Yucatan, what is the most fitting answer to your orders, and offer some advice that is very important for the good of all the neighboring lands. Your Reverence understands in all truth that I am not interested in this business but only in converting souls, thus in this way gaining much treasure. More, for in converting them I serve the interest of His Majesty, as I do by promoting intercourse with Yucatan through these lands and the recovery of these famous uncultivated lands that can result in great benefits to all for they are so fruitful.

I remain comfortable and satisfied in placing in the hands of Your Reverence this business, acquainted as I am with your holy zeal. This business is the cause of God, and in it may he guard Your Reverence. From Cobán at the end of this year of 1620.

After having discussed succinctly the distances and locations of the towns of the Manché and provided notice of the infidels who live on its borders, and with whom they treat and communicate, I was advised by some Indians who, beyond what I myself have seen, have visited each land and the route of each river. For this enterprise one needs to begin with the rising of the waters, following them downstream, and learn where they go and the requirements of this conquest by going upstream from the mouths of the rivers and determine their origin in rivers or mountain ranges and their route. The map should be clear enough to answer any question.[34] It is based on actual eyewitnesses, and when from hearsay, from persons worthy of trust who have volunteered information without having been asked for it. The foundation is of truth, and in the truth of what I write one should have faith. Leaving the manner in which I write, I will now turn to all these lands; I will emphasize some more than others.

I left Guatemala and turned right onto Lake Izabal, where I took a canoe at Xocolo and, following the coast, arrived at Tzoite. This is the town where, in my other essay, I noted finding three happy Indians of the Manché who, not doing well there and without women, went down to these towns. Also those of these towns who did not want to work went up to the Manché, like those that I mentioned of the town of Campin, all of whom fled from here in canoes. I came and entered the town of Xibun, where there is a different language from those in Tzoite, who speak the Chol language of the Manché.[35] From here I entered Çactan, and from Çactan entered Chinamit, both being on lagoons and rivers of saltwater.[36] From Chinamit, they took me by water to what is an inlet of an arm of the great lagoon [Chetumal Bay]. From there, going through the ranch of Pedro Hernández, I came to Bacalar. All this was by canoe. As you know, then I came to the city of Mérida, and from there to Campeche there was always a range of hills on my left-hand side.

From Campeche I went to Champoton. From Champoton by land I went to the town of Tixchel, which is a league from the water of the Laguna de Términos. I lodged in the house of the governor, Don Pablo

[Paxbolon], who had died eight days previously.[37] These and adjacent towns speak a language different from that of the Yucatec. This is where they make spoons of Carey, and where there are ranches of livestock and mules.[38] It is here and in Champoton that the fathers speak of the missions that they had founded in the hills with recently converted people and how there are many more beyond them. The fathers fearfully live among them and don't care for the others.[39]

I continued my trip by canoe inside the Laguna de Términos and crossed it all, seeing toward nightfall large ships inside the mouth. The Indian rowers continued past a wide river flowing into it. After the middle of the day, in some swamps on the right-hand side, there appeared land with wild livestock. I was then about three leagues from the tiny town under the priest of Tabasco called Atasta. Here, on the left-hand side, was a river, and I asked where it came from. They said that they did not know [but thought] that it came from the Lacandon.[40] From this town, it was a day to another river that they called San Pedro y San Pablo, whose abundant water entered the sea by means of two mouths. From a ranch of a Spaniard on the headland, one day more found us sleeping in Tabasco. From there to Villa Hermosa, and then to Chiapa, and from Chiapa to Sacapulas and Sacapulas to Verapaz, and thence there again, I went down to Xocolo, which is Lake Izabal, to obtain supplies for my convent. Here, I gave thanks to God that I completed the circle and now know how many leagues long it is and that one can complete this circle [around the Yucatan Peninsula].

After I had made this long trip, I intended to enter the towns that they call the Manché of Chols Indians with the same spirit as seen in my travels. Intending to convert these souls, I learned the language well and completely. Working as I did on my travels—with gifts, good works, and questions—I found out what I could of the climate and the disposition of the streams. I went in their midst writing down with their names what the Indians know. To this I added some gentle questions, and God offered me an Indian who lived in the town of Yol who had traveled much and told me much without prompting. He gave me proof that he was familiar with what I had seen. Putting in a notebook what he and others had said, and using an outline to determine if I was being lied to, I asked questions on the lands.

From those of San Marcos, and by these means, I had a long account of the lands of those of San Marcos where they killed the Father Friar Domingo de Vico. They martyred him with arrows and, as noted below, cut his head off, and it was never seen again. These Indians lived in Cobán. It was my intent to ask them afterward in Cobán the same

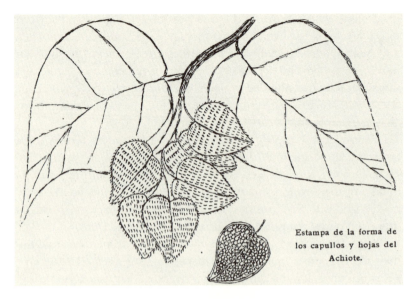

Estampa de la forma de
los capullos y hojas del
Achiote.

Figure 3. "They had cacao and achiote groves"
(Fuentes y Guzman 1933)

questions. I hid what I knew to see if they would lie about the first
explorer. I discovered that what they told me, and what I found from
those of San Marcos, conformed in all respects with the account that I
had brought with me. This made a great impression on me.

These Indians brought me a bachih that is among them—an old wise
man who is a hundred years old. He had seen the death of Father Friar
Domingo de Vico, been captured by the Lacandons, and knew all of this
land. For this, I placed in front of him a basket of cacao [beans in order]
to show [me] the manner in which ran the waters. He made lines of
cacao, and where there were towns put three cacaos together. Finally, he
also showed the ground by depicting it for me in response to my questions. He gave the proper names of the [river] mouths, headlands, crags,
hills, and resting places. I went [about] making small slips of paper and
placing them on the cacaos. I copied what the Indian said on a paper and
erased [his] depiction. He made it again, three more times this map. I
found it very carefully done each time. Always without any alteration in
name or changing anything from the first that he had made. Beyond
this, for further proof, I asked two other oldsters, who provided the
same marks for the rivers and in the same order the same names. In all
[things] they agreed with what he said. The first oldster offered his
person to accompany me if I didn't believe what he said was true. That

made me decide, and be certain, that there was no doubt because everywhere in all the land they showed me [where] they had cacao and achiote groves, they always began their testimony by using them to draw the features of a map.[41]

All the unknown lands on the route of the above-mentioned trip to Yucatan, those in the Verapaz, of the Lacandon and Manché together with Laguna de Términos, I intended to see in person. Beyond the inspection of the Manché, there would be a visit to another depopulated region, that of San Marcos, those lands that separate the Lacandon from those of Manché. Going from them to the Laguna de Términos, which is not far away, one always goes north and somewhat to the left. I want to explain the depopulation of these beautiful lands of San Marcos by recounting the death of our predecessor and glorious martyr, Friar Domingo de Vico.

The Martyrdom of Father Friar Domingo de Vico

Heaven endowed the father with knowledge of different Indian languages, the first being Mexicana, in which he was very fluent, using it to learn the others; the second being the Cakchiquel, which is that of Guatemala; fluency in the third of Sacapulas; the fourth being that of Verapaz [Kekchi or Pokomchi]; and the fifth [being] the Chol of those of San Marcos, which is almost the same as that of Manché and is the one that I know.[42] Also he was a very learned man and above all holy. He prescribed many books for the Indians, translating them into the languages of the Indians. Above all [he wrote] the work called *Theologia Indorum,* where he copied from the Bible all but the difficult passages.[43] In this work, he treated of the creation of the angels, the world, and the heavens for humans; followed by the life of Christ, a discussion of the sacraments, and many other things that I have not mentioned here. All [this was written] in the profuse language and copious vocabulary used by the same natives. Often in these times, on studying them, we find something new and curious that without the Holy Spirit it would be impossible to acquire, even though we study but a single language, and that we would never have discovered ourselves.

This father afterward traveled throughout all of these lands. On the coast of Lake Izabal, when the Indians abandoned him, he feared being killed by the [local] Indians. He and his companion made a prayer while waiting for death. Then he heard a voice saying that he would not die now but on this day in a future year. They would kill him following his trip and return to Cobán, where he was prior, in another year. He intended to enter the lands of those of San Marcos from where some had already been baptized by the Father Friar Alonso Bayllo, who also was a father at this time and a great apostle in this land. As is the custom, they then sought a blessing at the church. They prostrated themselves, and his prior asked that the prayer of the travelers go with the deceased without noticing that he kept silent. He said that all was well. With him was Father Priest Friar Andre Mozo, who began to learn the language in his company from the Indians of San Juan Chamelco, a town of the Verapaz. Don Juan and his people received them there without much pleasure. As Indians, they knew that the [San Marcos] Indians intended some treason and implored Father Friar Domingo that he call off his enterprise, but he knew now that they were waiting and went [to those of San Marcos].

The day before San Andre was the day marked by the voice. He [Friar Domingo] said that it was their imagination [they were not in danger] and that they [the Indian servants] should all return to San Juan; that he was very safe. The Indians in obedience to him returned to Cobán. One night, his companion went to feed their mules and could not find them. Feeling uneasy he went to the prior, telling him of the mules. He suggested that perhaps they went to drink or somehow got loose. Filled with foreboding, Friar Andre could not sleep, so Father Friar Domingo and he went to the church to pray and passed the night alone with God. Friar Andre, being tired, fell asleep dressed on his poor bed. At the hour perhaps of four, [to the] sleeping Friar Andre and vigilant Prior Friar Domingo began to come crowds of Indians with arrows who posted themselves near the church and house of the fathers. For this enterprise those of San Marcos had summoned many infidels, including for certain those of the Ahitza.[44] They remained there until Friar Domingo left on the coming of day.

[With] previous martyrs waiting in heaven to include them in their company, he went to go to their little house and saw the crowd of people with quivers and arrows. Seeing them waiting in the space between their little house and the church, the father asked them lovingly: "Children, why are you dressed with these weapons and arrows?" To which freely responded the ruler that he intended to [obtain] revenge for his insults. These were that the father had already admonished this ruler two or three times because he had two or three women and he [the friar] wanted him to leave them. Thus, he [the ruler] requested vengeance. Then the holy prior told them that he didn't have arrows because he feared nothing, but that he did worry over the damnation of their souls for doing so grave a sin as killing a priest. Then he continued for a time with a spirited and inspired sermon. The father did not stop preaching, and it seemed to the ruler that he was talking too much and [so he] asked the captain of the infidels to begin shooting. The Lacandon responded that you should begin what you wanted, and thus the ruler of San Marcos shot the first arrow into the middle of the [friar's] Adam's apple and throat.

With pain escaped from Friar Domingo a cry of "Jesus Christ" in a voice that woke Friar Andre. Seeing what was happening, he did not leave by the door where they were waiting. The arrows knocked off some of the reeds of the reed and mud wall, going through the house into the jungle. So filled with fear were the Indians by Friar Domingo's preaching that it incited them to shoot arrows at two sleeping Indian children of the Christians who had helped at mass. In front of all, they opened the breast and removed the heart, and there in the moment of sacrifice fell the holy prior. As is customary, they then cut off the head with an ax to carry it as a symbol of victory. They made a cup out of the head, and in their principal feasts drink from it.[45] Since Friar Andre didn't leave, they set fire to the house, and as it was burning and they didn't see him leave, they cast about to see if he had fled. They followed him, and on the next day overtook him and opened his head with an ax in two or three places so that he died.

The ruler, who we said was of San Juan, when he returned [home], feared for [the friars] and sent some Indians to see the prior and learn how he was. They found on the road the alarming spectacle of Father Friar Andre. Returning from their confrontation, they advised him of the disgusting find left by the enemy Indians. Some Spaniards in the entourage of the Spanish governor of the Verapaz followed the trail of those of San Marcos and arrived at the site, where they found the mutilated body of Friar Domingo without [his] head and they sent it to the convent.[46] All the fathers came to receive it and greeted it with many tears. They buried their bodies before the major altar of the church of Cobán.

Continuing in the pursuit, the Spaniards captured many Indians, suspended them from trees, and killed them from below with arrows. This incident, and the fear of punishment, depopulated all these lands of San Marcos. The Indians of San Marcos have cacao and achiote groves that grow in their forests, as do other trees, without planting. Such being the fertility of the land, the grains that fall on the ground that the squirrels or other animals don't eat, sprout at the base of the cacao trees. Moreover, since the corn ears begin in sixty days, one never needs to wait three months from the sowing of the maize until harvest. Thus, never in these lands does lack of maize cause a man to seek the help of others. So rapid is the sowing that within sixty days they can remedy hunger with new maize.

The intercession of the fathers stopped this killing and punishment of the Indians. Those who remained in San Marcos, some sixty houses, the friars pardoned and made a very good little town. After this conquest, the Lacandons attacked them every day. Since their own lands were a three-day journey from the other Christians and they were too few [to defend themselves], we brought them to the city of Cobán. Here they remain, although against their will, and they desire to open up the roads that would allow them to return to their land.

I advise that when this road is made, they don't take Indians from Cobán nor from San Juan [Chamelco] nor San Pedro [Carcha] because when I went asking questions on the death of Father Friar Domingo, all who spoke on the lands said they were content and agreed in everything with those of San Marcos. Afterward, they saw that I had a real interest in opening the roads and having them assist in the conquest. Therefore, they began to throw out many lies and exaggerate the work, difficulties, and costs. They having the very bad custom of making a thousand prayers as if already they had died, only so that they would not have to work.

Now I declared in the first notebook that I sent to Your Reverence the districts that border those of our fathers [the Dominicans], the towns that we have discovered east and north of Guatemala or Verapaz, those on the Bacalar coast from the Gulf to Bacalar, [and] those above the hills that run in a chain toward Campeche. Now, I want to present those closest to the Laguna de Términos and all the rivers, or the largest, that go to this Laguna [de Términos].

The River of Cancuén

The river of Cancuén is born in the last towns of the Manché and, before it leaves this land, goes rapidly from its birth until it joins with the great river of Sacapulas. It is no more than thirty leagues from its birth until the town of Yol, [or] three days by road. From Yol in a canoe, one can reach the mouth [of the river] in two more days. Here it goes very slowly for these are flat lands. It is the river that connects these lands of the Manché with those of Tixchel. Its strong torrent, fit for anchoring with land on both banks and without any swamps, goes from east to west until it enters that of Sacapulas. Then it goes north and enters the

Laguna [de Términos] on the right hand. One day from Yol, one sees from it a stream that they call Yaxcaba.[47] It is the location of towns and cacao groves abandoned by those of Xocmo when they fled from the Lacandon who used this river to attack them, as we will discuss below.[48]

Those of Xocmo moved to the left bank of the Cancuén. Going by means of the other large river, they settled on its southern side behind the hills of San Pedro Carcha. Just as Cobán is no more than a league from San Pedro, those of San Pedro have some fields next to the lands of Xocmo that they call Calic, meaning "fields of chile." In past years, the now dead ruler of Xocmo wished to make mischief and tried to capture three Indians of San Pedro who were in their fields, less than three leagues distant, and could capture only an oldster named Benito Chohil. They killed him and they even say wanted to eat him. This ruler was one of the oldest and most savage, but never attacked again because Coatcuxu, his remaining son, fearing vengeance, ordered a halt to attacks on the Christians.

He considered even success in making these attacks to be bad and he didn't want the burden of such a sin because we are peaceful. We have merchandise that we can bring there, and none will arrive if there is war. After this they came each day to Yol and other towns of the Christians. The town became peaceful and now has five baptized Indians. From there to Cobán the road is easy, and in proof of it, I walked with those who know it from San Pedro. It took a day to reach Chirreiquin, another to Chixut, and another to Calic. If we wanted, in those three days, we could have been sleeping at Xocmo. In proof of this, a baptized Indian called Juan Pana who lives in Xocmo, lacking an ax to work his field, climbed the hills that separate us and reached the royal road that goes from San Pedro [Carcha] to San Agustin [Lanquin, at a point] one day in time from Cobán. Waiting for travelers, he greeted them, said who he was and where he came from, and explaining his need for an ax or two, bought them in exchange for his cacao and achiote from a San Pedro Indian called Little Lazarus. Asked where he came from, he told them and said it wasn't far. This meeting was at the stream that crosses the royal road known as Tihix.

Subsequently, the current of the Cancuén River joins farther downstream a very large cold river that they call Hitzaha.[49] The oldster of San Marcos showed me this streamlet that those of Manché didn't want me to discover. It comes from the lake of the island of the Ahitzas, and the oldster used it in fleeing from the vengeance of Friar Domingo. He and two other Lacandons went downstream in a canoe on the Tuhalha and entered the mouth of the Cancuén.[50] After going upstream for two days, they entered this streamlet of Ahitza and rested in Tichi and slept in Muebac.[51] Early the following day, they arrived at the Ahitzas, which is an islet that they call Peten. It is a large rock, and another large rock of the Lacandons who border with Chiapa and Tzendales has the same name.[52] This oldster said that there is only one wharf, fortified with some walls of rough stone and mortar, of the Ahitzas. They called this entrance Ilibec.

In this way we have two roads for the Ahitzas. One goes through the Manché, as I said, by the stream of Tzibistun, and the other comes from the Laguna de Términos and the river of Cancuén.[53] I have said this having heard that soldiers intend to capture the rock [of the Itza], and in this case, now we have the means of bringing soldiers from Yucatan by the Laguna and these waters because the ships can go upstream on the Cancuén and on small boats up this river of the Ahitzas. I think this could be the best [way of doing this]. I want only to note here the flatness of these lands and that all these rivers are navigable for this is a great help because, although there are no roads, one can replace them with a canoe.

When in the town of Yol, on the banks of this river, I spoke to an Indian explorer. He said, "Father, I can tell you something about the lands on this bank north of us." I told him not to wait, that it is what I want to hear, and found myself a comfortable seat. He told me that he and some other friends out of curiosity wanted to learn more about who lived in this region. "We ventured out to this bank. Then we went, over some not very difficult hills, north of it. We walked five days; in truth, since there was no road, we didn't go very far. We discovered neither town nor trace of people. We saw flat lands, and it seemed to us that there ought to be towns there and [we] would have continued our trip if we had streams like here. This is what surprised us: that in the entire five days, we didn't find any rivers like those in our lands. I suspected," said the Indian, "that we were in the land known as Yucatan. Because I know who lives on this side therefore this land beyond ought to be Yucatan. That is what I had not seen, and I had a desire to see it and know it."

What the Indian said didn't bother me, nor that the land was high and hard. These appear to be the lands above the towns of Tixchel, where there are these small hills, from what I have seen the lands being tough and without communications by land or sea. I know that if God helps us to open a road, because I have verified and have evidence that this river enters the Laguna [de Términos], that these lands to the north are those that I have heard border with Tixchel and the coast of Champoton.

The current continues and joins the river Tuhalha, which is the Sacapulas.[54] The river of Sacapulas is now very large and slow, and two other large rivers now join it.

The one on the right-hand side, known upstream as the Çactohom, is that of San Marcos.[55] It is born behind Cobán and always runs to the north. Already it was large when I passed by it four leagues from its birth, having a pike's worth of water, but with stones, from its birth until it enters the Tuhalha.[56] This river is approximately thirty-five leagues long. I see that it goes straight north without winding. I intend to describe it and the lands of those of San Marcos. Afterward, it leaves the Manché. I asked for help from the head of our order in the Verapaz [for a] companion, and he sent me Brother Friar Juan Pardo.

Very talented, he was a mason and carpenter. He was quite familiar with these roads as he had also been on the Laguna [de Términos] and in Yucatan. When he heard what I intended, he suggested that even if it was a short distance, we should include four blacks in our company for defense if perhaps the Lacandons ambushed us. I selected the most rigorous time of the year and with the most water, and some protested, but my intention was that if in a time so severe and without open roads we could walk openly, certainly afterward it would be better. They said that it was impossible to cross the hills of Cobán and that other times there would be no pastures. Others spoke of the Lacandons. As I now realized that these were the devices of the Devil for impeding all good intentions, I didn't say more or respond other than [to insist] that I wanted to see these difficulties. Since no one could help me more than the Indians of San Marcos, I took with me two oldsters who knew most of the lowlands and three mules loaded with our small bundle of clothes, and in the name of the Lord, we divided the supplies at the end of September. Going always north, we walked four days through the hills where they told me it would be difficult. The mules made six leagues loaded in one day. I said to Brother Friar Juan that it was a much better road and the hills we passed no more difficult than those from the valley of Salama to Guatemala, it being a road so worn from herds that there is no difficulty. Nor did we see anything during the five days we walked on the roads. The hills were low everywhere, and I didn't see any swamp or precipice. One can avoid any obstacles. We saw the old sites of the settlements that were there before the death of Friar Domingo; and even after many years, columns of the church, the altars, and the stairs of the high altar were still standing at the site of those of San Marcos.

Twenty Indians came with us, and the first day was through an open forest with very flat hills. We walked four more days to the river below where they had some canoes. Here, we stopped because the people were tired and we proposed to go by water since the remainder was so difficult with so few people to open the road. We obtained a tree to make a good canoe. By joining it with another, which they had, we made it very good and large. In less than six days, I knew we would be near the waterfall or drop of the river that was approximately six leagues from here and downstream from there was an even larger river that joins in another day with the river of Sacapulas, which is the Tuhalha, and there it loses the name of the river of Sacapulas.[57]

Ycbolai and Çacacha Rivers

The river of Cancuén [Rio de la Pasion] and that of Çactohom all join to form one large [river] they call Ixbolay [Icbolay].[58] The water becomes brackish, the watercourse straightens and goes toward the north, and by it, downstream from the drop, are cacao groves. There are different fish that come upstream from the sea and on the left side nine hills they call Bolotenuz where there are salty waters, from which they make some salt.[59]

It was in these lands they often found Lacandons taking salt, and here is where they captured Old Santiago, tied him up, and took him with them. He told me: "Father, we left this stream of San Marcos going to the Rio de Tuhalha by means of a river that flows from the lands of Chiapa called Çacacha. We went upstream to the shores of the Lacandons. All the shore of the Tuhalha River on this side is theirs as far as where it meets the two large rivers from the towns called Cotzal and Chajul that descend from the hills of Sacapulas. All [is a] land of cacao and achiote."

Old Santiago was taken on perhaps all the rivers of Sacapulas, and all which flow north rise in the Verapaz as also [does] the river of the Lacandons and another that they call the Ixaccha where they killed Father Friar Domingo. More than a day's journey below Cobán the river of San Marcos enters a lake, and Old Santiago thought that by the river of the Manché, which is the Cancuén, the Lacandons go to the lands of the Manché.[60]

The Shores of the Tuhalha

The lands on both banks of the Tuhalha River are marvelous, have beautiful cacao groves, and are extremely fertile. As I said above, it is very flat, and has cedars and trees for making canoes and frigates. All the land is dry with hills but no marshes, nor as far as the site where Friar Domingo died, is any part of the river very deep. An old Indian of San Marcos said that it would support the founding of a convent, there on the banks of the Tuhalha, for they are very beautiful lands and near the sea at the Laguna de Términos and the Tzendales. These lands are close to Guatemala for it is only a three-day journey to Cobán and then five to Guatemala. He said that on the right bank one could do worse than make here a beautiful town for Spaniards. It would be extremely helpful for all because, starting from Cobán, it would be in the center of the Christian lands. A three-day journey from Sacapulas can provide poultry and meat. The fathers of San Domingo have two very large ranches in the valley of Salama, and it would take four days to drive the cattle to the villa and settlement. If the remaining Indians of San Marcos settled there among the same Spaniards in their own quarter to serve the settlement, certainly there would be no lack of maize. One could increase this town with people reduced from the Lacandon. One then would see this road open without waiting for their conquest. They would surrender in order not to lose their lands because they didn't want others to replace them. This town would be near the Tzendales so one should be able to reach the crag of the Lacandon from here. Since there is a route from Sacapulas, that way is better for they are closer, the lands more flat, and can support them with provisions and cattle.

Regarding bread and biscuits, they have it in house because I know that in the land of Sacapulas, one can prepare, sow, and harvest wheat for two cities the size of Guatemala, and this is, as we have said, three or perhaps four days away by road. They have supplies, when they need more ships and frigates, or more cables, tar, and resins for the ships.[61] These are abundant in the Verapaz, and because no one buys them, the Indians don't bother to collect it; thus, this [demand for them] would enrich the land.

Considering the many supplies those of the Laguna [de Términos] and adjacent regions provide to Tabasco, one can view this villa as a way of supporting many ranches whose abundant hides ships can bring back to Spain. It would be in communication with Yucatan. It would be the meeting places for Yucatan and Guatemala, Verapaz, and Sacapulas, the two Chiapas [provinces], and a port for frigates to Havana, San Juan de Ulua, Cartagena, and other places. Since the entrance of Laguna de Términos is much deeper, and doesn't have a dangerous shoal like Tabasco, it is a port where frigates can enter even in the middle of the night during a storm and be safe from harm.

The climate of the land is somewhat hot like Yucatan, and [the land] has a continuation of the same range of hills. Some say that one can walk perhaps thirty days in the forest by putting a cloth on the head, sleeping in the night air, and have enough sources of water with never a headache or pain. The city of Amatique (with its gulf) and those of Tabasco and Villa Hermosa are on bad sites that seethe with mosquitoes both day and night, [and as] all buildings are of straw, everyone is ill and so many die. They have no Indians for service and support of the ships and frigates. Certainly, they were selected on poor counsel and with little advice despite being a thing so obvious and in a place so well populated with busybodies.

One could alter the shipping of Honduras, and bring the ships of Campeche and Guatemala together. Even if they are not so many, they are four or five, and the other three of Yucatan jointly would make a very beautiful fleet. They could winter in running water where there are no shipworms. From here within a brief time they could bring help, more than 500 musketeers from Yucatan and Campeche. With the greatest ease, they can arm the frigates to help all and more if there were many enemies. It is no more than 100 leagues from Veracruz, where they can quickly provide support by sea or land as needed. In this entire plain, the enemy knows neither the mouth [of the river] nor the site [of the proposed town]. It is true that the ships can't enter the river or lake because of the strand, but neither will the enemy have access to the warehouses and treasure as happens every day in the gulf [of Honduras] and Amatique. When the Spaniards face them on the ground, they will have the most troops and have Indians to carry the baggage and provisions, thus ending the lack of maintenance that so discourages them. It is different in the gulf. Its port, not being like that of Amatique in a crater, the enemy can blockade to keep people from entering it.[62]

Even if the enemy has gained, and defends, the beach of Campeche, we are, from inside the Laguna [de Términos] and by roads, easily able to correspond and obtain advice and thousands of goods from the land for supply, or if it was necessary, 1,000 men from Guatemala. I would definitely not want to place them in the bad site that the ships now have in the port of Santo Tomás since, from the registers of the soldiers, one can say that many come but few return; most [were] always dying. One time, I saw provision being made for the convent including a guard. There were not ten of the infantry that could hold a musket, certainly a shameful thing when there are enemies.

The other drawback is that because of the price, the ships can never buy meat. From this port, they go to Havana to obtain it or warn other ships from San Juan de Ulua that they should bring it from Havana. This is sound advice because in Amatique and Trujillo, poultry costs eight reals each. On the other hand, here on this coast, meat has no value. For there are ranches where they slaughter the cattle only for the hide and tallow, and the highest price is twenty pounds for a real. Hens in all Yucatan, in all the Verapaz, are never more than a real and two roosters to the real. Furthermore, the people are happy with such food. Each day these merry people increase in number and riches, and sell at a low price. This extortion from this piece of land [Amatique and Trujillo] is nothing more than sloth and ill advised. In this all the pilots agree that soldiers whine, and grumbling merchants cry, so disgusted they are with losses that happen on this road from Honduras.

Taking, as I said, the harsh time of San Francisco to go downstream—a time neither of the cacao among the Lacandon Indians nor salt harvest—the explorers going downstream by canoe found nothing, neither trail nor people.[63] I waited eight and more days at this site for some loads of maize left in Cobán that could reach us only after twenty days. I had only biscuits and some jerked beef because we intended to explore beyond. But the unsleeping demon schemed to hinder it. The friar could find neither servant nor noble, no one to pay for their services. Thus, I regretted that those who had brought our provisions had not noted what remained before [leaving]. Being badly taught, the Indians of Cobán fled; and lacking provision, the people and blacks, crestfallen and melancholy, went all day looking for wild fruit to eat in place of bread.[64] There was abundant fish. We decided to return before the people became ill, and thus in four days, little by little, we returned to Cobán taught by experience for next time. If one is to serve God, one must prepare properly to achieve success.

It was of great value to conduct this expedition because from the center of this land, which we have seen with the two oldsters, I have always found the lands would be so much better with inhabitants. Understanding what they and the others had said, and learning how the rivers run and if they meet, confirms for me that this river enters the Laguna [de Těrminos]. Thus, it would be easy to see that it [the Çactohom or San Marcos River] joins the river of Sacapulas. That it goes to the Laguna [de Těrminos] all would know if they were navigators like the Indians, who say when arriving at the mouth of the Sacapulas River that they never go beyond because their canoes are [too] small to endure the tides of the sea and beyond this they don't know where this sea goes nor have they made a search. I will conclude this with the two arguments for proving that this [sea] is the Laguna de Těrminos.

My first argument is that on going straight north from Cobán, with the road that goes toward the coast of Bacalar behind me, I always come to the river of Sacapulas. It goes straight to the north indeed, looking from Cobán, toward Campeche and Mérida. The drainage of the side of Campeche supports this idea since no sufficiently large tributary enters Chetumal Bay.[65] This, in turn, implies that it turns straight to the west because, as is well known, in all of Yucatan there is neither a river nor drainage on the other side of the hills from those that go to Chetumal Bay.

The second and more obvious reason is that I have seen all the inlets of the Bacalar shores and none is so large that one can't see the other side from another. This is because they are even smaller than Lake Izabal. But these children [that is, the Indians] make the argument that they don't leave the mouth of the river of Sacapulas on seeing the sea because they don't know if there is land on the other side or only water. Therefore, this can't be Chetumal Bay from which one can see the land from all shores and certainly could be that of Laguna [de Términos].

I have proved that the lagoon is the mouth of Términos because I have shown that it could not be that of Bacalar; thus, it follows that it is of Términos because already you know that in all the land of Yucatan, there are no rivers, and that they all drink from the cenotes, deep wells, and pits where water is found at two or three fathoms. Because the land is so dry and deprived of water, the game and wild birds are so healthy that the doctors give them to the ill without any fear. The game birds are lean since they lack water, and easily killed since, as I have seen, the deer, turkey hens, and other animals come to drink at the reservoirs and cattle troughs of the ranches.

I want here to note the foresight of God for His little animals in that He cares to provide sustenance even though all the land of Yucatan has a foundation of stones and flagstones. The waters and freshwater rivers run so near the surface of the land, as I said, because of the stone flooring. Therefore, after heavy rains, little water goes between the flagstones and rocks, and not being absorbed by the ground or sinking in it, it lasts a long time. This provides the animals and game with water that had not seemed to exist, and there is an infinite number of game in all the land.

We have gone with the intent of presenting the evidence, and I have counted the mouths of the indicated rivers that are from Campeche to Tabasco whose shores I have followed and on these beaches of the sea there are no more than three river mouths. The first is that of the Champoton. Not counting the small streams that go toward the port of Ceiba but don't join it, this river of Champoton is a provider of water. I know that it was born next to the [adjacent] mountain range and that it thus could not be the outlet of the Sacapulas River. These and other Indians live in a town on the banks of a river that is not very large. In this town there is a shipyard, and they make very good ships, even ones that can go to Spain. If they founded the suggested town on the bank of the river inside the Laguna [de Términos], they could make them much more easily in a shipyard protected from enemies.

After this river, the coast runs twelve leagues to Tabasco. The mouth of Términos is thirty leagues from Campeche because from Campeche to Champoton is twelve, and from Champoton to the town of Tixchel (on the bank of the Laguna) is ten, making a total of twenty-two leagues; from there to the mouth of the Laguna [de Términos] is six, for a total of thirty.[66] In this lagoon enter many rivers; those here know of more than six, each of them with plenty of water. There is a settlement of Christians. Frigates go to the rivers, like that of the Acalan River and another that rises by the town of Atasta that is now under the priest of Tabasco.[67] It is twelve leagues from Tabasco.

Proceeding onward with the enumeration of the rivers, from Términos to Tabasco, there is the river of San Pedro y San Pablo. It has two outlets, and thus, could not be this [entrance to the river of Sacapulas].[68] One is much smaller than the other, being no more than or perhaps three times smaller. From here to Tabasco no one knows of any river, nor have I seen one in going through that land.

From this it follows that it would be one of those that enters the Laguna [de Términos] and has the most water. On looking for it toward Yucatan, its route goes south and somewhat to the west, perhaps because upstream it makes great circles and turns, which is why they call it in the land of Verapaz next to San Cristóbal Chihoy, meaning "in the circle," and here the Chol Indians call it Xoy, perhaps for the circular procession that it makes.[69]

The information available on travel to this land from the same Laguna [de Términos] is that they know nothing of these lands, and afterward we learned that those of Verapaz are also lacking [in information]. Thus, for fear of the Lacandons, when one comes intending to learn the description of the land, to appease the conquerors, they complain as we have said already. I [already] said approximately what is the route and that the bed of this river is larger than where the San Pedro y San Pablo empties its mouth. By making a circle in one's route and going toward the west, where the river appears to rise, and traveling about a day upstream, one encounters the two rivers mentioned earlier. The one on the right-hand side called Çacacha is the river of the Lacandon and comes from the lands of Chiapa. On it, they have a large rock that is their islet and scandalously they also say that one could come to their lands with small frigates.

Lacandons

These Lacandons are not many and are on bad terms with us now even though the captain who was among them is dead. He was the one someone killed in a town of the Mercedarian fathers, behind the Sacapulas, called Santa Eulalia.[70] That is how they came to attack all these lands, but lacking him they no longer come. He was a very savage Indian, with a face like a huge shield, and quite strong, coarse, and tough, although not very tall. This Indian peacefully entered one time in the towns of the hills of Sacapulas called Cotzal and Chajul when Father Friar Salvador Cipriano was the inspector. He [Cipriano] put him in prison and spoke with him. He told me this, and that also one time he caught eight and held them prisoner while waiting for instructions from the Tribunal. If the people fled, it was not due to attack but to treachery. They came again to frighten the people from their houses so they could enter to take cooking pots and cloth; whenever they found resistance or some of them fell hurt, then they abandoned the place and fled. Those of San Marcos told me the following:

"There were no more than twenty of us when a boy said that the Lacandons were a quarter league away. They had plundered a field, and had attacked an Indian and his wife with an oar. We began to keep watch all night, take walks, and sing and make noise with our arms and arrows to see if these Lacandon were as brave as it is said. They came at night, and as they saw we were on guard and that we waited for them, they didn't dare to attack because they didn't look for risk or danger, only to steal where they didn't find resistance."

More was told me by the friars of a Spaniard who was in a town of the Mercedarians.[71] At the hour of evening prayers, in that year of 1583, the Indians went to the forest to hide because they knew that the Lacandons were waiting for the night to enter and attack the town, and they did not dare to wait for them. The Spaniard smiled at them and told them that he didn't want to go, and thus stayed in the inn that night. He waited close by to see what would happen. He put on his sword. He put a good club by the door. Leaving the door half open, he heard some small noise of whispering from the people. Taking his club and putting his head by the door, he saw a line of them, one behind the other, and some apart and making little leaps like dogs. The first one softly came to the door of the inn, inserted his head, and began to howl like a dog. Then, the Spaniard who was waiting for him swung the club with both hands and hit him on the head, killing him without needing another blow. He then threw the club down, dragged the corpse inside, and waited for the arrival of another. The second one, who was farther behind, began to howl, and as he didn't see the first, he stopped what he was doing and waited and shouted what had happened to the others. They, some more quickly than they had come, left and did not continue the attack. Nor did they appear again.

In the morning, the Spaniard saddled his mule to go. The Indians came, and he told them what had happened and that, subsequently, they did not have to wait for them there. In this way, the Spaniard made them worry, and when one falls it depresses the others. Thus, there would be no need for the shedding of blood in their conquest. They would flee and hide, waiting for the invaders to leave. But since the invaders had support and others had their lands, they would come to an agreement to become Christians and do what was requested of them.

River of the Ahitza

Continuing on the route upstream of the Sacapulas River, we find on the left-hand side that it meets the river of the Manché, which I said was the Cancuén; by this river, one could also send frigates to the first towns of the Manché and in two days reach the stream of Ahitza. Joining on the left-hand side and going farther upstream [are] two other streams, one on the right hand and the other on the left hand; the first called Xocmo-xilba is where those of Xocmo settled and the other is called Yaxca-bilha.[72] In all the rivers the Indians travel by canoe, and it is very easy because all the land is so flat. One can perhaps go to the Ahitzas at least with large sloops and canoes to that crag that they call Pethen [Peten] and its gateway [of] Ilibec. All of these rivers, including those of the Lacandon and that of Sacapulas, have not been used [by the Spaniards] but are very easy because from the Lacandon they go in canoes and travel again upstream, passing through by the mouth of the Cancuén to the Tuhalha. This is why those of Manché fear the Lacandon and are their enemies. From this one can infer another advantage. One supposes that since now there are nine towns of Christians in the Manché that the Lacandons will not be happy. The same Indians of Manché led by Spaniards and with their support can help destroy them.

Now, continuing a little upstream on the Tuhalha, which is the river of Sacapulas, one comes across on the left hand another famous river joining it. Coming straight from Cobán through the lands of San Marcos one takes the river known there as the Zactohon until Indian canoes, which they call Ah Tzusuin, reach the place called Chaacchan. Then when it meets with the Sacapulas, they call all the Icbolay. On arriving at the peninsula that this river makes with that of the Sacapulas, all the lands look beautiful. The Indians of San Marcos have on them many beautiful cacao groves. [From] here, on this peninsula between the two rivers, one goes upstream for Cobán. There are nine hills, and next to them are many brines where they make salt. It is flat land and very solid, through which have passed Indians and Spaniards, and is known by all of those of the Verapaz since they came here to avenge the death of Friar Domingo de Vico. They all swore that it is most beautiful and fertile, and that there are forests of cacao and achiote without owners.

Furthermore, I found an Indian who confessed his doubts, saying: "Father, I have come to you to ask if it is a sin for me and those of us who are the bravest of these lands of Cobán and of the other towns, when we lack cacao or can't pay the tribute, to venture downstream to these on the plains of Tuhalha or Cancuén and return with a load of cacao, saying that they were from our lands." He said that since there is nothing but forests without any trace of cultivation, the animals eat this fruit and no one else collects it. One can see, that in this case, there flourishes an abundance of cacao that, when cared for and cultivated, can provide taxpayers with tribute of cacao and achiote, which in our times has a value like gold.

Mines of Gold

It is certain that there are valuable gold mines in these hills [as well]. There lives a Spanish black in Guatemala who was a servant of a priest of the cathedral when Cobán was a bishopric.[73] He said that after the land was secured, he went to Cobán with a Spanish friend and had permission to remove gold, but they abandoned the enterprise because the Lacandons came for salt and they could not take the risk of meeting them. I confirmed this with a friar of the convent of Guatemala who understood much of mines.

Once, when in charge of searching very carefully among the Indians of San Marcos, Cobán, or Manché for as many as possible of the small copper axes used in these lands in pagan times, I bought them even though they were expensive. When asked why I wanted them I didn't want to say, yet they insisted so I said they were not for me but for a Spaniard who had begged me to search for them. He is a founder, and knows how to make bells and other things. Once, in Cobán, I bought one for two reals and on melting, even though small, [it] yielded twenty-two tostons of gold [mixed with the copper]. Friar Feliz de Mata—a longtime father, oldster, and surely a saint—noted that many Indians in these lands [had] used trinkets of gold, which they placed in [their] ears and lips, and suspended from [their] noses.

Bonolhacha River

Now, I have spoken of how very large the Sacapulas River is, of the beautiful lands on its sides, and the other river where Friar Domingo de Vico died that meets it on the left-hand side, coming from the lake that is called the Bonolhacha.[74] Upstream from this is another called the Chituz that is born behind Cobán and passes six leagues from Cobán.[75] Moreover, there are two other rivers on the right-hand side, both large, that descend from the hills of Sacapulas from the towns they call Cotzal and Chajul. All this is enough to show how large is this river of Sacapulas. These Indians call the large river we know as the Sacapulas the Tuhalha. Many other rivers enter it, like the Hanlha and others [such as the] Holicha [and] Copalha. Toward the side of the Lacandon [are the] Chacailha and Poo. Perhaps there are others that, to avoid tediousness, I will not mention here. I have given enough to show how great is the river, and proved how it collects all the waters of these lands and brings them to the Laguna de Términos.

Travel from Laguna [de Términos] to Cobán or Sacapulas or from Cobán going toward Laguna [de Términos] is very easy and links those of Yucatan with those of Guatemala. Going upstream from one and downstream from the other takes less than eight days of travel; certainly this is true, for an Indian of the towns of Tixchel brought a Spanish speaker to Cobán.[76] He went downstream with those of Guatemala, identifying these lands and its lakes all the way to the mouth of the Laguna de Términos. In the same manner, a wise and old Indian of San Marcos had come with the Spaniards who had entered [the river] from the Laguna [de Términos]. The Indian advised them about the river mouths, recognized their lands, and although not naming the river of Sacapulas, facilitated [the preparation of] this report.

I had traveled by this river up to where died Friar Domingo de Vico.

One can go by land and horse, even without opening a road or making expenses, until a given longitude, and by water from there to Yucatan. It doesn't matter that this river has a winding course in crossing these lands and that defense from the Lacandon at these locations is necessary. This water is easy to follow because it is large, and those who go upstream just as those who go downstream can take their bearing and meet where Father Friar Domingo died, a three-day journey from Cobán. The untilled land, of which there is much with so few souls, will provide all that is necessary. Many of little spirit think that it is impossible to finish this enterprise and so don't start, or only believe it can be done by warfare. God grant that someday one will see it ended, and without any death or treasury expenses.

This I have written with zeal for serving God and my King. It is for this that we have come to these lands and left our dear country, to lead them forward to what our predecessors had made clear is the search for these lost souls and announce the word of God that had never come to them. It is this that has moved me to promote it and write about a year and a half in their conquest. If God carries me from this life, there will be a record of how little difficulty there is if one only has in his heart a little zeal for the honor of God. I trust our Lord will accomplish it if His Majesty and his Tribunals want to order it. In me, they have a chaplain, a guide, and an interpreter of the two languages of Cobán and the Manché, who will be the first in the dangers if there is a desire that I work on this conquest. God grant I deserve what my ancestors and fathers deserve, who with their work and blood bought the inheritance and right to the glory that God promised to those who legitimately fight [for him].

There are other things, our father, that I can write about their rites and some means to besiege these towns, which can make them more reasonable and so convert them, and thus I have left this history unfinished for when there is a place to write it and you order me to do so.

3

ACROSS THE OCEAN SEA:

MARTIN TOVILLA, 1630

In these days of jet-propelled travel, it is hard to imagine how difficult it was to cross the oceans in the sailing ships of centuries past. Martin Tovilla recounts what he recalled as "a happy voyage" that took not days, not weeks, but months of hardship and often misery. It was "happy" because neither bad weather nor enemies sunk any ships, and the inhabitants of the islands of the sea were watchful yet not hostile.

His stories of unknown islands, lost pilots, life aboard a galleon fleet, political intrigue, and natural beauty provide a proper setting for his ambitions as a would-be conquistador of Manché lands. Finally, with his landing at Santo Tomás and his progression along the coast to Xocolo and Polochic, we are back in familiar Chol Maya territory. But as the reader will discover, unlike Salazar, Tovilla only felt pity and gratitude for the "witches" of Xocolo.

Prologue

Curious reader: By edict issued in Madrid on the 18th of December of 1629, His Majesty, King Don Philip IV, our lord, ordered me to go to and govern this province of Verapaz. Obeying him, I put it into execution on the first possible occasion by embarking, in the year of 1630, on one of the two Honduras ships. For two reasons, I began to write this volume: the main one being that I not be idle, and the other, to [assist] whoever goes to these parts, [by describing] what happens in the Ocean. Arriving, I found the situation changed because of the harassment by the Lacandon and Ah Itza Indians, our neighbors, and thus continued forward, taking for the subject the origin of the present-day peace [and] writing at the same time on the conquest of the Manché.[1] This was my intention. Thus I beg you that if you read it, and if it seems to be too long, or impertinent, finish it without stopping, since it is lawful to ask you not to condemn it without reading it [in its entirety].

[Cadiz to Guadeloupe]

Chapter 1, Book 1:
Of the Voyage That We Made
for New Spain, from Leaving Cadiz to the Arrival at
the Islands of Guadeloupe

Twenty-eight times the sun had returned to the world, and ran its accustomed route in the hot month of July when, after making Christian preparations for a journey so filled with dangers to the soul and a supply of provisions and gifts necessary for the body on so long and troublesome a voyage, thirty-two vessels made sail for New Spain.[2] On departure, so beautiful were they that in the bay of Cadiz, the many masts seemed to form a peaceful forest. Even the wind was favorable. That day, we didn't go farther than to the end of the bay and through a dangerous strait with a large crag called Las Puercas.[3] We found ourselves in thirty-seven degrees, which is the latitude of Cadiz, and although [this passage] could have been a bad omen and sad portent of an event of what would happen to us, it wasn't, for as my history will show, it was a happy voyage.[4]

In truth, in going to deep water to join the rest of the fleet, we came very close to putting us in the Almiranta of Honduras in great danger, although we had little experience with such perils.[5] We only heard the angry voices of the worried pilot and disorderly crew: "Apart! Above! Cut the rope! Raise the prow!" and other remedies that seemed necessary by the experts. Hearing our prayers, heaven took pity on us, and the ship, with a very damaged prow and a diminished bowsprit lookout post, was quickly repaired for these are things of lesser importance for sailing. Our strong ship resisted the blow so well that it was left without any damage except for some glass that fell from a lantern.

This day passed in taking roll of the soldiers and other necessary measures. The following, we began to sail with a good wind astern, so favorable that in less than eight days (passing the feared gulf of Mares without any resistance, other than what is normally found elsewhere in similar areas), the Canary Islands came into view, 300 leagues distant [from Cadiz], which is not so far for this account.[6]

We passed eight warships that, in our defense, separated from us on

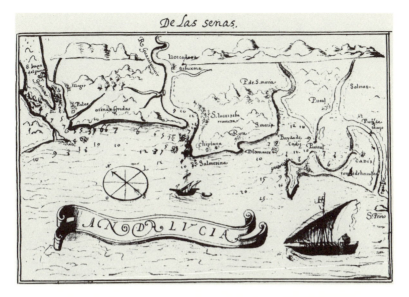

Figure 4. "We found ourselves in thirty-seven degrees, which is
the latitude of Cadiz" (Vellerino de Villalobos 1984)

the news that Don Fadrique de Toledo had now happily arrived on the
coast of Spain with the warships, galleons, and fleet, and that he had left
in Havana fifteen galleons to clean the sea of the corsairs, all of which is
very normal, and the remainder guarded the ships from the Indies. We
remained alone, but being that there were twenty-four ships, this was
numerous enough if not to protect us from all our enemies, certainly to
inspire resistance against fewer ships.[7]

We were now in the wide gulf of the Ladies, which is no less than 800
leagues long. The origin of its name is not known other than the quiet of
its waters, for it seems that the ladies, even though they were with all
their ornaments and embellishments, could plow through the water.
This is what my limited ingenuity comes up with for so deep an abyss. In
it, we saw something very difficult to credit: little fish provided with
wings to fly in the air. They escaped from the great ones who wanted to
swallow them by leaping into the air. They obtained in the air the mer-
cies that neither in the sea nor in their companions did they find. They
went elsewhere, quickly enough to save their lives.

Returning to our voyage, I said that Saturday, this being the 10th of
August, the day is celebrated in our Spain because of that wonder of
holiness, Saint Lawrence, and for the great victory that our Catholic
King Philip II had in San Quintin, the last being commemorated with

Figure 5. "He had left in Havana fifteen galleons to clean the sea of
the corsairs, all of which is very normal";
naval combat between Spaniards and Dutch
(seventeenth-century painting courtesy of Museo Naval, Madrid)

the sumptuous work and fabric of the Escorial [palace], the eighth marvel of the world. We wished to celebrate the holiday, not with great decorations and hangings but with many masses for on our ship came thirty friars of the Order of Saint Dominic who went to the province of Guatemala to renew their convents, and continue the work that had cost so much blood of martyrs and whose path *each day with their preaching had pacified more lands than Cortés with his valorous works.*[8] So pacific and obedient were these lands that unlike in other parts, it has been many years since they saw a rising of the Indians. Discovering new lands each day, they gave many harvests to heaven. Entrusting the pulpit to one of these holy friars, called Friar Juan Navarro (a native of the city of Ecija), at three in the afternoon he took it, preaching one hour, and I don't know whether it was the effect of our holy Spaniard or the good presentation of the speech that made many of us say little and listen with pleasure until evening. Before the hour of prayer, a gun discharged from a great distance. It was from one of our ships, and then hoisted on the main topsail was a signal made in sighting sails or some disturbance. At once the mast man climbed to the top and, nothing having happened to us, checked to see what happened to the others. The Almiranta halted to guard the ship on its right that had made the signal, which had seen a sail to the windward. This was very brief because it soon became dark. Thus we didn't know anything about it. Before seeing it, we believed there had been fighting between the passengers and owner of the ship. Next morning came the cry of another sail. Excitedly, each of us pulled out our weapons, and in our view to the windward near the ship that had seen it the night before, coming behind it was a large and well-loaded warship. They said it was English, but to us it appeared to be an East Indiaman that at more than even two leagues seemed to be a forest.

We could not investigate it because, as I said, it was windward. Thus we continued our voyage, doing for diversion a thousand different things, some being work and others amusements. The captain frequently marched a squadron of guards and taught the soldiers. They worked on cleaning their weapons and preparing the bullets. The pilot sighted the sun and took the latitude, giving orders to the sailors and cabin boys, who doing their duties, obeyed very quickly. Of the passengers, some prayed, other read or wrote. It seemed a small world because in such a small space (as in any ship, however large) went more than 300 persons who were never idle. Officials attended to their duties as if they were on land, although without the full uniform of the Main Street of Madrid. But in this small space, one could not ask for anything not there. Nor if absent, make it instantly appear with the aid of officials and gifts. Besides this, others amused themselves with card games, dice, and chess, with which they passed the days, even if they were hot.

The nights were quite cool, and better for the diversity of music, dances, and games, and was one of such joy for us that we announced the greatness of the coming day, for in the ship San José as happy husband of the Queen of the Angels one celebrated the glorious Assumption. For it we made a mountain of fire with innumerable quantity of rockets, bombs, wheels, and a thousand other inventions. There were more than 2,000 lights on the stern, prow, and from the waterline to the rigging of the ship. The display lasted more than two hours. We also saluted the following day, when the sun painted the horizons with his fire, with a salvo of artillery, muskets, and harquebuses from all the ships. To our surprise, they were all beautifully adorned with their bunting, streamers, and pennants, each being eager to be the first to offer a cannonade to the royal Capitana and the San Jose.[9] [The salute] having been made by us, we separated a good distance from the ships and ornamented it better so that we could place the altar where the Very Reverend Father Master Friar Pedro de Montenegro (who will be vicar of the friars)—learned, and of holy life and laudable customs—could celebrate mass. They said he and three others administered communion to more than 100 persons.

In the afternoon, Friar Antonio de Guevara, native of the city of Salamanca and college of Santo Tomás of it, preached as learned and elegantly as could be hoped from the son of this mother, and transplanted it into the eminent pulpits of this Religion, the mother of the sciences.

The remainder of the day we spent in amusements and diversions from the heat, which was very great. A short time after the sermon, a sailor caught a fish called a shark that was seventeen feet long and had a head as large as a bull, and so wild that it flung itself from one side to another in the ship, biting with its mouth, making a great noise, and moving its tail and entire body to defend itself. Quickly, to subdue it, they hit it on the head with some very large tackle. On opening it up, they found inside it three live tuna fish and many bones of men and other animals. They gave a portion to everyone on the ship and even then there were scraps left over, and the soldiers said that for fresh meat it was tough. Those days, it was amusing to see the many different kinds and names of fish. Among them, more than a thousand fish as large as oxen passed around the ships, appearing on the water like inflated hides, making a great noise and giving great bellows.

On the 25th of this month of August, a ship left us for the island of Santo Domingo. It had now arrived at its place, first obtaining permission from the general and making a great salute to the Capitana.[10] We had the great pleasure that afternoon of seeing some large birds who they say don't fly out far into the high sea, meaning that we were near land. Soon, we saw not what we were looking for but an unpopulated islet called la Fonseca.

Always, going from Spain, the degrees of latitude got less. On the 27th, the pilot measuring the sun exactly at midday with the astrolabe, found that we were on the fifteen and a half degree, which was the same as that of the islands of Guadeloupe.[11] To head toward the west, [he ordered] the sails changed. In this way, we passed four days on the same latitude for more than 100 leagues. At sunrise on the last of them, Saturday the 31st of August, we saw the land of an island called The Desired One, an appropriate title as it was what we most desired to see.[12] There was general joy and pleasure, with the giving of a thousand thanks to the Lord. The friars sung in a high voice the "*Te Deum laudamus*," and all joined in it.[13] All day, we were in sight of this land and another islet placed next to it called the Little Desired One, and in the afternoon, we arrived at another large one called Marie-Galante—in brief, the most pleasant view that one can imagine, even exceeding the gardens, landscapes, and fields of Flanders, Germany, and Italy.[14]

So fertile are the three uninhabited islands, and that of Marie-

Galante, that Indians of Guadeloupe come to grow maize and harvest some fruits, which was why, this day, a canoe with twelve Indians came to the ships carrying a white cloak as a sign of peace. The San Francisco de la Natividad was the first ship that the canoe met, the ship where the headman climbed aboard.[15] Then, the General ordered the Capitana of the fleet to launch a small boat, and with six oars on each side, it came very quickly to the canoe.

[The Indians had] all come nude, without anything to cover their shame, and painted with something like red ocher, which they use for making their idolatry and to protect themselves from the mosquitoes and from the sun for which reason they smear themselves very well with it. But it is certain that they use it more for ceremony than advantage. They were in the Capitana more than two hours, and said there were no sails of enemies in all these adjacent islands. They asked why there were no ships of ours in these islands for the last twenty-four moons (which thus, they call months and were very curious as to the reason). For which we satisfied them by the best tokens that we could provide them. We treated them well, giving them wine, which is what they most esteem and call water of Castile. They returned to the island Marie-Galante that afternoon for now it was close to evening, and we sent two small boats to obtain tortoises on the beach. We shortened the sails and waited offshore because due to the shallows and rocks, we could not go this night to Guadeloupe. We spent all this night, which was quite peaceful, looking at the fires of the island, the fishermen, and the Indians, and in this way we waited with much pleasure the good hopes of landing on the following day.

[Islands of Guadeloupe]

Chapter 2, Book 1:
How We Came Ashore on the Islands of Guadeloupe
and What Happened to Us There

As we had collected the people who had gone to fish by the island, before sunrise we made sail for Guadeloupe, going past some large peaks called the Friars and coming into view of some large mountain ranges that have the name Matalino because when Columbus discovered this land, he was in distress, the crews having decided that if they didn't see land in so many days, they were going to kill him. The time having been completed, they were getting ready to kill him that very day when this island appeared, and thus they called it by the name of Mataleno.[16]

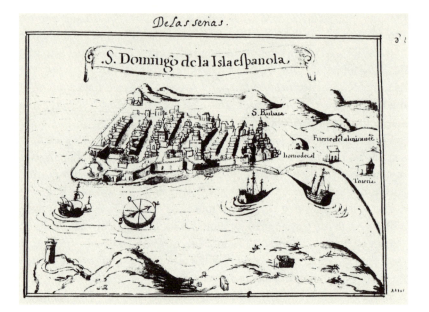

Figure 6. "A ship left us for the island of Santo Domingo"
(Vellerino de Villalobos 1984)

Figure 7. "We saw the land of the island called The Desired One"
(Vellerino de Villalobos 1984)

Figure 8. "In the afternoon, we arrived at another large one called Marie-Galante" (Vellerino de Villalobos 1984)

Figure 9. "Islands of Guadeloupe" (Vellerino de Villalobos 1984)

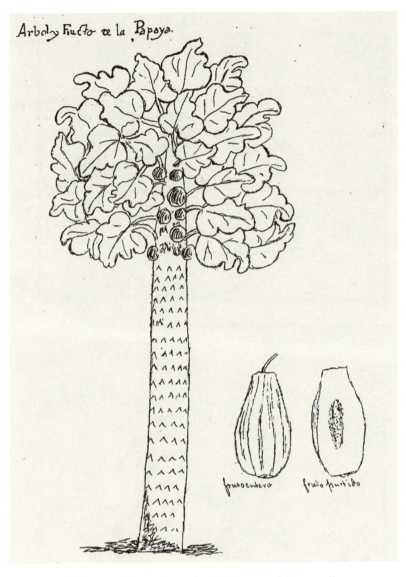

Figure 10. "In exchange for six I got . . . six papayas"
(Fuentes y Guzman 1933)

We arrived at noon to anchor between two ravines called Rio Grande and Rio Chico for one carries much less water than the other. They come down from some very high and pleasant forests in which one doesn't see a yard of land, it being so covered with innumerable fruit and fruitless wild trees.

Below were a large number of Indians in canoes. One of those, with fourteen people, or three women and eleven men, boarded our ship. None wore anything other than the down that grows naturally in the hidden parts, and they had none on the limbs nor arms and little in the way of a beard. Both men and women cut the hair short in the front, weaving it with feathers and [in the] behind [with] some large plants, very well combed and made into long braids. The unwed youths pierced the front of the nose and pulled a string through the hole, and the women [wore] a rope of red string around the belly to designate being maids, and those who aren't don't carry them. They have their head-men, which is whom they obey and obey absolutely. They brought all their bows and arrows, the points of a very strong burned wood that can go through a wooden board. They are so skillful in shooting that they kill many [birds] on the wing with them. Their canoe came well provided with different fruits, animals, and fish in exchange for knives, axes, beads, ribbons, and other ornaments, which are things of importance because they don't have gold or silver.

Thus, when they rowed their canoe to our ship, I met them and gifted them with hardtack and some snacks of Spain, and in return they gave me some very good ripe plantains, which is the best fruit that they have. I began to trade with some shiny butcher knives and yellow thread, which is what they love, and in exchange for six I got four bunches of more than one hundred plantains, six papayas, a sucking pig, and a handful of tobacco in a leaf, for which they didn't want any other thing. They brought sweet cane, hens and roosters—which they call male hens— tortoise, and spider crabs similar to the crabs of Spain, very tasty, and the ship became well provided, they leaving us well intoxicated and loaded with a thousand items given in exchange for what they brought us.

They asked us how many times will we sleep here, which is how they refer to the nights, and we indicated it with a finger. The headman, who was an old Indian—tall, lean, and frowning—said that they would bring more refreshments with the sun. At that they went, and we remained astonished to see people like this on this island without knowledge of the faith, such handsome men, such good faces, so strong and lusty, content with this poverty, satisfied not to learn more. They are the color of cooked quinces, with good features, and no bad understanding, no one being able to deceive them. The action of one of them astonished us. Someone offered him an ax for a tortoise, and he took it and examined it carefully, and then took out of a little reed box a small knife and made a great scratch that was very clear, and he thus knew it wasn't of steel and didn't want it nor [would he] give anything for it.

Figure 11. "The first of our people to land was a group of guards
from the Royal Capitana and the other three ships of war";
surrender of Dutch garrison on San Martin Island to
Spanish naval forces, 1633
(seventeenth-century painting courtesy of Museo Naval, Madrid)

The first of our people to land was a group of guards from the Royal
Capitana and the other three ships of war, and at the mouth of the river
they made their barracks arranged in squads because at times these
Indians had attacked. Many people died from arrows before they had a
chance to get freshwater. In 1573, the first time they came to this land,
they killed six friars of Saint Dominic who entered the land by following
the river upstream, as the forest is so impregnable and thick. They [the
Indians] used some narrow paths known only to the inhabitants of the
jungle.

We also had great difficulty with the ship Santiago, perhaps the largest
of the fleet at 1,100 tons, which became stranded on land through the
carelessness of the sailors who didn't properly set the anchors on the
bottom when the pilot ordered it. The Lord calmed the wind that hour
for if he didn't, it would have been broken into pieces, and its value was
more than 3,000 ducats. More, the Lord showed here his power in his
gentle way since for more than six hours, not causing any damage or
losing a jar, the boats of the other ships came alongside and unloaded
the 1,500 pottery jars filled with wine. That, and the rising of the tide a
little, was enough to set it free; a thing considered a miracle for it so
obviously was at risk.

So pleased was everyone in the ship escaping from danger that all celebrated in a festival with trumpets, bugles, hornpipes, and other warlike instruments every time the boats returned to their ships. The soldiers turned to their needs, drying their shirts and washing their clothing, and thus with more than a thousand persons washing and hanging, turning this beach into a snow-covered mountain range.

It happened to be that our ship was on the edge of the mouth of the Rio Grande, and therefore we had more time than others. To make good use of it and to give an account of these trees, I went ashore with another friend at six in the afternoon. Thus, we came to land to give our un-limited thanks to our Lord, whose mercy brought us here without hav-ing brought any storm or bad day, and collected the clouds that gathered above our tents. They irrigate so well that no day passes without receiv-ing the benefit of his powerful hand, and are the fathers of the plants that never lacks them on the accustomed hour, for which reason these hills know neither winter nor summer but are always a fine green color.

We went a good distance upriver to drink water not been made filthy by washing or soap, seeing a thousand different trees and plants, they so high and abundant that there hardly was room for the sun, for they greedily search the ground making a cover as if it was a well-woven carpet. Very much enjoying it, we picked some fruits, which not being known to us, we did not dare to taste. Nor did we see anything like those of our Spain. We came across some shrubs with some chestnuts as large as those that they fill with tobacco. We opened some, and they had very white, bitter meat that one could not eat. Therefore, we decided not to tire ourselves more in search of things that we don't know if they are good or bad, as we can't bring what we don't know back to the ships. We sat down on some rocks in the middle of the river and had a good cold lunch of extremely good sweets from Spain, and we drank of this water, which was very good, sweet, and cold.

Having done, we returned quite happy to the mouth of the river and ocean beach, seeing the many ladies who with bravery had landed this hour to enjoy the fresh air and bath themselves. I was certain as to how to respond to the result of my curiosity and my ardent desire to amuse myself. I saw then that I would need the eloquence of a Greek Demos-thenes for an enterprise so difficult, but I want (even with the risk of Icarus and piteous ruin) to trust in the word which fortune has given to those who have passed through it and describe this shady valley that, if the accounts of antiquity were not known to be fables, one would believe was the Elysium Fields, such was the pleasure, such was the happiness that all had.[17] Finally after so long a trip, seeing by the water a circle of ladies, it was their beauty as a reminder of Spain that touched us. Without difficulty, they removed water from the abundant river that, hurling itself over cobblestones, meanders among a thousand tiny flowers. There they ate lunch, eating with such pleasure stews, even those lacking the sauces and relishes that induce gluttony. There we saw those who care for holy cleanness washing their clothes with such dexterity that it seems it is their profession, rather than out of need or for their entertainment. These things continued until midnight, when we returned to the ship.

In the morning, other canoes returned much more provided than those of the day before, and I gave some Indians two knives for a good box and twelve arrows with their quiver. The owner of the ship bought all the provisions that came in their canoe, on which they left, and the Capitana and Almiranta of the fleet, having weighed both anchors, advised us to set sail.

[Guadeloupe to Trujillo]

Chapter 3, Book 1:
From Leaving the Islands of Guadeloupe and Arriving in
the Gulf, and What Happened until We Arrived at Trujillo

It was noon, Monday, when we made sail, and since two ships that delayed in leaving couldn't go that afternoon for lack of wind, it was necessary to wait for the morning breeze from the land. Therefore, we were stuck in the ocean waiting for them to leave the port. That afternoon, with the permission of the General and making the usual salute to the fleet, three other ships separated from us, one for Cartagena, the other for Puerto Rico, and another for the island of Santo Domingo.

The next day the two ships left in search of us, which since we had moved, they didn't find us until it began to get dark. When they were close to us, a good wind began to blow from the stern. It was so favorable that the following Friday, the 6th of September, we saw the land of Puerto Rico and continued to see it for more than thirty leagues. Saturday in the morning, we saw the land of the island of Santo Domingo, which has more than 250 leagues. This island stayed in sight until the following Wednesday. We passed also in view of others called la Beata and Altovela, and some high mountain ranges called Doña María in the Cabo de Tiburón.[18]

Thursday [September 12], we arrived in sight of the land of Jamaica, where at dusk we met a frigate sent by the Governor of the island;

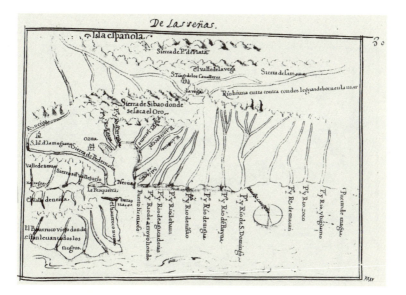

Figure 12. "Saturday in the morning, we saw the land of the island
of Santo Domingo, which has more than 250 leagues"
(Vellerino de Villalobos 1984)

because we arrived late, no news of the dispatches for our General
reached us that night. The next morning, a cannon fired by the Capitana summoned the officers for council. Each one launching their boat
into the water, the captains and masters came from all the ships. When
they were all together in the Capitana, he [the General] opened the
dispatch and read the letter of the Governor. The governor informed
them that there were eighty French or English sails on the coast of
Havana. So that they could pick a route that would not bring them into
contact with their enemies, they all voted and gave their opinions, and
most said that they should check the Isle of Pines and confer again on
Cozumel or Cape Catoche.[19] Thus, they agreed that the ships of war
going to the province of Honduras and Havana should accompany the
fleet until the next conference.

The commander of the Honduras ships (Lucas de Rojas, a native of
Seville) was very much against this. Normally, we separated here from
the other ships, and inside six days we could be at our destination in the
port of Trujillo. He argued long and begged that the orders be changed,
but in no way were they allowed to leave the fleet before arriving at the
Cape [Catoche]. Being warned that if they didn't stay with the fleet they
would be considered traitors to the king and be killed, they all returned

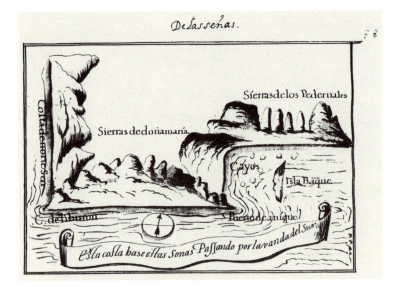

Figure 13. "We passed . . . some high mountain ranges called
Doña María in the Cabo de Tiburón"
(Vellerino de Villalobos 1984)

to their ships and each followed the required route of the fleet. The
following Saturday appeared Cape Perea in route to the Cayman Islands, to the complete disgust of those of us who were going to Honduras. We sent new petitions to the General, but the only response was a
repetition of the orders. The same happened to the ship supposed to go
to Havana.

We continued with good wind until Tuesday, not seeing the Caymans,
which was a very bad sign, and that day in the evening we had a storm,
which if it had lasted longer, it is very possible that we would have been
lost because neither the sailors nor the pilots knew where we were. In
this manner, we continued blindly for astonishingly more than three
hundred fathoms without being able to take soundings until Tuesday,
the 23rd of September, when we found ourselves in the morning in
twenty fathoms of water without having seen either the Isle of Pines, the
western end of Cuba, or Catoche, all of which was rather strange. The
pilots didn't know how we could have gone two hundred fathoms and
never found bottom.

From there, at four in the morning as we were taking soundings, the
winds let up and the General (Miguel Echazarreta, a gentleman of the
habit of Santiago) ordered us to immediately make our departure.[20]

Enjoying a small refreshing breeze, we immediately followed these orders. Firing three pieces of artillery and raising [sail] to the topmast, our own Almiranta changed course and turned back to go on our voyage. We continued all night, losing from view the fleet, which was [then] very close to Campeche.

By morning the next day, the wind had calmed down, and all of us went fishing for pollocks, of which we caught an enormous number, and it took five days to leave the Gulf of Mexico because there was little wind; moreover, after leaving it, so quiet was it that in fifteen days we didn't have two hours of wind. The shortage of food and drink greatly distressed the people because there was no more than a pint of water per person, and it was so hot that it was hardly sufficient to allow one to swallow one's biscuit. In more than ten days, for lack of water, we cooked nothing. All that was eaten was a soup made with vinegar and ocean water. Because the ration was not more than a pint, it was drunk without trying to clean our dirty and smelly selves.

Each day we celebrated three masses, which were a great comfort in this situation, and Sunday, the 6th of October, made a procession in the waist of the ship, making great pleading and prayers to the Lord to save us with wind from our great distress, for we didn't [have] in the entire ship fifty jars of water and we were more than three hundred persons needing to drink it.[21] They made customary and specific promises, each one believing oneself to be the author of this great misfortune and the cause of the Lord's punishment of the others.

Some begged for a little dirty water from some pitch-filled ponds on the deck of the ship. Those were very fortunate who could satisfy their thirst without noticing the filth in these ponds. The weather freshened this day, and Monday we had heavy showers, causing great relief, seeing how for twelve hours we were quite content and happy thanks to the wind and showers, but then it calmed again.

The following Tuesday we had a heavy shower, the Lord leaving the wind by the stern all this day until midnight, when it moderated. Continuing the next day, by twelve we had gone twenty leagues. At that point, measuring the sun with an astrolabe, we discovered it had gone down by a degree or a little more. This day, Wednesday, we made a devout procession after celebrating two masses and administering communion to all in the ship. Finally, a learned monk and professor in holy theology called Friar Rodrigo de Urosa took the pulpit, and all cried as he made a speech so holy and prudent that his points moved heaven to compassion, it being so well reasoned that it would have even affected bronze. Within an hour came from the stern a small breeze from the north so violent that in a very short time we traveled more than six leagues. Later, the wind renewed for two hours. We lost it because shortly before sunset we saw land by the prow. If we had come in the night, we would have gone into it.

The sailors and pilots climbed to the main topsail and quarreled over what land was it, for no one knew it. Some said it was the Rio de Lagartos, others Cape San Anton, and others that it was an island where they lost some galleons, and with these mixed opinions the pilot ordered the ship south and we went the length of this unknown land, not knowing its reefs and shallows.[22]

We continued until sunrise by this route, and all the next day we had a very quiet sea. In great happiness, forgetting all past work, that Friday we saw the looked for and desired land. It would be the twelve o'clock of midday when, after sailing from sunrise, the lookout called out, "Land! Land!"—a shout that filled us with joy and infinite pleasure. At once, our pilot climbed the mast and recognized two islands called La Guanaja and La Guayaba that were in sight of the port of Trujillo, and this confirmed our pleasure as they were messengers of good news.

We continued the rest of the day with all the sails, and at sunset took down the largest sail, foresail, and mizzen, leaving up only the topsail and spritsail, and thus we were stationary all night. Saturday, at sunrise, we ran into a strong sea wind that in a short time took us close to the land and we went through the two said islands to the great pleasure of all.

Concluding the passage in sight of the land of Trujillo, the pilots didn't know the port. They had neither been told of it nor had they ever been in it. When they checked the coast, they were more than two leagues to the windward of it. The ship tackled the other way to see if we could make some headway, but the work was useless because even going windward all this night and struggling against the wind, in the morning we found ourselves more than six leagues from Punta de Castilla, which is the name of the mouth of the port. There came this hour a little land breeze that pushed us out more to the sea, and in the afternoon we improved our position so that on sundown we could anchor close to the point. We discharged two pieces to inform the city that we were friends and needed help. They answered with one, and we cast anchor a league from the promontory for it was very small, and the pilots believed that we were going away from it and were windward of it.

On sunrise, we discovered the land so near us that it was impossible to use this wind for it was blowing the other way and the current ran rapidly. This caused us great annoyance, especially since if the wind changed or increased, we would go toward the Jicaques, who are those

Carib Indians that eat people.[23] But the Lord didn't abandon his creatures, and a rainstorm that came from the north saved us. In danger of drowning, and using the sounding line, we weighed anchor with it at ten in the morning. In less than two hours, with great work from all for the storm was very great and with all of us being soaked, we entered the desired port. With this work, we cast anchor at twelve and gave a thousand thanks to the Lord for his mercy in changing the [direction of the] winds, which at this time continue here two and three months. Those on the Almiranta had even more work than us since their ship was much smaller, and thus could not carry enough sail, and it took three more days [until they] made port. With these scares and tribulations we cast anchor, as I had said that day, Monday, the 14th of October.[24]

[In Central America]

Chapter 4, Book 1:
Of What Happened to Us on Arriving in Trujillo

The Captain, having cast anchor, allowed us to land with the Governor of this province. Captain Francisco de Vía Montán y Santander, a knight of Santiago and a great soldier with many talents, had come with us from Spain. The following day, I disembarked with all my retinue and we arrived on land, which is three leagues from the anchorage of the ships. We walked on the ground with great pleasure, very much wishing to finish with our sailing and not wanting to reembark for another port sixty leagues from here, near the province where I was going to be governor. This was the same destination of all the cloth going to the province of Guatemala. We lodged in one of the better houses of the place, which had no more than two rooms and was covered with leaves similar to palm that served as roofing.

This is a city and port of 150 households. In it, the people who are rich and important are mostly Vizcayan and Andalucian. Perhaps all the women are American born with a pale, sickly color and a pleasant manner. Entirely fenced and fortified, the city has a strong point of seventeen pieces of artillery, some small cannon, and a good armory.[25] Although there are few households, when it is necessary, help comes from the interior.

Indians of the five nearby [bay] Islands come to serve in the city and each of them get paid four reals per week for this. They are well-made Indians, strong, Spanish speaking, and well dressed. They have their rulers to whom they owe allegiance.

There are infinite numbers of cattle, one resident of the city, Mateo Ochoa, owning so many that he can't pay an exact tithe because in more than thirty leagues of savannas, which is what they call the plains without brush, there is no pasture for livestock other than his, no other ranches being near them. Many times, those going to Spain buy the livestock for eight reals per head, giving with them more than a hundred slaves at the same price. Supporting themselves with this livestock are enemy Indians who live in these immense areas, their lands beginning in some highlands visible from the city, and six leagues from it. This mountain range continues until Cartagena, more than 300 leagues of mainland filled with infidels and gentiles.

Beginning with the unloading of the frigates, which took more than eight days without counting the cost to the commander—that being no less than triple the cost of Spain—all swore to return to the ships and pay in goods of the land, which were indigo, hides, sarsaparilla, agave, cochineal, and other things of this type, since there were few coins [among the inhabitants]. They unloaded a great amount of cloth and wines, selling more than 100,000 pesos not counting the other items consigned to the persons of this city.

The Governor, whose predecessor awaited him, assumed office on landing the next day, and on the following Sunday, made a great party in honor of the Holy Sacrament in the principal church, whose avocation is Saint Mary. It had a very solemn procession and an elegant sermon by that Father Professor Friar Rodrigo de Urosa whom we had referred to previously. All of this was in honor of our arrival and to give thanks to the Lord.

The benefice of this church is the best in many surrounding leagues, and this I can't pass over in silence. It receives an income of 6,000 tostons and supports with 2,000 the benefice of two assistants, the holder then enjoying with much ease the remaining 4,000. The holder was Dr. Diego de Cañabate, a resident of Villanueva de la Jara in La Mancha, who was also vicar and inspector of the province.

The following Sunday, we invited the Governor to dinner to bring together the residents of the city and the vicar, who were on bad terms and suing each other. When everyone important was there, a quarrel began between the two heads [of the military] in the city—that is, between the Governor and the Commander of the ships, Lucas de Rojas. It is certain that if they had disembarked even half of their soldiers, the disturbance would not have ended so quickly. Therefore, after they badly treated the Commander, the Governor joined his people and went with them to the fortress, where he ordered them to man the artillery.

The captain of the people, Sancho Ruiz de Ayala y Villela, asked about the gateways and placed guards in them so that the Commander could not land people from the ships.

This night, the Governor made an important and good decision supported by a council of important people then in the city, these being the four provincial governors (of San Salvador, Nicoya, and Tegucigalpa, plus myself), two dignified monks (Master Friar Pedro de Montenegro, the new vicar of the monks, and Friar Jacinto Quartero, lawyer for their province), and the officials of the city. Unanimously, they voted that the Commander should go to his ships to defend them from the enemies who could come looking for the port; for the anchorage being three leagues away, they could not receive help from the city or fortress. To avoid great disturbances between the residents of the city and the soldiers, they should stay in their ships, for the principal intent of His Majesty in sending them was the defense of shipping and not those on land. Thus, that night, the Governor sent an order to the Commander that he and his people on land should go to their ships. He and ten persons that morning went extremely upset to the ships.

The following Monday at ten in the morning he set sail, for it appeared to be good weather for it, and seeing them going past Punta de Castilla, we went in a frigate to catch up with the ships, but at four in the afternoon the wind diminished and forced us to return to shelter in port. All night, we waited in the frigate with the monks for a favorable wind to go to the ships. It remained so gusty and contrary that no one slept, and at moments, we feared the great wind would cause the anchors to drag and we would wind up on the coast. We passed the entire night worrying, and on sunrise, went ashore. The Commander of the ships made his own arrangements now that the weather was so contrary. He landed with the captain of his Almiranta, Don Gabriel de Santiago, a competent and prudent gentleman and great soldier, and also a native of Valladolid. Without permission to enter the city, he waited outside it. Don Gabriel asked for it from the Governor, giving as a reason the sickness and illness of the Commander, who wanted to enter only to recover from them. Allowed to enter with no more than two servants and no soldiers, he could live only near the gateway of the city.

Remaining in this manner on land for two days, the Commander then returned to his ships to wait for a change in the weather, and I went with all my entourage because I didn't want to spend another night like that in the frigate or remain on land. Also, because one couldn't buy wheat bread or even *cazabe,* which is the basic food, since there wasn't any.[26] If someone had some, it was bad and so bitter that one couldn't eat it because it is of roots. Lodging with a roof of straw cost a peso per day, and everything was expensive. Only meat was cheap because one real would buy eight pounds of very good cow, and for sixteen a calf and a kind of sheep. The poultry cost a real and were not good.

We had our baggage on the ship, without it moving, for fifteen days. We spent most of the time on land for it wasn't subject to the night air, humidity of the port, and its toads and poisonous insects, who when they bit a person, he died. The soldiers spent their time in fishing, reading, games, and other pleasurable things. One of them invited me to go in a canoe, with his other friends, to the forest near the ships. We entered it, although with difficulty because of the thickness so filled with fruit trees, so cool from the water, so pleasant from the green herbs, and so perfumed from the many flowers, which in equal measure and at the same time satisfied all five senses. We wandered over a large area, admiring the fertility of these impregnable forests. My companions cut two very large palms, from which they removed buds as high as a man, like a column of alabaster, as tender and tasty as those of Spain. We came across a thousand different fruits, but none had the color or the taste of those of Spain.

We returned to the ships. On the next day, the 27th of November, we had such a furious storm that, being so close to death, we changed our joy for weeping, the games for sorrows, the amusements for sermons and strong pledges. The wind forced us to do so because although the ship was well moored with four anchors, it treated it as if it were a kitchen tub, now kissing the sky with the top of the mainmast on magnificent mountains formed not of clear but of foamy water, now raking the sands of the depths with the keel. We knew of no other remedy than to have prepared a piece of wood or plank to cling to if the ship ran aground. But the Lord was satisfied that we need not undergo such great pain, and although this wind lasted three days, nothing unfortunate happened and it mitigated a little, but we didn't go ashore until the morning of Saturday, the day of the blessed Saint Andrew. Still, we had some fear because of the silent surge of the sea begun as a result of the storm that formed at times great turrets of water and, finally, because of the undertow against which we landed. Here we stayed afloat with difficulty, and [landed] the women on the shoulders of four men, although even then they could not avoid getting wet.

With all this we were very happy to be on land and proposed not to return to the ship so quickly, but we could not keep this resolve since the following day at dawn, we embarked because the weather had improved and appeared to be appropriate for our voyage. We went to the ship, where the Commander called a council. Thus, the pilots spoke of the coast to those who came in our ships to obtain their vote on if we should weigh anchor and go with a small northwest wind. They decided to wait all day, and as it blew until midnight, we didn't raise the sail. The captain of the Almiranta and the Commander agreed with them, and with this agreement we waited, and the wind abated all night and next day blew very well, more than the day before the meeting [so that] on leaving the port, we would not need to lie in waiting for it.

We met Wednesday, the 4th of December. The weather was so favorable that in the same hour we raised the anchors. In twenty-four hours, we went forty leagues to the Puerto de Caballos. The next day was calm. In the evening it renewed, and we went twenty leagues to the shallows between La Cruz and Tierra Firme, a very dangerous locality for in places it was no more than four leagues wide. We went with great risk because of the danger of a contrary wind in this passage. If the breeze calmed, the water currents could force us on the coast. In this manner, we sailed all night without the pilots taking their eyes from the [compass] needle and, at dawn, found ourselves in front of the point of Manabique. Here, because of the depth of this bay, there was no risk. The rising wind filled all our sails, thereby making a daylight entrance necessary. There were two currents with dangerous sand that we passed with great pleasure, and filling our prayers, we anchored in the sought-for port of Santo Tomás de Castilla.

Chapter 5, Book 1:
Of What Happened to Us in the Port of Santo Tomás
de Castilla until Coming to Xocolo and the
Description of This Port

The next morning, the Spanish governor of the port and the vicar (who was a Dominican) would come to the flagship in a canoe. They received us very well for so desired and so lacking are the products of our Spain, especially the wine, that they lack it for celebrating [mass]. Many days, there can't be any mass for lack of it. They ordered us to disembark and, at the same time, fired three pieces of artillery toward the city, where they responded with other pieces. We stayed at the house of the Spanish governor for our jurisdictions would be next to each other.

They entertained us as much as possible in a city that only has the name [of one] for in all there were no more than eight to ten badly built huts of reeds, on a humid pestilential site next to a fort. To leave a description for the interested reader, I must note one admirable thing,

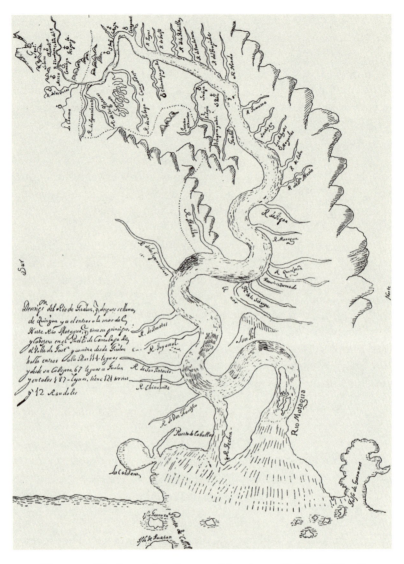

Figure 14. "In the good anchorage of the place called La Caldera"
(Fuentes y Guzman 1933)

this being some piers supporting the church (which also was of reeds) that had sprouts of more than a yard, as did the foot of the benches of the table where the friars ate. Because the site is low, surrounded by enormous forests, and filled with swamps, wherever one drove in a stick, by the fourth day it had sprouted.

The fort is there to protect the ships in the good anchorage of the place called La Caldera. There is an impregnable headland above the settlement that has seven large pieces [of artillery], three culverins, and two swivel guns, with which they command the headland and make it easy to resist any enemy attack.[27] His Majesty made this port a city with the aim of populating it, thus giving great prestige to the settlers of it, but more was not possible. Because of the reasons cited above, many people are very sickly and die here.

The vicarage, which is under the jurisdiction of the Bishop of Comayagua, could not support the priests sent by him, nor the Mercedarian friars, who also were here and abandoned it. The only supporters of the faith who are in this province more than any other are the friars of Saint Dominic, placing it on its feet, and they have great expenses from their farms but will not leave because there are towns of Indians who lack their assistance, lack the faith—to which they have little allegiance—requiring each day new efforts, and if they left they would lose what it has cost them.

The following day, a Sunday in which the church celebrates the Conception of our Lady, we found in the morning ready the preparations for the great holiday filled with plays, parties, dances, and games. When at eight in the morning the two captains with all their people, who totaled more than 200 men, disembarked, we converted [to peaceful use] the war instruments like drums, fifes, and reports of firearms, as well as the guns like the muskets and harquebuses; and besides the rich and expensive uniforms, they put on strong breastplates and glittering weapons. They were as skillful in the military art as if they had themselves invented it, and they were visible from above by their arms as well as by their gallant and elegant manner. Assembling both companies in columns of five, shooting intermittently their harquebuses and muskets toward the church, and on arriving at the entrance to the small plaza igniting the fireworks and shooting off the guns, they made a noise fit to cause the heavens to fall.[28] This done three times, the troops then went to their barracks.

They held mass and, on its conclusion, the Spanish governor went to dinner with the two captains, and thus we ate together this day and, although we give many presents, we missed bread for there was nothing other than some cakes of hot maize that were most healthy and prepared on ceramic griddles, yet so thin that it would take twelve for the average person to be equivalent to an egg omelet (of which there were none).[29] They were [nonetheless] very tasty, and we did not find them strange.

In view of the bad climate of the site, I gave orders to leave it, and the Spanish governor furnished a large canoe and four Indian rowers to take me to Xocolo, which was thirteen leagues from here, the first place of my jurisdiction.[30] The Indians put up a roof of palm leaves and it remained as an awning. They loaded all our cloth and we left at dusk. We said good-bye to all our friends and companions, including [the] captain of the infantry and various friars. They accompanied us to the dock, where they gave us a warm embrace as friendship requires, for after so a long voyage [together] they now felt like relatives. We entered the canoe. The Indians rowed with such great force that in less than four hours we arrived at the mouth of the river, which is four leagues from the port. Tying the canoe to some branches, we spent there the entire night, and on rising continued our voyage.

As a sign of luck, we met in the mouth of the river three canoes and, in them, two friars of Saint Dominic, one called Friar Juan Ochoa, vicar of Amatique and other towns of Indians, and the other Friar Antonio del Castillo, a Creole and prior of the Dominican convent of Cobán, capital of my jurisdiction. We rested a long time, made the customary courtesies, and exchanged presents, giving them a bottle of wine for we did not carry any other thing, nor in this moment could we give anything else of such value. Imitating the Lord in payment, they filled our canoe with good preserved foods, chickens, cheese, and other things.

We had good luck with such a good meeting since it foretold good relations with the church. With a loving good-bye they continued on their way, which was to the port to obtain supplies for their convent and carry some gifts for the friars who came from Spain. I, speaking with the said superior, agreed to wait for them in Xocolo, where in three or four days they would return so that we could travel together.[31]

I did not expect the pleasure I enjoyed all morning going upstream, which was the most pleasant and delightful that men could imagine. In the three leagues to the lake, there was continuous shade and crystalline waters fenced in on both sides by two cliffs so lofty that I could hardly believe my eyes. In this manner does nature surpass art, for humans could not equal these works.

We arrived at midday at the Golfete, which is three leagues long, and with a favorable wind using the sail, in less than two hours we left astern two friends on a small beach who, having seen us off, took a small canoe to bring them to their frigate.[32]

Two servants and three or four chests came with us, making it extremely crowded on the badly loaded canoe, for it carried much of value on the edges. This small vessel made from the best cedar, with a length of twenty-five cubits and a width of eight, was no larger than can be made from a tree.[33] On this occasion, it carried more than fourteen chests, some jars of wine, and fifteen persons. All of this could have caused us some injury for it had rained the night before and the Indians were careless in bailing it. There was some danger as we saw water three or four times flowing into the vessel. People made promises and offered prayers to our Lord that it would not happen in the two leagues to Xocolo of freshwater lake what didn't happen to us in two thousand of wild ocean. The Indians, their efforts strengthened by the gifts made them and restored at the oars, rowed with such fine vigor that in less than two hours, we unexpectedly arrived at Xocolo.

Then, when those of the town learned that their governor was on the beach, they rang the bells and lit festive lights, running to the wharf with torches of resinous wood, which is the wax that they use there. We disembarked, kissing a thousand times the ground and embracing it, not yet believing we were on it, because in all our sailing we didn't have the frights and surprises that we had that afternoon. They carried us to the houses of the city council, and although they were very bad, they seemed to us sumptuous palaces for we knew our bed was planted on firm ground. The Mayor came, as did the city council, to bring us some gifts and give us welcome. It certainly greatly saddened us to see the poverty of these people, whose usual dress was always barefooted, with cotton shorts and shirt on which was a piece of white cloth, which they call an *ayate,* in place of a cape, with a string on the left shoulder like those of the Jews.[34] The very powerful and rich brought hats, although they never wore them in the presence of the Governor, nor did they bring more than what we mentioned. We were in this town three days until the arrival of the prior of Cobán, and then on his arrival, continued our voyage as we will give in the chapter that follows.

Chapter 6, Book 1:
Of the Voyage Made to Polochic, of the Arrival There, and What Happened up to Assuming Office in Cobán

New palm leaf thatch replaced the somewhat maltreated old one as an awning for our canoe, and at eight in the morning of a Wednesday, we and the superior of the convent of Cobán who had embarked in a somewhat smaller boat began rowing through the placid waters. We crossed three leagues of the bay for, although not following the land, it saved us three leagues. The waters were similar to a vat of oil, and they guaranteed us their peacefulness and tranquillity. Afterward, we repented since in an instant a tempest rose that required us to cut the sail with a slash, for there was no time to loosen or lower them. It was great luck and done on my orders because otherwise there is no doubt that we would have capsized and drowned. The boat put us in great danger. It moved as if it was a nutshell on the foaming waters, now rising to heaven, now [falling] to the depths. We lost sight of the smaller boat, and this caused us great grief for we believed that they had sunk. They would have if they hadn't taken greater care than us and took shelter on land.

At nightfall the wind calmed, and we went to a tree-shaded beach where we met and landed, each one telling what had happened and the fright that they had undergone. All night we moored by the land, and the following day returned to sailing, crossing five leagues of the lake. There being a small, fresh breeze, we raised the sail and helped the rowers. Raising our spirits and lightening our hearts, in less than three hours, we entered the less dangerous mouth of the river.

In three days, we went upstream twelve leagues until, on reaching a wharf, we could go no farther by water. Certainly, the beauty and tranquillity of the waters, the elegance and abundance of the trees, the abundance of fish, the differences and abundance of the birds and animals of the forests, through which run the crystalline waters, diverted and entertained, thus raising [our spirits] from our recent difficulties. We arrived at the wharf, and now as we had so often looked forward to, landed for the last time. The monk, helping us all, took a cross and sung the "*Te Deum laudamus.*"

We were there this night, a league from a town, and had many presents that the punctuality of my predecessor had provided, knowing already that we were coming. I had a peaceful night. It is not possible to indicate the pleasure that we all had, having now concluded so long and troublesome a journey, which in the past took less than fifty days, but for us lasted more than one hundred and forty.

The next day arrived the city officials of Polochic, which has up to thirty, bringing mules, horses, and Indian burden bearers to carry the clothing. We were quite happy because in more than 2,000 leagues we had not traveled by land. We found the houses well adorned and there were the usual triumphal arches.[35] We dismounted and went first to the church, being pleased that the parish priest (who was the same that came with us) prepared it so well. We were in this town four days, resting and obtaining the necessary supplies for our trip.

We left better provided than we came, and being Doña María, my wife, was somewhat indisposed, they carried her in a chair on the shoulders of Indians. But they could not continue in this way for the road was bad. I gave orders to have her carried in a hammock on the shoulders of the Indians, and with which it was as if she were lying in her own bed because these hammocks are a form of bed.

We had much pleasure and gratification. In all the towns, they received us with trumpets and clarinets. We had triumphal arches, dances, and entertainment. They did everything to amuse us and not remind us of the miseries of these lands, because they are, for lack of gold and silver, the most miserable in the Indies. Although they say they had some mines, the monks always made the natives hide them for their preservation, since many died in mining. It is why none can be seen. The laziness of the Indians, and because there are few rich among them, makes the land so miserable.

They say that there are Indians who walk around barefooted, men as well as women. For them, even among the most rich and important, all their finery and expensive clothing consist of a blouse and some underpetticoat without a shirt or other clothing. The women have only a piece of colored cotton cloth to put on their head for entering the church, and in leaving restore its fold so it can serve some other use.

In one of the towns that we came to, called San Pablo de Tamahú, on the second day of Christmas, we had news of some Indians of the Manché, of those now baptized who had rose and apostatized in the year 1628. Their neighbors, called Lasa [Ah Itza], burned five Indian towns, killed four Indians and the father who administered them, and burned the houses because they returned to the faith, and were returning to their towns and were in them. This gave me great concern and I sent a request to my predecessor that he frankly give me an account of the truth of this matter.

At this time, certain news had come that the father had not died but that all the others had, and that if the friar had not hidden with some Indians of the town in some canyons, he would also have died. Being in a reed house, when he heard the noise and clamors with which they entered town, he broke open a wall. They fled for the forest, where they stayed until the next morning, as the traitors had left, returning to see the damage made to the town and its inhabitants.

All this the Governor, my predecessor, wrote to me, and on hearing of my arrival in the province, notified [in] Guatemala the President of the Royal Tribunal, Don Diego de Acuña, knight of Alcántara, commander of Hornos, and a member of the council of war of His Majesty, Governor, and Captain General of all the district of the Tribunal. My predecessor told me that he was glad of my arrival and not certain of the death of the monk; that he would prepare that day what I requested; and that he was going to give an account of what happened in this province and the requirements for its preservation.

I came to Cobán by way of some good towns, some with 300 and 400 tributary households. Coming to the city of Cobán, which has more than 400 tributaries, it pleased me to see a good town for Indians, a splendid monastery, and a sumptuous church big enough for 2,000 persons to hear mass in, whose foundation we will discuss in its appropriate place.

We gave a thousand thanks to the Lord on seeing the help and devotion given to the divine cult by the natives, and how well indoctrinated they had been by the monks of Saint Dominic—whose convent it was—who with enormous work and personal attendance, taught and catechized every day, filling the duties of priests of the souls according to the order they had from His Majesty, as we will discuss further on, and with the permission and order of their General. They had kept these Indians so firm in the faith and so constant that never since the beginnings of preaching of the Holy Gospel have they rebelled. Only [in] one group in this city, called San Marcos, did they martyr two monks of Saint Dominic on their lands, which are very close to those of the Lacandon. Even they said there were those who helped them. As we noted previously, those of this province are good Christians, and punctual in obedience to the Governor and the monks who administer it.

4

BORDERLANDS:

MARTIN TOVILLA, 1635

When Tovilla was named governor, it was not merely of the Verapaz and Manché but what was in those days the "land of Sacapulas." His account of their inspection allows us to look at the Manché from another direction: its southwest frontier. Viana described the Verapaz highlands and Salazar the Manché lowlands; now, Tovilla tells us of the Quiche frontier and the lands at the headwaters of the Usumacintla.

In doing so, he explains how the Spaniards administered their lands using a system in which whippings were a common punishment and the natives were expected to keep careful records of all fiscal transactions. Tovilla gives the specialities or oddities of the towns. We learn, among other things, about the hunting of deer, salt made from dirt, and how wheat came to bring prosperity to an Indian community.

Life was not merely a matter of rules and work. Festivities also had their place in the recollections of Tovilla. A form of pre-Hispanic soccer was still being played with a rubber ball in the ruins of Utatlan. Tovilla describes the jousts in the squares of the capital of Spanish Central America and the glitter of fake jewels in a reenactment of the Spanish conquest. His comments on pagan rituals and deities, trade routes, political alliances, and wars among the Indians beyond the Spanish frontier provide a different, nonecclesiastical viewpoint—that of a professional soldier and secular administrator very much concerned with the things of this world, not just preparations for the next.

Chapter 22, Book 1:
Of the Laws Used Today for the Governing of These
Indians of the Province of Verapaz

The first judge who came to inspect this province was Doctor Sedeño and after [him] Doctor Argüero. Then, entrusted and sent to inspect it by Jerónimo Alfonso de Prada was Licenciate Juan Maldonado de Paz. Having spoken with the headman in each of the towns, he [Maldonado de Paz] made these laws to govern the natives of this province.

The Licenciate Juan Maldonado de Paz, of the council of His Majesty and his judge of the royal tribunal of Guatemala, inspector general of these provinces of Soconusco, Zapotitlán, and Verapaz, orders the mayor and city council of Cobán in the province of Verapaz, and the inhabitants of the town, to keep the following laws:

1. First, since His Majesty is the patron of all the churches, monasteries, and hermitages of the Indies, and as such his royal arms ought to be in the best and most preeminent place, I order that in the churches and hermitages of the town and others of this province they be painted and placed at the right side of the entranceway and main altar, and removed from wherever it was, the cost to be paid by the community.

2. So that the Indians of this city and the others of the province know what belongs to our holy faith concerning Christian doctrine, I order and require that in the churches of the town, every Sunday and holiday, the Indians always go to the church of the town with their women and children a half hour before the saying of mass, so that the master sexton can instruct them in their mother language in the Christian doctrine.[1] So that the devotion of the Holy Sacrament and Conception of the Virgin our Lady go forward, they should teach the doctrine before beginning and after ending [the service], saying, and the others with him, in their language: "Praise be the Holy Sacrament from the altar" and "Virgin Mary our Lady conceived without original sin"; the penalty being that Indian men or women who fail to come, if not being legitimately employed, will have their feet placed in the stocks for three hours the first time, and for the second time be left for six hours. On the third time, the head [shall be left] three hours [in the stocks], and then the person whipped in public by the justices of the town, the same punishment being given to others when many Indian inhabitants and families don't know Christian doctrine.

3. So many boys from their infancy know the Christian doctrine, I order that all the Indians send their sons each day so that the master sexton of it can teach for an hour in the afternoon the doctrine after the prayer in the church; also, that they send their daughters to the wife of the master of the church so that she can teach the doctrine an hour before prayer. The master can punish and bring to instruction missing boys, and his wife the girls, without their parents or other persons interfering on threat of the penalty given in the previous law.

4. To raise the Indians properly from their infancy for service to the church and the offices of the republic, I direct and command that the master sexton of this town teach them to read, write, and count, and to play flutes and help in mass. He [the master sexton] shall be, because of these and previous laws, exempted from all service and tribute, and shall be paid by the community for whose benefit he is busy.

5. Because on the esteem and respect that the Indians have for the priests that teach them depends the doctrine that they teach, so that these go forward, I order that all the Indians have great respect and obedience to the priests that teach them as ministers of God, the *tatoques* and justices above all to set an example for the others.[2] Those who lack respect should be punished severely by the justices. If this is not done, all should be punished by the Spanish justice [that is, the Spanish governor] of this province, and [if not done] the penalty ordered on reviewing the acts of the administration of the Spanish governor shall be very heavy.[3] Despite the risks and inconveniences that might result, it is important for the tranquillity and instruction of the Indians as well as the preservation of royal authority.

6. Moreover, I order that the justices and tatoques take particular care with the repair and adornment of the church, and this with considerable honesty, spending each year from the funds of their community for necessary things up to twenty tostons, the costs being approved by those who administer the fund and the expenses being recorded in the book of the community.

7. The abuse and old custom that the Indians have from their paganism of selling their daughters, that being more than giving them away for marriage, is very damaging, and of great inconvenience for the service of God and tranquillity of the towns. Because parents order the marriage of Indian ladies against their desire, as if they were slaves, they live in perpetual hatred due to the lack of loyalty and love in the marriage. From this follows considerable harm. To remedy this, I direct and command that no Indian man or woman can receive any service in return for marriage with a daughter. The penalty for such service being fifty public lashes in the pillory of the town, that he shall be unfit to hold offices in the government, and that he pays what he received into the exchequer of His Majesty. If he was a noble, he would become a commoner. Moreover, I order the justices to enforce the penalty of this law on the transgressors. The governor of this province should take particular care to always execute it least he suffers a heavy punishment on review of the acts of his administration.

8. Moreover, I order that the mayor and councilmen of the town meet

in their city government building on the first day of the new year, as is customary, and freely elect those officials of the government who they understand would best serve in those offices, without noting petitions, kinship, or anything other than the common good. Those thus elected should be installed in their offices without need of other confirmation. They shall be fined ten pesos if they don't jointly read these laws in the mother language so that they know them henceforth.

9. Moreover, I direct and command that the elected make an inspection of the expenditures and receipts of the past year from the community funds, they being fined ten tostons for each missing inspection. Also, they are responsible for the accounts passed to them.

10. Moreover, I direct and command that the Indian justices do not give or execute any sentence on request without sufficient investigation. Nor can they fine any Indian more than a toston for each transgression. Half of the pecuniary fines should go to the exchequer of His Majesty and be written that day in their records. The fine for disobeying this order is four tostons for every transgression.

11. Moreover, the mayors or other justices can't detain a woman for civil debt, or try for adultery against married women against the wishes of the husband and then continue also against the adulterer, or if the husband consents to it, continue against all three. They can't accuse any woman, on the penalty of deprivation of office and a fine of ten tostons for the exchequer of His Majesty.

12. Moreover, I direct and command that when some Indian man or woman of this town is ill, a judge of it shall stipulate his testament in front of the notary public of the town and witnesses. If he [or she] had children or legitimate descendants, [he or she can] leave them as inheritors of his [or her] goods without disposing [otherwise] more than a fifth part. If there are no children, and if he [or she] has parents or living ascending relatives, he or she can't leave it to them for heirs without disposing [otherwise] more than a third. If without either, he [or she] can freely dispose of his [or her] goods. With this will be prevented the abuses that prejudice the rights of the rightful inheritors. The executors should discharge their duties within a year, and if negligent, it should be executed by the mayors. A copy of the original testament shall remain always in a book of testaments, prepared at the cost of the community, and in possession of the notary public who gives one or more [copies] to the executors or inheritors.[4] To correct any damage, the original goes to the governor of this province in case it is not discharged, or if the mayors and Indian justices had been negligent.

13. Moreover, I order that when the Indian man or woman dies leav-

ing minor children or inheritors, the justice makes before a notary public of the town an inventory of all the goods and entrusts it for the minors with the tutor or guardian whom the deceased had named [prior to death]. If one has not been named, one should nominate the governor, who is of good conscience, creditable, and diligent.

14. Moreover, when the Indian man or woman dies leaving a husband or wife, the spouse obtains what had been brought to the matrimony and half of what was acquired during it. If some Indian man or woman dies without making a testament, their legitimate children or descendants inherit; and lacking them, their parents or ascending relatives; and if they lack all, the closest relatives who have an obligation to distribute for the soul of the dead the fifth part of the goods that have been inherited.

15. Because the town has the power to give rations to those who administer it, help in the works of the church and expenses of the community [for the] priest, and sustain the poor Indians and ill, I direct and command that all the Indians of the town make a community field in two different parts, making a sowing of a bushel or less. This they should cultivate, harvest, store with much care, register, and order for the benefit of its community. The mayors should sell the maize in a public auction before the notary public of the town, who should then register it in a community record book for review by the governor, bringing it to him and the mayors [as proof of] what happened. Moreover, the penalty is that they pay from their own goods what they lack and be punished for the crime. I order that they don't name Spanish judges to supervise the harvest of the fields because their salaries use up the money for the others.[5] To better help cultivate the field of the community, I order that they don't make another for a *cofradia*, or any other thing, for that of the community is for helping the repairs to the church and other things as indicated.[6]

16. Because the Indians sustain themselves and pay their tribute [by] raising poultry and pigs, it is necessary not to require them to go searching [for grain] outside the town. [Therefore,] I direct and command that each married Indian, widower, or bachelor, although exempt from tribute, make one or two fields of maize of a sowing of a half bushel. The mayors should take care to inspect them twice a year, and punish with whipping those Indians who are defective in the sowing and care of the fields, dividing among themselves the inspections so that the duties be equal, with the warning that they would be punished by a Spanish judge with the same penalty that I have ordered for the errant Indian for any deficiencies in the sowing and care of the fields of the Indians of the town.

17. Moreover, I direct and command that each married Indian, widower, or bachelor have their own house and not live two in one, even if parents and son or son-in-law, and that they have houses well roofed, with beds, images, and rosaries. The mayors of this town shall every third month inspect the houses of the Indians and punish with whipping without taking money from the negligent in any of the above mentioned, providing what is necessary so that they don't lack in the future. Moreover, the penalty would be that all were punished by the governor who inspects it with the same penalty, without putting them in prison or charging prison fees for the defects, on pain of paying double for the exchequer of His Majesty and upon investigation of the acts of his [the governor's] administration.

18. Each married Indian lady, widow, or unmarried lady should have twelve chickens and a rooster as well as a male turkey and six turkey hens. They should also have another rooster to provide an allowance and help to remedy their needs.

19. Because of the need for money for the community, as I have shown, I direct and command that they have a community box for their money that has two different keys, one in the power of the native governor or oldest mayor, and the other in the power of the steward, and if there isn't one, of an alderman. All the maize that comes from the community field, and the tribute that the Indians newly married or settled pay since the last assessment, should be sold in the public auctions noted in the fifteenth law and the proceeds placed in the box, without any entry being possible for a private Indian. In the presence of the notary public of the town, they shall register in the book of the community what enters as well as leaves it. Whoever removes community money, or has in his power any such money contrary to what this law requires, shall be given fifty lashes, be deprived of office for four years, pay twenty tostons for the exchequer of His Majesty, and return the money to the community box.

20. Moreover, I direct and command that the money of the community cannot be spent by the mayors, tatoques, or other lesser person, or any large amount, without permission of the Lord President of the Royal Tribunal if not used for the repair of the church, as stated in the sixth law, and in the paying of the allowances of the priest that administers it. Or in the support and curing of the poor Indians who are ill, as in the fifteenth law, except up to the amount of twenty tostons each year with permission of the governor of this province, all expenses to be noted in the book of the community. On penalty of deprivation of office, fifty lashes, and twenty tostons for the exchequer of His Majesty, no

expenses shall be incurred contrary to the intent of this law and all moneys shall be placed in the box of the community.

21. Because the duties that the Indians accustomed to apply among themselves are of great inconvenience for the tranquillity of the town, causing much pain to those of the commoners who are the most poor, I order that in no manner do they apply, nor can they be collected on small or large amounts for any reason, nor in any manner, even if they ask for them under pretext of charity. Moreover, [there is a] penalty of 100 lashes for whatever Indian applies them or collects the duty, removal from the office of justice, banishment from the town for four years, and [a fine] of twenty tostons for the exchequer of His Majesty. All of these requirements shall be enforced by the governors lest they be penalized during the review of their administration.

22. Because His Majesty has ordered that the tribute of the dead or absent cannot be collected from the living and present, although the living have inherited it, I order and request that the goods that the dead passed on to their heirs be without any load of tribute, other than would be owed to His Majesty or encomendero by the dead at the time of death, because what would have been paid if they lived had been paid from the community treasury.

23. To avoid great inconveniences and pains to the Indians resulting from drunkenness and offenses to our Lord, I request and order that no person bring wine to this town for selling to the Indians, on penalty, if he was a Spaniard, of 200 pesos for the exchequer of His Majesty and loss of the wine the first time, and for the second, the fine doubles and banishment from this province [is required]. If not able to pay the fine, he shall be expelled in shame to the city of Guatemala. If he was Indian, mestizo, black, or mulatto, on penalty of having the wine seized for the exchequer of His Majesty, and 100 lashes and banishment. Because the same drunkenness and pain is caused by a drink they call *miscol* or *guarapo* that the Indians make from roots with plantains, maize, sugarcane, and other things, I order, under the penalty of 100 lashes and banishment, that no Indian or any other person can make it or drink it.

24. Moreover, no person can bring to this town or sell to an Indian cane syrup, sugar pastry, concentrated honey, brown sugar, or other kind of sweets on penalty of losing it, if he was a Spaniard, and [a fine] of twenty pesos for the exchequer of His Majesty; and if black, mulatto, mestizo, or Indian, the same fine and 200 lashes, plus four years of banishment from this town and province.[7]

25. Moreover, I direct and command that no Indian can sell lands, except to another Indian, without permission from the governor of the

province, and sale in any other manner is invalid, and even with their permission such a sale to a Spaniard is invalid.

26. Moreover, I direct and command that no Indian without permission from the Lord President, or Inspecting Judge, can dress in clothes as a Spaniard, or have a sword, dagger, lance, harquebus, or firelock.[8] Nor can he ride a horse with saddle and bridle. Moreover, the penalty is loss of the dress or arms, saddle, bridle, and horse, half of the value going to the exchequer of His Majesty, and the other half for the judge and informer in equal parts.

27. Moreover, I direct and command that no person can sell anything on credit [worth] more than ten tostons to the Indian nobles, and eight to the commoners, and that the Indian that obtained something on credit cannot buy any other thing on credit until paying for the first, the penalty being loss of what was sold, and the justices shall make a decision on this as indicated below.

28. Moreover, I direct and command that henceforth no Indian can serve as muleteer and tradesman for more than a month's wage and, up to twenty tostons, for buying and selling merchandise. Until providing the service and being paid the amount, [an Indian] cannot do more on penalty of losing what has been given, and the judges shall thus carry this out.

29. Moreover, I direct and command that no merchant—neither Spanish, black, mulatto, mestizo, nor Indian—can sell in the streets and houses of the Indians any merchandise, or keep it in a house of an Indian, but [must] sell his merchandise in the inn where he is staying or in the market, not staying more than three days in the town, and not return to sell it in less than four months. The penalty being twenty pesos for the exchequer of His Majesty and what he sells if a Spaniard, and if Indian, mulatto, or mestizo, besides the fine, fifty lashes and four years of banishment.

30. Moreover, I direct and command that the justices and tatoques take care in opening and repairing the roads and bridges of their district, and the rest houses, community houses, and inns, so that the passengers would be well taken care of and not need to stay in the houses of the Indians. They will provide sustenance and necessary supplies conforming to the established rates without maliciously detaining them. Moreover, carelessness will be punished by the governor and at their cost they will repair the above noted, repair costs to be paid by the judges and tatoques and not taken from the community.

31. Because those who teach the Indians when they come to the towns bring a bed that is usually carried by Indians, against the royal edicts that

prohibit it, I order that with the community funds they prepare a mattress for this purpose in the house of the parish priest and no other thing.

32. Because ordinary service is the easiest way for the Indians to assist, falling on most, I direct and command that no Indian can be excused from the services of the government or others by having been mayor, alderman, or head constable, or having some other position in his town, but on ending his term of office, must help with the services like the other natives. He should have helped before his term of office. The Indian justices have been and will be obliged to require them to do so. Moreover, the high justices of the province can punish them for negligence with jail, warning that if this is not done, they will be so sentenced in the review of the acts of their administration.

33. Moreover, I order that none of the justices [or] tatoques of the Indians can either receive more [than their salary], neither cloth nor other merchandise for barter or benefit, or buying and selling it in the towns. Neither can it be given nor can it be asked for in judgment. The penalty being that it is lost, half being placed in the exchequer of His Majesty, and the other half divided equally between the judge and informer.

34. Since the presence of blacks, mulattos, and mestizos in the towns of the Indians is very prejudicial to good instruction and their customs, and to their finances and honor, and by edicts of His Majesty is prohibited in the towns, I direct and command that no black, mulatto, or mestizo enter them or reside in the towns, or pass through buying or selling anything, not even permitted items, the penalty being their loss, 100 lashes, and four years of banishment from this province.

35. Because the inspections that the Spanish judges make in the towns of the province are to make things better, to conserve and augment them, and not for their destruction, they being intended for a good purpose, I direct and command that the governor of this province and other judges making an inspection do not have more than a notary public, head constable, translator, and a servant, each one coming with their own bedding. The judge can bring a woman to prepare the meals. The community book shall record the cost of what the Indians provide for their sustenance. They [the inspectors] and their servants shall lodge in the community houses, those of the city council, and inns, but not in any private Indian house. Anyone who violates any part of this law shall be fined twenty pesos for the exchequer of His Majesty and it shall be considered important in the review of the acts of an administration.

36. Because the weakness of the Indian men and women is so well

known, I direct and command that no person or house can give or send Indian girls to grind or prepare maize for the meals of the justices and priests, or for any other reason. The mayors of the town should send maize to the house of the wife of the sexton who is in charge of the girls who perform this task, and an Indian man should take it to the kitchen where it is made into tortillas for the justices and priest. They should send Indian women millers of more than forty years in age. The penalty [for violating this law] is 100 lashes and deprivation from government office for four years by the governor or Indian alcalde who does the contrary. For the Spanish judge of the province who does not enforce this law on the transgressors, [there shall be a fine of] 200 ducats for the exchequer of His Majesty and it shall be considered important in the review of the acts of his administration.[9]

37. Because the dances that the Indians do in their festivals cause much expense from renting feathers, clothes, and masks, and since they lose much time in rehearsals and drunkenness, halting them would benefit their finances, pay their tribute, and sustain their houses. They bring to memory the sacrifices and old rites of their paganism and other offenses to our Lord. For all these reasons, I order and require them to cease so that the Indians only celebrate their town festival on the prior evening and actual day, that of Corpus Christi and Christmas.[10] In them, they should neither rent nor bring masks, feathers, or clothing other than what is normal for Indians. Nor should they act out the old histories of pagan times, with or without long trumpets.[11] Nor should they do the dance they call the *tum ni uleutum*.[12] Neither the Indian nor Spanish justices should permit it on penalty to any Indian of 100 lashes and deprivation from government office for four years. If the Spanish justice does not punish the guilty, he will be fined 200 ducats for the exchequer of His Majesty and it will be considered a grave charge during the review of the acts of his administration. Because they are dangerous to the conscience of the Indians, I ask and strongly charge the parish priests to have particular care to persuade the Indians to halt the dances and expenses. They [the Indians] should keep the Christian law that they profess.

38. To stop the fights that follow detention, and punishment of the fiscals of the churches and others by the Indians, I direct and command that neither the fiscal of the church nor any other person of the town detain, whip, or punish any Indian man or woman except for the children under twelve years in age, whom they are directed by the priests to give a dozen lashes for being defective in Christian doctrine and service for the church. Because, as noted in the law, the girls of any age are

punished by the wife of the master sexton, and other delinquent Indian men and women are punished by order of the secular Indian or Spanish justice and not by any other person, there is a penalty of 100 lashes to the Indian man who without orders from the judges detains or punishes any Indian male or female, and if it was a Spaniard [who does likewise], 200 ducats for the exchequer of His Majesty and perpetual banishment from the province. If the governor doesn't enforce this law, he will suffer the same penalty of 200 ducats. It also will be considered a grave charge during the review of the acts of his administration.

These laws are given to the mayors and aldermen of the town of Cobán and its inhabitants. They should keep and comply with them as written, and the Spanish governor of the province of Verapaz should keep them, complying with and executing each and every one of them.

Done in the town of Samayac on the 19th day of the month of December of the year 1625. The Licenciate Juan Maldonado de Paz. By his order, Juan Palomino de Vargas.

Chapter 23, Book 1:
Fruits of This Land and Festivities
of the Indians

I have already spoken in chapter five and six of the clothes of these Indians and how they go barefoot, unless very rich and important. These are the rulers, principals, or *calpules,* who are the heads of the principal lineages. These [people] wear shoes without stockings, and if they wear some cloth, such as pants and doublet, it is with the permission of the president. The laws I have seen say they can't have mule trains even though they are rich, but the permission is easily given, and today there are in this province, as in others, many rich Indian muleteers. This damages the royal revenue because although they move much merchandise, they don't pay taxes; up to now this practice has not been noticed, and thus not remedied.[13] Indians ought to pay more than a thousand reals of duties each year, but with the paying of their tributes, which don't come to even sixteen, they remain exempt from all the others. Wine should be prohibited to them because it makes them so extravagant that fathers would sell their sons for this. They get drunk extremely easily, and when they are so, don't [even] respect their own mothers.

Their government is in the proper form of Spain. On New Year's Day, they elect mayors and aldermen, a steward, scribe, and other officials, among them the head constable, jailer, and other constables, there being more than thirty who serve each year. Having made this election, they bring the results to the governor to confirm it, which they do if there is no defect in the official elected by his predecessor. Each year, the governor inspects all the towns of his jurisdiction and requires the obeying of the laws, which if not done, so lazy are they, they would not sow a field or work an hour, and so [would] die of hunger. The married Indians pay to His Majesty each year in this province three reals, a half fanega of maize, a fowl, and if it is a place of cotton or cacao, in products of the land.[14] The widowers and bachelors pay half, and the widows no more than a chicken, although from twelve years old in this province they pay one toston plus each one gives a donation, or alms as they say, and it has become the established form in which they pay and they always pay it. With what they pay, His Majesty provides for the parishes. Although they also give a little for the support of the monks who administer them. Also paid from this is the salary of the governor, which is 1000 ducats in this province. They have their community strongbox for the surplus, kept for repairs and ordinary expenses, and to pay the salaries of the head constable and scribe during an inspection.

This land is so rainy and the Indians so lazy, as I said, that although they can extract some products to enrich themselves—such as bark, liquidambar, copal, and other things—they don't do so. Nor do they want more than a tortilla of maize and a little chile and salt, with which they are more content than if they ate turkeys, which are quite cheap: the price of a large male one is six reals and the female is three, and chickens are one real. It rains, as I said, nine months of the year, and in the three dry months of summer, February to May, they make their plantings of maize. There is also in some towns a harvest of very fine and highly valued feathers, with which they paid tribute to Moctezuma. Remesal said that they value them more than gold and silver of other provinces, which does not surprise me, for they are very attractive and, although they are no more than three *dedos* wide, some [are] more than a vara long.[15] The Indians pay very well for them to use in their dances. And the way of obtaining them is in the summer when it is very dry; in some drinking troughs or pools of water that they have purposely made, the Indians place some traps that when they [the birds] come to drink, they leave the feathers stuck, as they have very long tails although they are small as doves, and the best and most fine feathers are those of the tail. They value these birds so much that they never catch them, but each year harvest new feathers, and [so] they have great interest in them. Not every one can collect the feathers but only those who have sites inherited from their fathers, and the dead, have these watering places. And because this curiosity is worthy of being known, I have discussed it at length.

They don't keep any of the yearly holidays other than Sundays and the first day of all the *pascuas,* the four holidays of our Lady—Birth [Christmas], Purification, Annunciation, and Assumption—all the holidays of our Lord Christ, the holiday of Saint Peter and Saint Paul, and the patron of their town.[16] They don't fast more than the Fridays of Lent and the prescribed fast days.[17] They eat in all the vigils, and [both] Spaniards and Indians [use] lard [on] Fridays in place of the oil in all the Indies. They have their fiscal who teaches every day in the mother language the prayers to the boys, and his wife to the girls, as will be told. They preach to all of them during the festivities in their language, and in this way they teach and catechize. They make great dance parties during the festivities of their town, and the things of the church they do as they do in Spain. In the processions of Holy Week, they whip men as well as women, which they [later] halted.[18] They carry their images and devices very devotedly. They are ingenious and handy for all whom they teach, and in this province in particular there are great number of expert blacksmiths, carpenters, shoemakers, and tanners, for a hide of cured bull is worth eight reals, as are those of native animals. Thus, this province has no need of things from outside. Previously, many came to it for some things, especially one item obtained in the two towns of the hot lands called Cahabón and San Agustin [Lanquin]. This is the achiote with which they make the chocolate. As it gives fine orange coloring, this trifle is of great value and is sold where it is collected for five and six reals; in Guatemala it is sold for eleven, and is taken in large amounts to Mexico where it has [an even] higher price.

Chapter 26, Book 1:
Of the Site of Guatemala, and of a Festival
That Was Made There on the Birth
of the Prince of the Spains

Although I have no intention of this history being lengthy or saying more than is pertinent to it, at this point it seems to me an insult to the noble city of Guatemala if nothing is said of its grandeur, of its gentlemen, descendants of the conquistadores, of its site and climate. Even though the little time spent could not do it justice, nor my limited talent provide understanding, speaking succinctly in order not to tire the reader, I will tell of what I saw and learned during my first few days there.

I arrived at a good time in this city, when as I noted previously, they were celebrating the birth of our Prince.[19] The one in charge of these events was Don Luis Alfonso Mazariegos de la Tovilla, my cousin, who at this moment was the mayor of the city. During three days, they enacted the conquest of a great volcano in the middle of the plaza and the taking of Moctezuma, who was in charge of it when they captured him, the Indians of Tlascala helping the Spaniards.[20] It was something very much to see because the Indians who celebrated these festivals were of the outskirts of the city, and as they were among Spaniards and interacted with them every day, in the Spanish manner so gallant and graceful that no one would consider them Indians. Those who helped Moctezuma were so well dressed according to their usage, so filled with jewels, so costly and genteel, so covered with very costly feathers, that without doubt they would look well in the luxurious plaza of Madrid, and could appear in front of Their Majesties and serve to entertain them. The plaza where they had the festival was so well embellished, so adorned with costly hangings, so filled with beautiful and gallant ladies, that it astonished me to see in a land so remote the practices, clothing, manners, and speech of what properly belong in Madrid.

More plays came to the Royal Tribunal and chancery with so great a prince and brave soldier as they extol, so worthy ministers as they govern, so important and ancient gentlemen as they celebrate, it seems to me they could not—although they ought to—have had such qualities. Counting the festivals from this day, they made eight in a row, ending with a game of reeds with costumes so costly that it seems to me they would have impoverished Margarita and removed all the pearls from its river.[21] They concentrated in so brief a space as that costume all the diamonds of China, taking away the value of emeralds and rubies, that they seem to be the heads of brilliant stars or a cowl congealed of fine diamonds, so that they seem to be all one. The gowns, cloaks, and sleeves were so filled with pearls that one could not see another thing, nor could one form an opinion on what was there. As I said, nothing was of gold or other costly stones. These gentlemen, although rich, demonstrated more the spirit than the power.

At the beginning of these brilliant festivals, the President, accompanied by the Royal Tribunal, the city council of the aldermen, other gentlemen of the game, and encomenderos of the province with capes and caps, made an entrance into the plaza. His Lordship and all the other gentlemen made a procession, and having done, went to their seats. The other gentlemen went to their houses to change into the costly black clothes with their shining costumes, and soon entered with a great number of trumpets, clarinets, beasts of burden loaded with reeds, and thirty-six pages on horses with the shields of their owners. After this entrance came eighteen pairs who divided into squads of six, all very qualified gentlemen, descendants of the conquerors. Having entered and divided into squads, they joined in a skirmish, each one remaining in their post, and began to play at war with such skill and so well placed on their horse that it seemed that each one was the original horseman. None was distinguished above the others because generally all appeared so expert and gallant that one could replace any with the others. After a game lasted a good time, the assistants released the bulls, giving a pleasant end to the festival. I was pleased to have come on such a good occasion to the city.

[The city] has its location on not very fertile flat plains, drained by some canyons and with water drains inside its streets. The houses are not high because of the quite common earthquakes. There are powerful men of 300 to 400,000 pesos, and merchants of 100,000 pesos, whose traffic with indigo dye is very great, and there are many dye works in its jurisdiction. The district of the Tribunal extends over 1,700 leagues. One can measure the excellence of the province by how many times the ships of Honduras were lost, merchants losing 100,000 pesos, and many 50 and a great many 30, not once but many times, yet none ever went bankrupt.

Also the city has good exits, and there is an old city close to it. At this site previously there was the city, but it was depopulated because of being flooded one night. They say that a blasphemy of a woman was the reason. . . . [22]

There is a volcano on the border of the city, two leagues from it, which is always burning, and at times on very dark nights, with its brightness one can read a paper in any street of the city. In the year 1617, ash rained for three days over more than forty surrounding leagues, and it burned all the harvest and pasture of livestock, and the sun did not appear at all for three days, it being so dark as if it were night. Many roofs fell thanks to the weight of the ash, and I would not mention this here if I had not seen the testimony of the notaries, not counting innumerable persons who have mentioned this to me. I didn't think this chapter would be this long, nor that to give an account of all these particulars would take this effort, and now I will return to my soldiers who were waiting for me. [23]

[Inspecting the Province]

Chapter 7, Book 2:
Of the Inspection I Made in My Province, and of the Differences and Climates That Were in It

On the 21st of July, I left the city of Cobán to make an inspection of the province, accompanied by my scribe, chief constable, and interpreter, who are the persons necessary for it, their salary being paid from the treasuries of the towns. The first towns where we began were those of Rabinal and Cubulco, said to be the most cheerful of the province.[24]

As they have ranches very close with many animals, they met me more than two leagues from the place with fifty Indians on horses and good mules. They adorned the entire town with arches, dances, and parties according to their usage, but lacking trumpets and clarions, these being always left a half league from the town when receiving their Governor.[25] They dismounted, and then came the mayors and aldermen. Then they called to the remainder of the city the council, the aldermen, and important men, and gave a long speech that the interpreter said was to welcome me, expressing the pleasure that they had in their town the Negotiator of the King, which is their manner of referring to my office. They brought me a gift of turkeys, a calf, cheeses, and plantains, and after I had responded, asked permission and returned to their houses.

The following day, I ordered the entire town to meet in the plaza and proclaimed the order of the inspection, indicating that all who had questions of the mayors present or past, or of any other person, should come forward and they would receive justice. That if any live in sin, they should so declare. Or that if treated badly by some Spaniards, and if some person had come to [illegally] sell in this town and other things of this type, and above all if the mayors had made a very prejudicial assessment. That they should request remedy for all done against the royal laws and punishment for the culprits. Having made this proclamation, they all went to their houses, and on the next day, I began the inspection in the following form.

The mayors, aldermen, and all the important men of the town joined me and went by horse, for it was a large town and hot, the scribe and constable joining me on foot. With the trumpets in front of us, we left the house and began to inspect those of the Indians. The constable entered each of them to see if they had beds on which to sleep, tools for making their fields, and an image before which to pray, and if they had poultry and the other items required by the laws, and if the houses were well roofed and in good condition. Those that were not in compliance with the law got twelve lashes, more or less, as decided by the Governor. If the lack was of poultry, they whipped the woman. Also required was a good-looking blouse and petticoat, and a white piece of cloth with which to go to mass, and if they didn't have them they punished them. For doing less, I whipped them in the street by the doors of their houses.

This I did because some judges do evil in inspections within their jurisdiction by putting the Indians in jail for little or no guilt and requiring two reals for jailer's fees. In this manner, because they don't tolerate anything, they obtain much money from the towns. If there was a fowl less than twelve or a house somewhat badly roofed and other faults of this type, they pardoned no one, leaving little or nothing to pay [tribute]. I tolerated much in this first inspection. I excused them on the second if the lack was not excessive or due to their laziness. I did not whip them. In this manner, we visited this morning fifty houses and in the afternoon others, but according to the law, not more than a hundred houses in a day; sometimes seeing an entire town of 400 Indians in less than two days, and thus placing them in order.

There is no day of judgment for them like this before which all tremble. Each one prepares something to give to the Governor, perhaps a hen or rooster, perhaps cacao or chile or eggs, and none leave without giving something of what they have, and the ones with some wealth give reals of silver, keeping in this the ceremony of the Jews not to appear without something. In this way, they never speak to the Governor or to the monk who administers them without carrying something.

We took four days to inspect this town, and then examined the records of the mayor for the community funds of the past year that they were responsible for and settled their accounts; all the surplus funds entrusted to the mayors of the present year and that which they collected from the natives (in agreement with their assessment) being used for what is necessary, which is to pay for the support of the monk who administers [the parish], since other expenses in monk-run parishes His Majesty supports from the royal treasury. They give their support according to what is possible from the town in maize, poultry, and money, and this besides the tribute that each Indian pays to His Majesty or his encomendero. If the town is of an *encomienda*, each one gives a half fanega of maize and two reals, and together with the goods of the community (for some have ranches of cattle or mules, others sow fields of maize and cotton), they pay the support and salaries of the inspection, and provide wax for the festivities of their towns and the monuments and church festivals.[26] Although they have some expenses and steal what they can, always there is more than enough money in the treasury of the community, and especially in towns that have a large ranch for cattle and mares. We took six days with the accounts of the ranch and town, and in them we were well treated with game and fish, because they are Indian nobles and pride themselves on being very polite.

We went to another town called Copulco three leagues from there, and on the fourth day, we inspected it and examined the accounts for it since it was smaller than Rabinal.[27] The colder highlands of Sacapulas started at this town. The valley itself was quite warm.

Continuing my travel with all my people, we climbed the highlands of Sacapulas, which are very high and rough. There are in them five good and pleasant towns with the climate of Spain, although never with snow. They harvested in them all the good fruit of Spain, like quinces, apples, peaches, figs, and some small pears. They often hunt deer, partridge, pigeons, quail, and rabbits. There are wild pigs called *quequeos* that have a navel in the middle of the spine, and if they kill it [the pig] and don't remove it [the navel], it damages the meat so one can't eat it.[28] Deer are common and large. Perhaps all have good bezoar stones. The Indians capture them on foot, a thing that is incredible, and to prove it they came with me because I wanted to see them take some. They did it one afternoon with more than 200 Indians. They went from all sides into the heart of the forest and enclosed a large piece, leaving us on the foot of the mountains in a small savanna, and after more than two hours they brought down three deer to the plain. Shouting, running, and harassing them on both sides, they burst into song on taking two of them, allowing the other to return to the forest. They were very large and both males. [When the Indians] opened them, they found good bezoar stones although not very large, and one had one like nut. They estimate that there are many in this land and those of these mountains are the best. On this there are in reality many opinions, some authors saying because it freezes, and others saying the contrary.

In this manner, all of them hunt and throughout the year these Indians supply themselves with meat. Thus, they eat better than those of lands who lack this ability. Although now all know it well, in the beginning of their conversion they hated the cow because of its great multiplication in all these provinces. Since the lands are temperate, the grazing good, and few were killed at the beginning because the Indians didn't eat them, they filled the valley in a few years and one found many wild cattle even in the forests.

They [the Indians] also harvest in these mountains in a town called

Santa María Cunera much and good wheat.[29] This is because they have a great, irrigated, fertile plain. Also they sow in the mountains. It has only been thirty years that they harvest it because although from the beginning it seemed as land well suited to it, the land lacked proper preparation due to the laziness of the Indians. Sowing came only after a monk who administered that parish required them [to do so]. In the beginning, it took great effort to make them do it, and they received so little profit from their own oxen that they shot them (with arrows) in order not to work anymore. The monk did not rest until they had learned well how to do it. Thus, each year they sowed more and made mills and ovens until today, with the good harvests, it is the richest town of the mountains; having seen what it brings, everyone sows this plant.

The other three towns are higher up, bordering the lands of the Lacandons. The one that comes the closest is Chajul de los Reyes. For ten years, they [the Lacandons] have not come to this part because of the twelve harquebuses, with munitions for them, given to the Indians of this town. Using them once to make a noise with them when they [the Lacandons] came to their town, they did not come back. I found in this town of Chajul an Indian who, a little before, had fled from the Lacandons. I examined him in his own language and, as we were planning an expedition to Ah Itza, obtained with the truest possible verification of what the Indians speak since they were the greatest enemies of the Lacandons.[30] Thus asking him some specific questions, and the monk who administered the parish serving as interpreter, he gave me a long account of all, and I had it written down to send it to the Royal Tribunal, as was done and seen in this place.

Chapter 10, Book 2:
Continuing the Inspection, and of the Climates of
Some Towns and Peculiarities of the Land

I finished the inspection of the towns of the mountains, and went down to Sacapulas, which has 400 houses and is the capital of the province that they call Sacapulas. In it was an expensive monastery founded by Father Friar Domingo [de] Vico on the 8th of November 1553, the prior then of Saint Dominic of Guatemala, with the permission of Bishop Don Francisco Marroquín and the decree of the Royal Tribunal. They ordered Francisco de Bolaños, high constable of the Tribunal, to delineate the site and lands for the monastery, and so it was done. It is . . . [page torn] from this town is so different from those of the mountains that I am amazed to see in such a short distance so very different climates. This is caused by large canyons between them that prevents the movement of air. A good, large river with many fish passes by it. It is that we heard called downstream Conuntehila, which is here nothing but [the] Tuhal.[31] The kings of the Quiche used this town in pagan times as a jail or dungeon for those captured in the wars that they continually had on their borders, for these kings of the Quiche were very powerful, as we will discuss further on.[32] They placed the captives here on a large crag all night, and in the day they used them [as laborers] to make salt, which they produced in great amounts since it was important for their king, and thanks to this business they were much more powerful than their neighbors. Because of the lack of salt in these provinces, it was highly valued, although in others the Indians didn't use it.[33] They kept from Pagan times their manner of making it. It is extraordinary and quite different from what I have seen elsewhere.

I have seen many saltworks, and had in my charge and administration the best of Spain, which are those of the kingdom of Murcia. There are, in them, different saltworks. Most prepare it with the summer sun, although there are others that are mines, from which come already prepared that called stone salt. Also, I have seen salt made from seawater, much firewood being spent reducing it. The way these Indians make it is different from all others and incredible. As Pagans, they were people more inventive and clever than those of other provinces; and being something they didn't have in other parts, and the expensive buildings of their kings show it, I will not omit speaking about the salt.

This town of Sacapulas has six wards, and in each one there is a headman called *calpul*, because when the fathers joined them, as they were in small villages, they brought four or five to each town to make one that was large.[34] Thus, each ward of these kept the name of the village where it came from. Their old lands they keep today, and use to make their fields and for other necessities. The ward of Sacapulas, as the most important of this town, was the original lord of it, and the native lords own the saltworks and enjoy them without allowing the other inhabitants to work salt. It is next to the river, measuring four leagues long and two stone's throw wide, the soil being very clean and well swept.[35]

In different places, there are more than a dozen saltwater wells of about a yard in depth, with which they water very well the ground each afternoon, and having dried by the next day, they irrigate it again.[36] This they do three or four times, and in the afternoon they collect the well-salted, sun-dried earth. Covered up in case it rains, the next day they spread it out in the morning and irrigate it three or four times, and in the night they gather it again. Having done this, they take all this land, put it in some very large baskets with some large earthenware jars for catching water beneath, and pour very hot water over all of this earth, distilling it little by little until there is no more liquid on the earth.[37] Having done this, they take this lye, which is what they call the distilled and cleansed water, divide it among some little flat bowls of unpolished clay, and as pans placed on a stove, they heat it until it boils.[38] When it begins to boil, they add a little liquefied maize flour.[39] The result, after coagulation, is a very white but not very salty loaf. All this work that's done and they do gives twelve or fifteen loaves for a real, this being the cost of the firewood used in preparing them. Certainly, this is a clever stratagem and shows great ingenuity to put it into practice. Moreover, the Spaniards are not so phlegmatic, although they can execute whatever they want to do. In the end, the Indians work much and obtain their necessities with it, and it continually goes on. For the curious who would be amused in reading of it, it seemed worth noting so extensively. Going on, I consider the extent of the grandeur of the kings of the Quiche.

Chapter 11, Book 2:
Of the Grandeur of the Kings of the Quiche, the Site of Its Capital, and the Other Neighboring Settlements

This province of Sacapulas has fourteen towns, which I will discuss here, six being in the mountains—including the capital—and eight others.[40] Although it gives me much pleasure to mention it in passing, this volume isn't large enough to list the particularities of each one for it would increase this history to an intolerable size.

The people of these fourteen towns, many others that have vanished, those that survive near the South Sea, and many that were eliminated when they joined them together, were subjects of the kings of the Quiche, who as I said in the previous chapter were very powerful. Thus they received what came from them.

We came to a town called Santa Cruz del Quiche, having passed two others with few people, but quite comfortable because they have very great lands in the temperate zone. They harvest wheat and many fruits of Castile. There are rams and sheep. The two towns they call San Pedro Jocopilas and San Anton Ilotenango.[41] Near the town of Santa Cruz are the ruins of the palaces of the kings, where with mature understanding, to erase from memory the places of sacrifice where they had their idols and other houses of this type, the fathers of this time did not want to place the town. Having finished the inspection, and having a free afternoon, I spent the time with an Indian called Don Joseph Cortés, the grandson of the native king of this province, who gave me an extensive account of all these buildings and those who served their kings in the manner that follows.

Entirely by flat road, this site is less than a half league from the town. One enters it by a narrow way on which one can't bring horses. In total, it is little more than a quarter league square and is near some extremely deep canyons. Part of this is natural and part the work of man, so that if one doesn't take this way, it is impossible to enter it. When the Spaniards obtained the land, there was a drawbridge that made it almost impregnable.

In those times, Balanquiçe was the king who was the most powerful of all in these lands and from his name came, although corrupted, the name of Quiche for the province. He reigned skillfully, and those who governed his entire kingdom were twenty-four lords in the manner of the grandees of Spain. These never left this site, for they always accompanied their king, and all esteemed them because all government was in their hands. They had inside very sumptuous palaces, and built in each one a grandiose tomb, more than 14½ yards high, with many paintings on it. When someone died, they buried him clothed and made the same ceremonies as did the Indians of the Manché—that is, they placed food on top of the tomb. They did not demolish his house but did no more than whitewash everything again and, with great skill, paint some histories of their past. They whitewashed all the streets and palaces, inside and out, and painted new histories when the king died. They had three or four wives, and the eldest inherited, all the others being sent to war as captains or [put in] other high offices. There never were in this community, besides the king, more than these twenty-four families. These kings were very rich because the tribute from their vassals was in the products of the lands where they lived: cacao, vanilla, cotton, feathers, achiote, deer, jaguars, lions, fish, quail, turkeys, and worked stones for their buildings.[42] They had famous captains who continually warred with their neighbors, whom other Indians called Cakchiquels, and those they captured they sent to manufacture salt or used them for service in the palace, in which they fed them much maize porridge to fatten them like pigs.[43] When some were very fat, they sacrificed and slaughtered them on a large stone that today is still there, broken.[44] The day on which they made this important celebration, the king took the form of his nagual [that is, changed into the animal], which was the eagle, and the other twenty-four also took theirs, which were of lions, jaguars, bears, and deer.[45] In this form, they danced from morning until afternoon around this stone. At the end of the dance, they killed the wretch who had been awaiting his death, tied on the stone, throughout the ceremonies. Their priest arrived, opened [the breast], and removed the heart. He presented it to the queen, and from the remainder they made various stews, eating them the next day in the presence of the rulers. This form of transformation still continues, especially among those of the Manché, where it is frequent. I never would have believed it, but many trustworthy persons have assured me that it is true, in particular friars for whom nothing is hidden. They say it is done with witchcraft and the knowledge of the devil. There is no doubt that this is true.

They have skillful games, and even today there survives a very good building where they play the ball game in the daytime. They play with balls of rubber, which is a kind of tree gum, moreover so hard and light that a small bounce on the ground jumps about 3½ yards high. They can't play it with the hand, and thus they say they have some armlets of the kind they use in Italy for the game of football, and with them they play as they wish.

When the Spaniards came, the king left this site with 30,000 soldiers to defend his land, on the borders of which were some plains where today there is a town called Totonicapan.[46] He went in a day (as he was a great sorcerer), flying over the Spaniards, shooting arrows, going so low that a soldier hit him with a lance and he fell to the ground dead.[47] Then all his people fled, and the Spaniards gained the entire land.[48] In this town there still is today descendants of these kings and twenty-four so powerful families, and they have become so poor that to eat, they do their own work and sustain themselves by bringing firewood from the hills. Although His Majesty, the king our lord, had given pensions to the legitimate descendants of this king, Judge Pedro de Agüero, while inspecting the entire land, eliminated them. It seemed convenient to do so because the pension was in tribute paying Indians and because they didn't recognize him, as from what I saw they ought to, as a lord. This is my opinion because the very notable buildings here can't be ignored, and I continued with my inspection elsewhere.

I went to another four leagues away called Santo Tomás del Quiche [Chichicastenango]. It has more than 400 houses, all rich Indians, half of them merchants and most excellent great workers. Their inhabitants own more than 3,000 mules with which they trade with the coastal province of Suchitepeque on the South Sea. They are, I said, rich, because they bring to it a large amount of baked bread, cloth, and other things, and remove from these lands cacao, cotton, and vanilla, which are the most valuable goods in these lands.

They harvest in this town the fruits of Castile, including apricots, seen nowhere else in this province. They obtain a very fine although small amount of cochineal. The Indians, finding the harvest so small, don't want to cultivate it.

I went to another town called Zacualpa of the Holy Spirit [consisting] of more than 400 houses, and it is the encomienda of Don Fernando Ruiz de Contreras, secretary of the Council of the Indies of His Majesty.[49] They obtain in it the best pomegranates of the Indies and as good as those of Seville. There is much forest hunting for deer, rabbits, quail, and some large birds that they call *cololes,* who are like the partridge of the kingdom of Valencia, yet have even more breasts. I was inspecting them when a messenger came from the Manché with letters of Father Friar Francisco Morán and some testimony of those Indians who had fled from the Ah Itza, [both of] which I dispatched to the Royal Tribunal and President as I explain in the following chapter.

[Manché and Lacandón]

Chapter 3, Book 2:
Of the Rites and Ceremonies That the Pagans
Had and Still Have in the Province of Manché,
and of the Way of Understanding Their Months and Years,
and an Apostolic Brief of Paul III in Which He
Declares Them Rational Animals

Having made my good-byes to the monks and soldiers, I left accompanied by four with their harquebuses if it be necessary to punish some Indians of the towns through where we are passing. This day, I met forty of those of Yol who accompanied my messengers, and asking about the others, they told me that they had not found them. I gave orders that they take my letter for my lieutenant to the town of the Spaniards. The letter told him what to do, and I continued my travel to the first town, called Ahixil, where I found some Indians who had fled the day before from our settlement.[50] They came from a tiny town called Noxoy that I had burned because it was idolatrous and moved the people to the town of the Spaniards.[51] They asked pardon for their flight, saying that having been discouraged—that being [a] common [excuse]—when they had made some mistake, and fearing the Indians of Ah Itza, they had fled into the forest. Allowing this, although of little profit, having seen among them a priest of their idolatries, a monk reclothed them, it being more to pacify them so that they don't return to the forest, which is how they make war. I didn't punish them with the hope that the monks, who in truth still had baptized few or none, could continue to help them regarding their errors on the obligations of Christians. I was the entire day in the town of Ahixil with the monk who administered it (he being Friar Jacinto de San Ildefonso) since I couldn't leave that afternoon because it was continuously raining, and having only walked until midday, did no more than four or five leagues. I will inform you very gradually of the rites and ceremonies that these Indians kept in their paganism. As some of our subordinates and people have doubts on if they were rational or irrational animals, I provide the definition of Supreme Pontiff Paul the Third:

Brief of His Holiness Paul the Third

To all faithful Christians who can take notice of these letters. Paul, third Pope of this name, wishes you good health in [the name of] Christ our Lord and sends you his apostolic benediction. Master to the highest degree [of] the human race, the excellent God that made man not only made him the recipient of goodness like the other creatures but gave him the capacity to do maximum good so he can fix his eyes on it and possess it, even if invisible, and nothing can prevent him from reaching it. The creation of man, according to divine scripture, was to gain life and eternal happiness, which can only happen through the faith of Jesus Christ, our Lord, forcing one to confess that man should be in a condition such that he can receive it. Whoever has the temperament of man is capable of receiving thus the Faith. Therefore, it is not possible that there be someone of so little judgment that he can understand it and not be able to receive it. From this it follows that Christ our Lord, offering the same truth that one neither can deny nor can be denied, said to the preachers of the Faith when he selected them for this office, "Go to teach all peoples," he said, without exception because all are capable [of receiving] the doctrine of the Faith. Seen and envied by the Devil, enemy of the human race, who opposed all good works that prevent the people from coming to his end, he invented a way never heard of until now of preventing the preaching of the word of God to the people, and so keeping them from salvation. He incited certain soldiers, who with the desire of continuing to receive benefits, alleged that the Indians and other people of the west and south, who in these times it has come to our notice are used for personal service like the mute animals of the field, are incapable of receiving the Holy Catholic Faith.

We (who remain angry at this treatment) in the land that is in the power of Jesus Christ our Lord and with all our forces looking to bring together all those who were outside, the sheep that we are responsible for, consider that the Indians are true men. The Indians are capable of the Christian Faith. According to what we have been informed, they crave for it with much desire. Desiring to remove the said difficulties with adequate remedies, and with apostolic authority, by this our words or their translation signed by some public notary and stamped with the seal of some person with an ecclesiastic position who can verify their identity with the original, we determine and declare (contrary to whatever else is said or anything contrary to it) that the said Indians and all other people henceforth who come to the notice of Christians, even though most are outside the Faith of Jesus Christ, in no manner can they be deprived of their liberty and ownership of their goods. Legally they could and should use and gain the liberty and ownership of their goods. Indians in no way ought to be made slaves. If the contrary happens, it is without value or force. We determine and declare by the same apostolic authority that the Indians and other similar people can be called to the Faith of Jesus Christ by preaching the word of God, and with the example of the good and holy life. Dispatched in Rome, on the 10th of June of 1537, the third of our pontificate.

These Indians of Manché, as we are going to tell, have many idols and three who are their principal gods, which they call Man, Canam, [and] Chuemexchel. When they sacrifice and celebrate festivals, they make a great arbor in a canyon, and the married ones smear themselves with a red ointment and the teenagers with black. They set up an altar on which is the idol, and then comes the priest, the one called *acchu* dressed in well-painted vestments made from the bark of trees, and places on two sides of the altar two pans filled with smoke. In another pan, the priest collects blood that they all sacrifice from the ears, arms, and thighs, and offers it to the idol when requested by [the priest]. Then they leave all together and, in another room, get drunk with a very strong drink called *chicha*. Those who serve this drink are all maidens very well adorned with feathers, necklaces, and garlands. They go on these binges for two or three days. The children confess to their parents when they are very ill, and the questions are no more than to say that the sins committed angered their god and have sent him to punish them, and he has confessed all that he did. If they get well, it is a sign that they told the truth. In death, they bury them inside their house and abandon it to fall, and burn the fields of corn and cotton. If they bury the corpse elsewhere, as sometimes happens when not burning the house, they take a little dove, remove the head, and cast it on the ground, and if the dying one returns the head[52] to the house of the deceased, it is a sign that the Devil asks more of this house, and they leave it and move to another location. They bury the dead dressed and all his utensils—such as the axes, knives, cooking pots, gourds from which they drink, and everything else that they had—and in the ground is placed gold, like in Peru. In other places they found in these tombs, which they call *guacas,* great treasures. These are the only place to find them. They raise a great mound of earth, leaving on it a living dove with maize for it to eat. They shout each day for nine nights to all the [dead] relatives that they should not return, that here is something to eat.

They don't have more than a single wife, and [after] their parents agree, they marry with the intervention of a priest or any other person. According to the stories of the old ones, for a shrinking moon they say that the lion or ant eats it and climbs a very high tree to eat it, but when the moon waxes they say that it is free of the teeth of its enemies. They circumcise everyone, and the children wear many strings of animal teeth and fish shells on the waist, neck, and limbs.

All those of the Manché speak the same language, which is Chol, have the same rites and ceremonies, and divide the year into 18 [months] of 20 days each. Each of the 20 days has its own name like those of the days of the week. They call the month *uinal,* and the 20 days of it they divide into four parts. Each is one of 5 days, and the first four of each part change each year to begin the months. These are, or so they say, those that take the road and carry the month. Thus they go in a circle. They record 18 months of 360 days, at the end of which they have 5, called of the great fast. These are nameless days. With these 5 days they complete the 365. The only error in this count is the ignoring of the leap years. This shouldn't astonish us because for so many years we made a mistake, until the church corrected it, adding a day each 4 years in the month of February for the 6 hours each year beyond the 365 [days] of the count of the sun. They end these 18 months on the 28th of June, which is the last day of the month, and then enter the 5 days of great fasting until the 3rd of July. This vigil, for which there is great veneration, goes up to the 4th of July when begins the first day of the year according to its count. They have a sign for sowing in each month, for seeds like vegetables, without a disagreement of a single day.

Those of Manché have continuous war and are often defeated by those of the Ah Itza because they are few and those of Ah Itza are many. For many years they, the Itza, came in the *yazquin*, which is the summer, to take prisoners. This they did in 1630 when they carried off more than 100 persons. Thus, they returned with those whom they had taken a fancy to. After the Manche became Christians, the raids intensified because, since they border their lands, they didn't want them teaching Spaniards the roads as they [expect the Spaniards] to greatly punish them for the insolence and evil that they had made.

In the year 1624, they [the Ah Itza] killed Captain Mirones along with twenty soldiers. He had come from Yucatan, which is the land of Spaniards closest to them. They had received him in peace, saying that they wanted to be Christians and give obedience to the King our Lord. One night he and his soldiers, believing them and being careless, were captured when sleeping. They removed their arms and tied their hands. The next day they impaled all, placing in the middle the captain and a monk from San Francisco who was with them.[53] Many say Mirones was guilty, that his greed and bad treatment are what prompted the Indians to engage in this treason. That it was nothing other than carelessness and a little fear among a numerous people who did not know the Spaniards.

As said, they feared the punishment that they merited for so great a treason. They came with intent of doing away with all those of the Manché. [Stopped only] by finding Spaniards, if the Virgin had not made her miracle, these barbarians would have committed millions of evil deeds.[54] They have kept their paganism so many years since the discovery of the land, being in all directions surrounded by Christians and Spaniards because of the many large rivers that surround them, and being isolated on a great lake. They were those who gave help to those of San Marcos, as I have said, to kill Father Friar Domingo de Vico, who died a martyr in their power with another monk, his companion, and two other children, as will be told in the chapter that follows.[55]

Chapter 8, Book 2:
Of a Declaration Made to Me by an Indian
of Chajul of the Towns of the Lacandons,
Their Lords and Ways of Living

More than twenty-two years ago, the Lacandon Indians in an attack made on the towns of the Christians captured, among others, an Indian of the town of Chajul de los Reyes of nine years in age who, since one of his relatives was a Lacandon, they did not sacrifice like all the others.[56] Although raised among his relatives—and they treated him well to make him forget his native land—despite his young age and the many years he was there, a love without equal in him forced him to search roads he did not know, and traverse forests and mountains where the least that impeded the way were wild beasts, tigers, and lions. Perhaps it amused him to see them, preferring them to the rough crags and forests that towered over the habitations of even the wild beasts, causing him dread in valleys a little less difficult where he gained some rest. At the end of fourteen days, through rivers, swamps, bogs, and mountains, eating the few fruits and wild roots he could find in so rough a land, he arrived at his town, where all the inhabitants received him well, especially his relatives who, with the signs that he gave them, recognized and welcomed him.

On my orders, he gave a long description of all these lands. He was very difficult to understand because the Indian didn't know a word of his mother language, and my interpreter didn't understand his because it was of the Lacandons. Therefore, I looked for an old Indian who knew the language of the Lacandon, and begged the Inspector Father of these towns (an honest monk named Friar Lorenzo de la Bellaroca, a native of Sardinia) if he could help a little with the work and clarify the testimony of the Indian who knew these lands. We asked for the testimony in the following form.

I gave my questions to the monk in the language of Castile. He translated them into the language of this town to the oldster, and the oldster repeated them in the language of Lacandona to the Indian. The response was in the same manner, and thus it took more than a day to prepare the report.

I learned that these lands that the Lacandons have were many although not very populated, and those who deserve the name Lacandons didn't have more than two towns, called Culuacan and Cagbalan, and from one to another was a trip of eight leagues. The town of Culuacan has more than 140 houses, each one with an entire family, there being in it parents, children, sons-in-law, daughters-in-law, and grandchildren. This town has four lords called Bilbaao, Julamna, Acchicel, and Cagtei, and the priest known as Cuichilaquin Aeque Urabal.[57] The other town, Cagbalan, has 300 houses and four lords to whom they are subject.[58] These lords are Cabnal, Tunhol, Tuztecat, and Chancuc, and the priest is Cucit Cazqui. These two towns always live in peace with each other and help each other in their wars, which are commonly with those of the Indians of the Ah Itza.

Although he [the oldster] had not been in Ah Itza, he had heard it said that up to 300 houses, with a great number of Indians, are in the middle of a lake; that there ought to be in each house, including large and small, more than fifty persons. Although he heard mentioned the towns of Aquischan, Xocmo, Manché, Yol, and Noquichan, he had not visited them.[59] These were of those we call Manchés, most of whom were not Lacandons. Those of the towns of Culuacan and Cagbalan communicate with the Indians of Tabasco, and they provided some axes with whose blows they make their fields. By going through unpopulated forests filled with wax, honey, and other fruits of the lands, it took thirty-five days to reach the settlements of Tabasco. In this direction, the route leads to the northwest, to the borders of Tabasco. To the north are the lands of the Ah Itza, with whom they have many wars, and in them the captains don't use anything more than some lances with the length of an *estado* [2.17 yards] and a butcher's knife on the point or a very sharp flint shaped like a lance tip, and all the other people have bows and arrows with points of flint.[60]

The land of Verapaz is from these towns to the south, and from them the way takes sixteen days, the first two by land, then four by water, and another ten by land. There are some good saltworks where they obtain salt. By these saltworks there is a great river, and farther down three or four join it, making it very large. There are great falls, because of which canoes don't go down it. I heard it said that some Indians from these towns had once gone far downstream until the river was so wide that one couldn't see land from one bank to the other. They saw two canoes so large that they seemed like hills with people inside and thundered like when lightning strikes. By which I infer that this river goes to the Laguna de Términos that divides Yucatan from Tabasco, and that the Indians saw a ship firing its artillery, which seemed to them to be thunderclaps.

This is the account that this Indian gave me, and it seems to me to be true because he ended saying that three years ago, he was with some 140 Indians making salt in the saltworks when 4 Spaniards, a friar, and other Indians came and they hid on the other side of the river between some crags and broken ground, saying that the friar was a woman on seeing his long cowl. That night, all joined with Bilbaao and Julamna and discussed killing them in their sleep. Forty went to spy on the Spaniards and returned, saying that the trail was very large and that there should be many, for which reason the lords advised them not to kill them. They were sorry they didn't kill the Spaniards when they came the next day. What the Indians said was true because that was the year when Captain Juan de Santiago Velasco, governor of this province, my predecessor,

went with forty Spaniards to explore these lands. Velasco sent two days before the main party a captain, ensign, two other soldiers, Father Friar Francisco Morán, and some Indians to explore ahead and determine the best route. All four [Spaniards] arrived at the saltworks in the company of the friar, as we will see in the following chapter.

5

COMING OF THE SOLDIERS:

MARTIN TOVILLA, 1635

Friar Francisco Morán was a rebel. The fame of the Dominican order in Guatemala rested on the idea of peaceful conquest, without warfare or bloodshed. This is clear from the earliest days of Dominican activities (see Saint-Lu 1968), and seventeenth-century friars such as Salazar supported this notion.[1] Morán, however, prompted by invasion from the north and rebellion among the Indians, wanted to bring in soldiers. Threatened by his superiors with expulsion from Guatemala, he appealed to the secular authorities for help, which they were only too eager to provide.

Governor Tovilla was a willing accomplice in the Morán scheme for the reconquest of the Manché. He was more than happy to request soldiers and enthusiastically undertook the task of logistical support for the expeditionary force, raised with permission of the head of the colonial government. More than that, he participated directly in the campaign, and the reader finds him leading a troop against Ah Itza raiders.

None of this was of any use. Tovilla required more force than the government was willing to provide, and the lands of the Manché yielded up little support for an invading army. A lack of discipline resulted in Spanish corpses and wounded decorating the battlefield while the newly reconquered Manché fled back into the forest.

The defeated soldiers left the area. With civil war in the homeland, no support came from Spain. All efforts to reconquer these lowlands ended, and the secular authorities would abandon them until the 1650s.

[The Expedition of Velasco]

Chapter 9, Book 2:
In Which Continues the Account of the Last and Gives a
Description of the Travel Made by Captain Juan de Santiago
Velasco with Other Spaniards in the Exploration of the Land

Captain Juan de Santiago Velasco, lieutenant of the Captain General and Governor of the province of Verapaz, left the city of Cobán with a company of forty Spaniards, among which was Captain Francisco de Valdés and Ensign Alonso de Escalante. Going as marshal was Don Pedro de Urbina, and for sergeant major, Don Sancho de Guinea (it seems to me to be many heads for so few feet). They went under order of the government of Guatemala to make an exploration by land and see if one could go to Yucatan by it. If they came across any Indian settlements, they were to capture or reduce them, because two months before Lacandons had come to the fields of the town of San Pedro Carcha (four leagues from Cobán) and carried off seven Indian captives, leaving two children sacrificed by removing their hearts. Given this royal order, they followed the route of these people, who as I said left from Cobán going straight to the north. After three days on the road, they discovered a great river called Conuntehila, which in our language is the same as saying "water of painted birds."[2] They all made camp, and the lieutenant of the Captain General gave orders that the captain, ensign, two others, and some Indians should go to the river to see if it was navigable, because if so, they could make canoes or rafts for all the people.

They made two small boats, and with Father Friar Francisco Morán (then the prior of the convent of Santo Domingo of Cobán who left his house to provide heroic help in this work), went downstream for three days. Although they found many rapids, since the canoes were small, they easily went past carrying them on their shoulders. At the end of three days, they arrived at some large and good-quality saltworks. From there, they sent letters to the lieutenant of the Captain General giving an account of all that had happened until then and of the good saltwork site on their route, and that they waited there to continue their travels. After two days, a new order arrived at the saltworks requesting that they return. Weary of waiting, the very spirited captain and ensign replied that if Velasco wouldn't send supplies, they would continue without them. They received another strict order requesting their return on pain of a charge of treason and losing their life. They thus obeyed and returned against their will. All this time, Father Friar Fray Francisco Morán was with them, inspiring them and persuading them to continue forward; in truth they had more than enough desire, but the laws of the militia forced them to obey. They returned to their superior, who then ordered all to return and leave the exploration for another occasion. Despite many requests from both the father and the officials, Velasco gave the excuse that there was much water, few supplies, and illness among the soldiers. But as told by one who was there, there were many supplies, and if they had continued forward, without doubt it would have been a good success since the land was very good and provided with much hunting, fish, honey, and little edible palm trees. No doubt God, by his just judgment, kept the conversion of these souls for another time.

As I said, the 140 Lacandons saw all this, and they were the ones who carried the Indians from San Pedro and sacrificed them. In Guatemala, the President and judges badly received the governor, for he had returned without doing what they had ordered. The officials agreed, after hearing the testimony of the members of the expedition, that it was sufficient to avoid punishment. It is certain, as I said at the beginning, that the many heads had different bodies. This caused the discord that kept them from rapidly pushing forward the exploration from its first days, for they had forgotten that they could carry only few supplies. The marshal, Don Pedro de Urbina, was ill and, as a person of importance for exploring the land, carried in a hammock. As a great pilot, he was able to calculate the latitude of the location where he was and the route being followed with the astrolabe. When measuring the sun, he decided to decrease or augment the route by a degree. Thus, he traveled sixteen leagues without having gone three to the base of a mountain range of which they had no knowledge. These and other excuses of my predecessor, I will quietly leave until serving the Lord by finishing the exploration of all this land.[3]

[The First Campaigns]

Chapter 24, Book 1:
Of the Trip That I Made to Guatemala and What Happened to
Me, and the Memorial That I Gave to the President

Having been a month in Cobán and received some offerings of gifts that are customary on such occasions, as well as having been provided some things for good government during visits of the monks and neighboring towns, and having been well informed about the Manché, I left for Guatemala a place forty leagues from Cobán and thirty from my jurisdiction. The [province of Guatemala] is quite large, has more than forty towns of Indians, and is more than 100 leagues in extent. I brought an interpreter to understand the language, and in each town there was need for one, for there are none used everywhere, in this province [alone] there are five different [languages].[4]

Some towns I like very much, especially that of Rabinal for it is large and situated in a land of good climate where it does not rain as in Cobán. It is a rich town, where there are Indians who have three and four cattle and horse ranches. Before coming to this town, there is a large valley with a tiny town called Salama. I want to say "edge of the water," because an extremely pleasant river drains it.[5] The fathers of Saint Dominic have here a ranch called San Nicolás, which is of the convent of Cobán, and it has more than 4,000 head of cattle and horses, with a great breeding of mules. Also, the convent of Guatemala has a huge sugar mill called San Jerónimo, and another ranch of livestock that supports more than 150 slaves who work for the sugar mill. This is of great profit for the convent and a great help in defraying expenses. There is in this valley much hunting, and fishes similar to those of Spain. It has rabbits, partridge, quail, turtledoves, pigeons, and a great abundance of deer. In the river are *tepemechins,* a fish similar to trout, and they gave me many in the town of Rabinal. The mayors, aldermen, and more than 100 well-dressed Indians on good horses welcomed me two leagues from Rabinal.

I went to Guatemala at a time when it was preoccupied with the great festivals honoring the birth of Prince Don Baltasar Carlos de Austria. I visited the President and Judges, and gave the letters of recommendation from Spain and decrees brought from our lord, His Majesty, the Catholic King Felipe the Fourth. I presented in a box to the royal officials my patents so that they would register me and pay me my salary. That being done, I offered my proposal for action in the pacification of the Manché, giving to the President the memorial that follows:

Illustrious lord: Don Martin Alfonso de la Tovilla, governor for His Majesty of the provinces of the Verapaz, Rabinal, Golfo Dulce, Sacapulas, and Manché, says that for the conservation of the said provinces and better service of both Majesties, after taking possession of his office, he spoke with some monks with experience in these provinces—such as with Father Friar Alonso Guirao, who had been prior of the Order of Saint Dominic, and with Father Friar Francisco Morán—of the manner in which they can conserve the towns that were reduced in the said province of Manché and those that still await reduction.[6] With their accord, I offer Your Illustrious Lordship the following points. At the request of Your Illustrious Lordship, I will give them as concisely as possible.

First, it would be useful if Your Illustrious Lordship would order posted in this city a proclamation that whoever would want to settle with his house and family in the most advantageous site and province would receive a grant to build his house and divide the lands for ranches, maize fields, and cacao orchards, increasing the other privileges that Your Illustrious Lordship would want to use to inspire them.[7] There should be at least twenty, with harquebuses and munitions of war, to serve as defenders of the peaceful and not attract the rebels, protected and sheltered from the Spaniards. They should persist with courage and not dare, on fear of punishment, to do so here. Being Your Illustrious Lordship can give the title of lieutenant of the Captain General, offer it to them. So that the person with the greatest experience should offer his advice on selecting the site most convenient for the population, Friar Francisco Morán should go with them.

To do this at little cost to His Majesty or his royal [government], if it appears convenient for the support of the people, they should borrow for a year 100 head of cattle from the ranches of Rabinal, 500 fanegas of maize, and 1,000 poultry from the tribute that His Majesty has in the province of Verapaz.[8] This should be sufficient to support them while they prepare the fields and obtain produce for their sustenance.

At first provided and then paid afterward, funds would come from the tribute newly reduced [that is, conquered] Indians would pay. They can sell for slaves those whom they have captured in war, and those who have rebelled in their idolatry and don't want to continue in the Faith. This is especially true for those of the town of Yol and Xocmo who have apostatized many times and took arms against the faithful. Your Illustrious Lordship, not only can I meet expenses but obtain even more.

Given an enactment of this proposal, the Governor would give an account to Your Illustrious Lordship of the faithful Indians who from then would be tributaries and provide from the products of the land a moderate tribute. Above all, I ask and supplicate Your Illustrious Lordship to quickly support my recommendation to take advantage of the weather of the summer, it not being possible to do this throughout the year without great difficulty as well as the inconvenience we have experienced each day from the Indians and their sacrifices, as have been made in past years until this of 1631.

The arrival of Father Friar Francisco Morán from the Manché, who asked the Spaniards for help in the defense of these provinces, greatly aided me with this request. He is a man of exemplary life and customs, and a great worker of the conversion of souls, costing him sixteen years of unending work in this province, which has been pacified four times. He has, by his own hands, reduced to the faith and baptized more than 2,000 persons, entering these forests without waiting for assistance. In 1627, he came with three other Indians to Campin, a town of Yucatan near these forests and towns of gentiles. He found an affectionate reception and gifts showing that the Lord protects him in the reduction of these souls. He knows all these languages, understanding and communicating with all.

He came, as is said, on this occasion more than fifty leagues on foot because he had entered the land to pacify the rebels. When he arrived at San Miguel del Manché, he found it as I have noted previously concerning the death of the Indians, and therefore, he decided not to return until he could stop these barbarians. With this resolution, he arrived in Guatemala [intending to] go to the President and Judges of the Royal Tribunal, and asked for the head of his order, who was on this occasion Father Friar Juan Jimeno, giving an account of his intent. Friar Jimeno contradicted him with great fervor and said he would assign him to Chiapa if he did not return to the Manché; that it would take away the glory of these achievements if Spaniards intervened or provided secular help for it. The monk replied, saying that he would not be returning only to die, and that although he and his companions had tried for twenty years many times to pacify these Indians, it was of no use to baptize Indians who then apostatized since, with little fear of punishment, each day they idolized. Thus, he should assign him wherever he wishes, but for these reasons he had no desire to return to the Manché. With the reporting of this conversation to the President and Judges, certain of his holy zeal and disinterest, they ordered him detained. They then met and issued the edict that follows.

Chapter 25, Book 1:
Of the Edict That Provided for Spaniards
to Go to the Province of Manché

To you, Don Martin Alfonso de la Tovilla, governor of the province of the Verapaz and my deputy in its district, whom I have entrusted what you have requested. Know that I have provided the edict with the contents as following:

In the city of Santiago of Guatemala on the 11th day of March of the year 1631, His Lordship Don Diego de Acuña, Gentleman of the Order of Alcántara, Commander of Hornos, of the Council of War, Governor and Captain General of the provinces of the district of the Tribunal and Royal Chancellery, who resides in this city and is President of it: I say that the Indians of the province of the Manché in that of the Verapaz, after having been reduced by peaceful measures to our Holy Catholic Faith, baptized by the monks of Lord Saint Dominic, and given obedience to His Majesty, revolted various times against it. They went to the pagan Indians by conquest, and to the forest, resulting in many deaths and sacrifices among the Indians. Because with great danger to their souls they go into the forests to avoid their obligations to Christian religion, service to His Majesty, and the tribute that was charged for this manner of reduction, the convenient and necessary remedy appears to be to establish in the most convenient part of the province of the Manché a town of preferably twenty honorable married Spaniards, or mulattoes or mestizos, with their arms of muskets and harquebuses, fuse, gunpowder, and balls, so they can control the settlements of the reduced Indians of the Manché and defend them from those enemies, the pagan Indians of the districts of Ah Itza, Yol, and Lacandon, who continually harass the Manché Indians. Because these Spaniards, mestizos, and mulattoes can't come without support and help with costs, lands for their fields, raising of livestock and maize for their sustenance, having consulted with the Lords of the Royal Tribunal, I intend to request, as in fact has been done, that Don Martin Alfonso de la Tovilla, governor of the Verapaz, recruit twenty married residents to establish the said population wherever seems most convenient, for which the royal treasury will provide fifty tostons to each one for moving expenses, and among all 500 fanegas of maize and 1,000 poultry of the tribute Indians of this province pay to His Majesty, providing whatever they obtain in the auction of the produce. Two hundred cattle obtained from the ranches round about and loaned to the settlers, divided into equal parts, shall give about two to each married couple. The towns of the Manché shall make houses and give ordinary service. Since the lands of the towns of the Indians will be next to those populated by the Spaniards, they shall demarcate the boundaries of their fields. The money, maize, poultry, and livestock thus given come from what they would have paid to His Majesty from the tribute that the Indians of the Manché shall pay beginning in the year 1632. Indian rebels, Lacandons, Yols, and Ah Itza, that the Spaniards take by war can be enslaved to serve them for ten years, or until His Majesty orders otherwise.

Inasmuch as for the present, reduction of the Indians of the Manché has been the interest, care, good zeal, example, Christian behavior, and disinterest of Father Friar Francisco Morán who administers them, neither his superior nor any other prelate can remove him from these duties, nor other monks assigned to it [the Manché], without order of his Lordship, in conformity with the decree of royal patronage that I administer. Thus I decree and I sign.

So it takes effect, I order it given, implemented, and proclaimed today. This edict is legal, and insofar as it affects someone, they should guard, comply, and execute it in its entirety as it states and declares. [Anything] contrary to its meaning and form shall not go nor be allowed nor take effect nor take place, for which I give notification as is required. Made in Guatemala on the 15th day of March of 1631. Don Diego de Acuña. By order of his lordship, Don Cristóbal de Escobar.

Immediately, I requested that this edict be proclaimed in Guatemala and people recruited. Given the aid that His Highness ordered, they gathered the harquebuses, muskets, gunpowder, and balls. It took ten days to do all, prepare all, and name an adjutant to command and quarter the twenty soldiers being dispatched. I remained behind to arrange for all the munitions. The day on which they left, I made a long speech ordering that there should be no disorder on the road, molesting of any Indian, or the taking of anything without paying for it. I gave ample authority to my adjutant to punish any crimes en route. In this manner, the twenty said Spaniards in the company of Father Friar Francisco Morán left from Guatemala, being ordered to always obey him and be guided by him in the above-noted actions.

Chapter 27, Book 1:
Of How the Soldiers Advanced, the Selection That They Made
of Officials, and [How] I Assumed the Title
of Lieutenant of the Captain General

On the fourth day after I left the city, I caught up with my soldiers, and was pleased on seeing how content and proud they went and that they had not demanded or done anything that caused a complaint among the Indians, who are very timid and intimidated by the news of Spanish soldiers coming to their lands. Having seen them [soldiers] only once, they [the Indians] seem to think that 1,000 males will follow making some excess. I arrived at the city of Cobán, where I made a selection of officials and accoutrements of banners, drums, harquebuses, gunpowder, and balls. Sunday of Santa Susana, the 30th of March, we went with great merriment to the convent of Saint Dominic, where Father Friar Pedro de Molina, prior of the convent of Saint Dominic and a native of the city of Jerez de la Frontera, consecrated the flag in my hands, making a great salute with the harquebuses and muskets. They made a demonstration, and since they were boys and quite inexperienced, discharged some practice blank shots. They did well with the harquebuses and then went on horses, of which they had bought good ones, and taking lances, skirmished gallantly in the plaza. I gave them orders that they should depart for the town of those condemned, in conformity with the edict, to slavery for ten years and, above all, always follow the advice of Father Friar Francisco Morán.

They arrived at a town called San Agustin [Lanquin], the residence of Father Friar Gabriel de Salazar, who then was vicar of the convent of Manché. I rested much, and with generous heart and liberal spirit, they gave us gifts and provided some things that we lacked, in particular for each one, his [own] baggage carrier to serve him and take care of his horse. I wrote how joyful it was to see the good people who went, which in truth it was, although few would argue that it was little more than a promise of things to come. I also wrote [ahead] of my arrival in these towns to prepare them, since I had stayed behind to arrange for provisions, because one could not hazard something so important for the demon with his cunning provided a thousand difficulties for the Indians. The major reason was the lack of maize, which is the wheat of the land, for three times the fields had an invasion of *chapulin* (what they call locust). At once I made other towns dispatch a large amount of it.

Continuing ahead, in two days I came to the soldier's camp. Because with these difficulties the Indians were somewhat slack, there was universal pleasure among the monks and soldiers on seeing me on the 5th of April of that year [of 1631]. I ordered then the issuing of a proclamation that all in the town with bows and arrows should come to a meeting that afternoon; and I selected 100 of the most handy and strong to go with the Spaniards to capture the Indians. The very brave Captain Don Miguel Juárez of these 100 Indians, the governor and ruler of this town of Santa María Cahabón, always aided the monks in their expeditions.[9]

Monday, the 7th of the said [month], I dispatched the Spaniards on ahead because it would take three days travel from there to reach the enemy town and Indians. Foreseeing a need for a supply of provisions, because the conditions were most difficult, I returned two days afterward to Cobán to forward cattle and other supplies. I provided orders to the captain of the Spaniards (who was Juan de la Mutilla Ortega, a native of the city of Alcaraz, my homeland) by virtue [of my] being lieutenant of the Captain General, as given in the following patent.[10]

Philip, by the grace of God, king of Castile, Leon, Aragon, the two Sicilies, Jerusalem, Portugal, Navarre, Granada, Toledo, Valencia, Galicia, Mallorca, Seville, Sardinia, Córdoba, Corsica, Murcia, Jaen, the Algarve, Algeciras, Gibraltar, the Canary Islands, the East and West Indies, the islands and mainland of the Ocean Sea, archduke of Austria, duke of Burgundy, Brabant, and Milan, count of Augsburg, Flanders, Tyrol, and Barcelona, lord of Vizcaya and Molina, etc. In virtue of my royal personage, I give the title of Captain General of the provinces of Guatemala to Don Diego de Acuña, Gentleman of the Order of Alcántara, Commander of Hornos, of my Council of War, President of my Tribunal and Royal Chancellery, who resides in the city, and my Governor General in its district, whose powers are as follows:

. . . By virtue of what I have provided, Don Diego de Acuña, Gentleman of the Order of Alcántara, by my President of my Royal Tribunal of the province of Guatemala, and agree to at the same time being my Captain General of it, for the present I select, name, and give power and authority to use and exercise the said duties of my Captain General of the said province during the time that he serves as my President of the said Tribunal, in all instances and things belonging and part of the said duty, according to and in the manner that it is done, they can and should be as my other and Captains General of similar provinces, and islands of the Indies.[11] I so inform the inhabitants, residents, and dwellers of the said province of Guatemala who I have for my Captain General, and who is responsible for all said duties that touch on and pertain to it, and you should obey, respect, and attend to our summons, reviews, and musters with your persons, arms, and horses, providing it on the occasions necessary of war as on the others when required for instruction and training in the things of war. You should guard and respect all the grants, gifts, exemptions, and liberties that you should have and enjoy, and you ought to be entirely and completely guarded by reason of the duty of the Captain General, without lacking anything. Given in Madrid on the 20th of June 1626. I THE KING. Don Garcia de Avellaneda. Licenciate Don Rodrigo de Aguiar y Acuña. Licenciate Alonso Maldonado de Torres. Licenciate Fernando de Villaseñor. Licenciate Don Francisco Manso y Zúñiga. Licenciate Don Francisco Antonio de Alarcón. I, Don Fernando Ruiz de Contreras, secretary of the King, our lord, having so written by his order. Registered, Don Antonio de Aguiar y Acuña, by the principal chancellor, Don Antonio de Aguiar y Acuña, his lieutenant.

Therefore, I have made Don Martin Alfonso de la Tovilla, a person of satisfaction and confidence, my governor of the province of Verapaz. In the past year of 1623, he went to serve, being promoted three times beyond his ordinary appointment in my states of Flanders and afterward being named chief administrator of the saltworks of Murcia.[12] Captain Pablo Ruiz Alfonso, his father, served me more than forty-four years, and in Portugal, was superintendent of the people of war reorganized between Duero and Mino and went with them to Lisbon, deployed the artillery in the castle of San Juan that evening, took part in the battle in the suburbs, fought with the cavalry, and captured a royal standard.[13] Captain Fernando de la Tovilla, his great-grandfather, served many years, and in 1525 Emperor Maximilian knighted him for special service as a valiant soldier.[14] Gonzalo de la Tovilla, his grandfather, served with a pike in the affair of Baza, where he achieved distinction, and the other special services that he and his ancestors have made are given further on.[15]

In the province of the Verapaz there are a number of pagan Indians who normally fight with those of peace and make surprise attacks, and for which reason in it and its jurisdiction there is a lieutenant of my Captain General for the defense of the natives and inhabitants of it. Respecting the ability, competence, merits, qualities, and services of Don Martin Alfonso de la Tovilla, we have named him lieutenant of my Captain General so he can exercise the duty and office in the province of the Verapaz, its borders, and jurisdiction on occasions of peace and necessary war in my royal service, and in defense of the province, natives, and inhabitants of it. Grasping the banner and with the drum and fife as the lieutenants of my Captain General gather the infantry of our jurisdiction, ordering that they all appear and be prepared with their arms and munitions, he agrees to provide all of them with all that is necessary for peace, quietude, and the protection of the province, its borders, and jurisdiction. Concerning the militia, he will name whoever he feels is appropriate as officials of the companies and give them their orders. All this is to better serve me and defend the land.

I have made him subordinate to the President, Governor, and Captain General so that all the above mentioned, annexed, and dependent will comply and provide all the things that those who are lieutenants of my Captain Generals—in my name, my kingdoms, and my domains—can and ought to be provided. I so order his dependents and subordinates to obey, and I order the captains, ensigns, officials, and people of the militias of the province and its jurisdiction, and the others selected and named, that they should obey him and respect the lieutenant of my Captain General, and they should come and personally appear before him in peace and war at his summons, following which appropriate penalties can be executed on the transgressors. They should guard and comply with all so ordered. That he should gain all the honors, exemptions, liberties, privileges, and immunities that by reason of the duties ought to have and possess and ought to be guarded and possessed by the other lieutenants of my Captain Generals of the cities, villas, and ports of my kingdoms and lordships. All shall comply on pain of punishment and a fine of 500 pesos of gold, half for my royal court and half for the expenses of war. Given in the city of Santiago in Guatemala on the 30th day of March of the year 1631. Don Diego de Acuña, [by the hand of] I, Andres de Escobar, secretary of the chamber of the King, our lord, and his Tribunal and Chancellery of Santiago in Guatemala. Written by the order of its President and Captain General. Registered by his chancellor, Don Pedro Marin de Solorzano.

Chapter 28, Book 1:
Of the Arrival That They Made at Yol and of the Letter
That Father Friar Francisco Morán Wrote and the
Other That I Wrote to the Royal Tribunal

Having made the entrance in this manner and arrived at the town of Yaxha, they were ordered to make a halt. They entered the forests on the morning of Holy Wednesday, that being the 16th of April, and walked four days through difficult terrain, crags, and swamps. Finally, on the morning of the Sunday of Resurrection, they arrived at the town of Yol.[16] Since the houses were very scattered, they could capture no more than fourteen persons, for all the others fled. While they were walking toward these groups, I was working harder than ever in preparing the supplies, dividing the cattle they had removed from the ranches, and other necessary things for the support of the people. On the 1st of May, the day of the blessed apostles San Pedro and San Pablo, in the town of San Pedro [Carcha], a league from Cobán, I received this letter from Father Friar Francisco Morán, who had arrived with the people:[17]

> Our Lord has given Holy Easter to Your Honor, for whose health I offer my inquiries: I am very much at the service of Your Honor, and with concern and desire await your arrival, because the rains have not yet begun. [On] Easter, after four days of going through the forests without much to eat, the soldiers and I were happy to make the scoundrels of Yol sad and put them in pain; for on the morning of Easter we were in their fields, which were exceptionally good and filled our needs, leaving those who had fled in great want. We captured fourteen, both small and great; the others, considering the great crime that they had committed and fearing punishment, left all their household goods except the lightest and fled into the forest, which is all swampy and filled with spines. It being rainy this day, neither Spaniards nor Indians could go in pursuit. We burned their houses. We took all the maize that the Indians could carry. We destroyed the fields, and not counting what the Indians of Cahabón [took], the soldiers carried away many axes, machetes, mirrors, clothing, and other things. I had the strength to walk with a stick behind many who did not try to do more than take what was in the houses without attempting to capture the Indians. It was a miracle to be with them after four days walking through forests and swamps without path or trail, guided by no more than a boy who had come from this settlement.
>
> Left well punished and taught the need for being peaceful, we felt they would want to die since we didn't leave them anything to eat, nor iron to cultivate the land. Besides which we brought back the husbands of some women who would not abandon them, and various other children, grandsons and son-in-laws of a headman, as well as a married daughter and a daughter-in-law. From these we learned that all feared the punishment made on those of Yol and had to make peace. All the Indians who were in their towns when the Spaniards entered this land with me were peaceful and quiet. Those who separated came together. Praise to the Lord for overcoming this difficulty. Those who fled on seeing soldiers are now

pleased and contented with the good luck, and eager to see you in the town, where we will go to rest and wait for Your Honor [on] Thursday.

After I read this letter, and others of the captain and soldiers, I gave an account to the Royal Tribunal of everything and how I would be leaving the next day for Manché. This account is as follows:

Sir. In conformity with what Your Highness ordered, I came to this province with twenty Spaniards from this city and arrived at Cahabón with the intention of entering it with them to punish the Indians of Yol and Xocmo for the crimes they had committed in the death of the Indians of Yaxha.[18] It seemed to me best to start with them so that the others would see we intended to punish the restless and rebels. Because of the great hunger in all of this province, it was not possible for me to go forward before going thirty leagues to the towns of San Cristóbal [Verapaz] and Tactic, which had harvests of maize, to obtain supplies. Therefore, as lieutenant of our Captain General, I picked a captain and ensign for the said twenty Spaniards, giving them harquebuses, gunpowder, balls and fuses, drums and banners, and other necessary munitions. I then ordered them to make an expedition in search of the Indians of Yol. In support of the orders of our President, to go with them, I sent 100 Indian archers from Cahabón, whose captain was Don Miguel Juárez. I also provided them with a banner, drums, and some lances. I sent Domingo de Ramos with orders to accompany the Spaniards and always obey the orders of the captain of the Spanish soldiers.

They stopped in Yaxha, a three-day journey from Cahabón, and prepared some supplies. On Holy Wednesday, they entered the forest in the company of Father Friar Francisco Morán, having a boy who guided them to where those of Yol had fled. It was in the Lord's service that after four days through forests and swamps, they found them on the morning of Easter Sunday, and when the Spaniards came they fled, leaving their houses without worrying about what was inside them. They apprehended fourteen persons, both great and small, and a headman and his daughter and daughter-in-law, and they removed many axes, machetes, mirrors, and some clothing. They obtained much maize. They destroyed the fields, which were very good, and burned the houses. All this made the Indians happy and pleased with the results of the arrival of the Spaniards, and I am sure that the missing Indians of Yol will arrive in peace.

I am leaving this morning for the Manché and have arranged to have the collected maize and other food sent [to the Manché]. It was not possible to obtain cattle from the ranches of the friars, and therefore, they came from others in this jurisdiction. Because I am providing a long account of all to our President, I am not going to say more here. May our Lord guard you, Your Highness, for the good and defense of your subjects and punishment of the infidels. Made in Cobán on the 2nd of May of year 1631.

[Toro de Acuña]

Chapter 1, Book 2:
Of the Trip Made to the Manché and the Settlement
of Spaniards That Was Made There, at the Site
Named Toro de Acuña

As noted in the letter to the Royal Tribunal, I left for the Manché. On arriving at Cahabón, I prepared defensive arms against the arrows of the Ah Itza or other infidels. I made a three-fingers-thick leather bag shaped as an overcoat, tied shut from the bottom, and stuffed with quilted cotton. It was proof against arrows. They in no way could pass through it. I also made my own helmet of plaster in the manner of a cap or hat that covers the entire head except for the eyes and nose, where only the eyes remain exposed, and on which I placed a visor of steel. It pleased the Indians of the town to see good armor, for although growers of cotton, they do not use it in this manner for defense from arrows. Previously, their bow-and-arrow warriors dressed in hides.[19]

With me came fifty Indian archers; I did not count the bearers of other things. Although freed by many proclamations, and the fact that a horse can carry more and go longer without a rest, since pagan times no one has been powerful enough to remove the loads from their [the Indians] shoulders. If one says something, they reply that their feet are more valuable than those of a horse, since a horse gets weary and they don't. With this they prepare packages of 75 and 100 pounds, and carry them 50 and 100 leagues if it is necessary. Their hero is the one who carries the heaviest load. With the heaviest loads, they travel less than 8 leagues [or about 30 miles] each day. They go by roads and hills so rough and mountainous, filled with loose rocks and slippery places, that mules can hardly pass, and by horse it would be impossible. Therefore, with two Indians in the lead to guide them, everything went by foot on their shoulders via the most slippery slopes.

We came to a little stream, five leagues from Cahabón, and there we passed the night. The next day, we went most of the morning on the worst road for it had many swamps and marshes. It astonished all the Indians. We came to a depopulated site, and subsequently in the following days, there were six [of them]. We all slept in settlements of Indians newly congregated after the general assessment of the year 1628. The first that I reached was Yaxha, and they were now as savage and barbarous as before baptism.[20] I took possession in the name of His Majesty, counted the town, and registered the inhabitants. I issued decrees and fixed prices, providing these orders the first time that I saw them, because the men didn't use more than some bandages that covered their shame, and the women some little underskirts that served the same function. I went to the other towns, looking at the arrangement of the land to see where it might be best to place a settlement of Spaniards. Although it was all good and very fertile, suitable for cacao and achiote, which is the silver that they produce, it was so hilly and hot that it did not seem to me suitable.

I arrived at a savanna or valley that was three leagues long from north to south and more than one wide from east to west, all cleared of trees, where there was a village of Indians called San Miguel del Manché. The fathers had there placed the convent of this vicariate. It seemed to me extremely good, because in more than sixty leagues there was no other site like this level savanna. It had all the things necessary for a great city. There was water as well as firewood, timber, and lime; and lands to make its fields. Most important, the good river called Petenha was eight leagues from the site.[21] Going with this river, it was two days to the port of Santo Tomás de Castilla. This is where the ships that come from Spain unload, making the site easy to supply. All these things, and being the frontier with the enemies, made me elect this site as better than some other.

I found there my soldiers; they and the monks met me a league from the settlement, all pleased with my arrival for they were eager to learn from me where I would establish the town so each one could work on their farm. They carefully examined the layout of the site, and finding it suitable, marked the location of the church and plaza, and then for each one a site for their houses, maize fields, and other necessary things. I made a large cross, and the next day we carried it in procession with great solemnity accompanied by trumpets and shots from the harquebuses and muskets, and having arrived at the cemetery of the church, arm in arm with the blessed Father Friar Francisco Morán and other monks that were there singing the hymn "The Banners of the King Go Forth," we raised it, having first placed three coins of gold, silver, and iron under the base of the cross, and then like a cornerstone set it in place. We closed the hole by putting a step around it and great arches of branches and flowers. All the Indians of the town helped us, and we made them come with wood for the church. They and the others of the region made it in four days, and it will serve until they make one of stone. In important places in these parts I have seen many that were not as good. Joining the Spaniards, and with many words, they asked that we choose for patroness of the settlement the Holy Virgin, our Lady, so she will help and favor us in our good intentions and a work as holy as the salvation of the souls of these barbarians.

So that the church would always have the decoration, cleanliness, and service necessary, we established a livestock ranch, and I was the first to give money for it. In my land appeared a miraculous image whose name was our Lady of Cortés (because the kings were accustomed to calling a parliament there), and therefore, we desired to give this title to our patroness. We celebrated the Holy Birth as if it had happened in the city of Alcaraz, and I gave an effigy of the image and some sedan chairs to carry it in procession and a frontal for the high altar.[22] Hearing of the good offering, the soldiers all swore, and each one with a liberal spirit offered what they could, with which we endowed for the Holy Virgin, Mother of God, and our Lady a ranch of twenty-two cows and some feet of cacao. I, in name of His Majesty, assigned a row of houses in the plaza for the same church and named stewards to care for the goods of the church, offering to the settlers for the miraculous Holy Virgin grants on this very same night. For all those who would soon do so, and govern in my absence, I provided an edict of foundation in the following form:

> Don Martin Alfonso de la Tovilla, governor for His Majesty of the provinces of the Verapaz, Sacapulas, Rabinal, Golfo Dulce, and Manché, lieutenant of the Captain General in all of these. So [by the powers vested in me] in the city of Guatemala, I issue the edict with the following meaning (this is the edict [I] previously referred to in chapter 25):
>
> All of which the edict ordered I have obeyed and complied with, according to and in the form and manner ordered, having collected the people in the city of Santiago de Guatemala and brought them to this province over a distance of ninety leagues, and looking for the best site within it, consulting with Father Friar Francisco Morán as a person of experience and the settlers, and [having]

tallied their votes, it seemed to me to be convenient and necessary to pick the savanna where sits the convent of the monks of the Holy Lord Domingo. It has enough water and highlands, and is on the frontier of the Ah Itza and Lacandon, from whose location all the surrounding towns discovered up to now can be protected and defended, and those discovered will have the same benefit.

Therefore, for the honor and glory of our Lord, Jesus Christ, and the exaltation of our Holy Catholic Faith, today, the 13th of May of [the] year 1631, I have designated the site where the church and royal houses will be built, and have named the site Toro de Acuña in memory of his Illustrious Lordship, Don Diego de Acuña, gentleman of the Order of Alcántara, Knight Commander of Hornos, of the Council of War of His Majesty, Governor and Captain General of the province of Guatemala, and President of his Royal Tribunal. His order and authority were important for this work, and for this reason, his Lordship, Illustrious native of the city of Toro in Spain, has added his surname. Copying the name of the miraculous image of Alcaraz de la Mancha, the patroness of the church is Santa María of Cortés. This is the effigy that is on the high altar of the church. I have also designated the site for the convent, incorporated into the church, and the houses of the settlers. I adjusted and marked all the lands that are on the western edge of this settlement up to the old site of San Miguel del Manché so that the Spaniards can make their corn and other fields, leaving all that falls on the eastern side of the town for the Indians, without placing them among any Spaniards. I gave in the name of His Majesty for this settlement all the old site of the town of Manché with its cacao orchards and [square] feet of achiotes, and all else that there is in it for the construction and repair of the royal houses. So that all these take effect and go forward, that the population and inhabitants have what they need to govern and preserve it in peace and justice, I have elected and named for my lieutenant general in all this province the ensign Pablo de Cales, for he is a worthy and experienced person. In order that the settlers have normal service from Indian *tiquitines,* like the Indian millers, I order that the Indian mayors and councilmen of the neighboring towns provide those needed and those that my lieutenant asks for, as additional service for the construction of the houses, they being paid in conformity with the royal tariffs and not in some other manner.[23] Done in the day, month, and year. Don Martin Alfonso Tovilla.

With this and the title that I gave from my lieutenant to the ensign Pablo de Cales, they all remained very content, and I would see how proudly they all engaged in the manufacture of their houses and other necessities.

Chapter 2, Book 2:
Of a Miraculous Event That Happened to Us Through [the]
Intercession of Our New Patroness, the Virgin of Cortés

While the settlers were carefully making their houses and my lieutenant engaged in the fabrication of the church and royal houses, I was torturing some of the Indians captured in the expedition to Yol. After a few turns, they made a full confession of all we desired to know, which was where were those of Xocmo.[24] As we were going to pacify the province, it seemed to me that some gentleness would attract them. Thus, I dispatched two of the same Indians to meet their companions and bring them, promising to pardon them if they came and did not cause trouble.

Their women and the children of the messengers remained in our settlement as a guarantee for their return. Saturday, the 17th of May, we wanted to celebrate the holiday of our new patroness, saying a mass with all solemnity, which would be the first time it was sung in this location. With the help of trumpets, harquebuses, and muskets, we celebrated the holiday as best we could, aided with much devotion from all the Spaniards and Indians. Finishing mass, I gave thanks to all the monks, and in the presence of all the Spaniards said that those who didn't want to pay what I asked them, the Virgin, our Lady, would quickly see that she would repay them with obvious advantages. As no one wanted to owe anything, all of us paid everything instantly; just as quickly we were saved from death, for this night we were surrounded by 1,000 Indians of Ah Itza.

The Holy Virgin, as thanks for having been chosen by us for our patroness, was watching carefully over her servants. When all my soldiers were off duty during the second part of the night, I awoke and touched off a false alarm as a precaution. I had intended to set off the alarm not at this hour but much later. This intention I communicated to the three monks because I didn't want to disturb them or make them uneasy. As I said, a little after midnight I awoke, and although it appeared to be early, perhaps by two hours or more, our Holy Patroness, since now was the time, made me rise and equip myself with a breastplate of steel and my bag of cotton so the soldiers would believe what I was saying. I shot off a musket, and caused the bell and a trumpet to sound. Then I shoulted in a loud voice: "Treason! We are surrounded by 1,000 Indians of Ah Itza!" I went from one place to another with my sword and a shield, and as the soldiers arrived, I ordered them to go around the place with a trumpet and shoot many harquebuses, and I so ordered those who were with me. [This was] done so eagerly and in such loud voices that the soldiers and monks who had been prepared, very certain [that something was happening], came with spears and stayed by my side.[25]

The commotion, bell ringing, and trumpeting lasted more than an hour, at the end of which I ordered everyone together and made a long speech, telling them that if some disaster had happened I would be very confident. Noting that we remain undiscovered, I pointed out that we are amid our enemies and 100 leagues from Spanish towns. I reminded them of the disaster that overtook Mirones with the Indians of Ah Itza, as we will present further on.[26] Although they had come quickly, we still could have all been killed, and that henceforth each night, we would post a guard at my house. That what they had experienced [shows] it is important to keep three-hour watches from four to four so we do not find ourselves dead or tied up in the hands of our enemies. With this the monks gathered. I ordered the soldiers to return to their houses, and I returned to my abandoned bed.

The same day, Sunday morning, we came to hear the mass and a sermon preached by Father Friar Francisco Morán, which although presented in the language of the Indians, all the soldiers assisted him, and on it ending everyone went to their houses. Soon after, an Indian came loaded with arrows, bows, and other loot, saying they were of the Ah Itza and that they were from very near, for the night before they had their outposts at the edge of the forest. I convoked a meeting and certified that it was true. Then I ordered at once the sounding of an alarm and gathering together in the church of all the women, children, and oldsters. Leaving them with two soldiers and two monks to guard them, I went with my soldiers and about thirty Indian archers in pursuit on the path they had taken. The trail of arrows, bows, and quivers began at 100 paces from the houses.[27] From the entrance to the forest up to two shots of a harquebus from the last houses, which is where they camped the night before and prepared for their assault, there was an infinite number of mats made from the bark of trees that they brought to cover themselves, bows, arrows, maize, *piñol*, tortillas, tamales, rope to tie up Indians, gourds of tobacco, little leather caps, and wooden earflaps, all of which they had abandoned there.[28]

It is clear from the evidence that they fled with great haste, leaving the effects that we could collect. From what some Indians who had fled from Ah Itza said, when we were sounding the alarm in our settlement, some had been spying on us to see if all was quiet and others were making a prayer to their false gods. For we found placed below an arbor an altar, the clothes of their priest, and three large idols—one the head of a pig, another of a lizard, and the other a bear covered with copal—as well as many small saucepans with the incense used to perfume them. They also had many other tiny idols of wood. Besides these they left two [of] horsemen with something of a crest and many different-colored feathers in place of tassels, and a well-made shield as protection against arrows. I ordered that no one should touch them because I would return to collect them to send them to the Royal Tribunal.

Picking up one of these horsemen and the shield, I followed the road in pursuit. Although it was muddy and filled with marshes, none of these made any difficulty for me. Being first, I hurled myself into the rivers with the sword in my mouth to give inspiration to my people. We walked all day in this manner without any of us having eaten any meal. Moreover, certain that there would be 1,000 Indians, we only carried weapons. All went on this road covered with the above-mentioned things and many bloody tracks, especially due to some sticks in the rivers, which hurt one each time one passed them by. As it was a narrow and spiny road, and they were many Indians, they could not pass all together. Most of them flung themselves into the water, leaving on the banks all that could hamper them. We thus continued until arriving, before a great storm, at some huts that the Indians had defended that afternoon. They were more than 800, and leaving them, we took a different road to our settlement. I gave an order to my soldiers to return because there was no way we could kill them. I sent twelve [of our] Indians to follow their trail and mark the roads for another time. It now being the rainy season, these roads were impossible because of the great rivers, swamps, and marshes.

We returned to our town and gave innumerable thanks to our patroness for having freed us from so obvious a danger. The next day, all the Indians and Spaniards (I being the first to start this work) began fortifying a parade ground with good stakes to give the women and children some protection if the enemy comes. With these and other things that needed ordering, it seemed time to return to Cobán. The rains had begun, and I wanted to inspect all the province, and as will be seen in the chapter that follows, give an account to the Royal Tribunal of what happened and send, even though few have any value, the spoils from the barbarians.

Chapter 6, Book 1:
How I Returned from the Manché, How Some of the
Colonists Returned, and a Letter That I Wrote to Them

The trip from Manché to the town of Cahabón took several days because of the roughness of the roads and the great waters that appeared
so suddenly. In some places it was necessary to use rafts, in others
swimming, and in others the water always [came to] the seat of the
saddle. Since it was a new route, one did not know the roads to avoid,
resulting in all these inconveniences. Of more help to me was a letter that
I received there from the President and Judges; their thanks for the good
success of the expedition to Yol cheered and comforted me. They said
that I should continue and that they had great hopes from such good
beginnings.

I wrote, giving a long description of all that had happened since I was
here last, and sent four loads of relics left by the Ah Itza, as well as all
their idols, bows, arrows, mats, earflaps, and things of little importance.
With this, leaving well arranged the means of carrying provisions for my
Spaniards, I went to the city of Cobán because I would need to make an
inspection of the province that up to now I was not able to do.

As the Devil is always watching to obstruct the welfare of souls, and
seeing how great has been the assistance of the Spaniards in this province, he didn't lack a plan to sow discord among them, placing on them a
thousand difficulties, and the greatest appears to be hunger because
provisions could not pass by road due to the great waters.[29] Thus it was
that a week after arrived some four Indians with the pretext that they
lacked sustenance and remained alone without a monk to say mass
because, since I had come, Father Friar Francisco Morán with four
other Spaniards had entered the land of the infidels. The other monk
said that since the rivers had swollen and the roads were so bad, one
could pass neither on foot nor horse, and so they had lacked food for a
week. I thought to bestow sufficient commission on someone to take all
the Indians what was necessary from the towns, so they made rafts and
houses on the roads to supply provisions, which could come perhaps
with the great rains. Being told that when these four returned all might
leave, I sent an order requiring, on pain of death and treason to the
King, that they return to the demarcated site. I sent them with Captain
Juan de la Matilla, who had remained with me to prepare some things,
and wrote this letter to cheer them:

> Master soldiers: Can you not see that the Devil, being interested in
> the loss of souls, has done everything possible to turn aside and

dissuade the important work that you have begun? Do you imagine that he has no work beyond disunion and destruction. For without our esteemed victory, would we deserve the glory and rewards that we await from them? Even now, one can take as an example Father Friar Francisco Morán, who although favored with preeminent positions, as he always had in his order, he did not stay in his cell to give orders but always exposed himself to work and dangers. I have not shrunk from those that have presented themselves. Thus, in the trip from Manché, I went on foot through swamps, through rough and painful roads, just as in the pursuit we made of the Indians of Ah Itza I was always in the lead. Thus, what the Lord gave us in this work dwarfs the strength of giants. Consider the bad consequences for the victory that he achieved with his companions and their honorable fame and rewards if Cortés [in the conquest of Mexico], considering that he had a million Indians for each Spaniard, refused to go forward. For now neither will the Lord show less mercy on forsaking his own cause, nor His Majesty the King, our lord, be less liberal than his ancestors in providing grants [that is, rewards] for conquerors; nor is the work of greater importance nor the hope for grants, nor should Spaniards be more timid.

These examples are good enough to show that we should finish what we have begun, and we can see that the time has now arrived to reduce these souls to the authority of the church. By the signs he has given, our Lord will guard this enterprise, giving us the victory. By working miracles so that the incredulous and blasphemous will believe by seeing it with their eyes, our Lord caused more than 1,600 Indians to flee, without even seeing us, in fright. One way to make a better effort is by obedience and not omitting by the smallest amount any of the orders of your superiors, for the soldier who deserves the most reward is the one who erroneously obeys but succeeds despite instructions and orders. All of this is to say, what I myself ask and His Majesty orders, that you should not abandon any part of the demarcated site. I will offer to send these papers and letters of Father Friar Francisco Morán to the Royal Tribunal. I am writing to the Lord President asking that grants be conceded on just petition, for the splendor and progress of our grants is important to me. If this request has no effect, I will personally come in January, with 50 other Spaniards and 400 Indians, to finish with this ghost of Ah Itza who so troubles these new Christians; until then, trusting in God that He will spread the fame of your works, you can postpone making shields and cotton jackets for your defense. You are well aware that this exhortation of mine is enough to bring you tranquillity. The more so since if someone violates the royal orders, they can punish them. I am sending this order, as is well known, to my lieutenant. If not already required to do an inspection of this province, I would come directly to see you and assist in the great service that we will make to our Lord in it. May He grant you and me health so that we will see us triumphant over the devil in Ah Itza. Cahabón, July 6th of the year 1631.

This letter was of great benefit because it, and the arrival of their captain, quite pleased the soldiers. Thus, they unanimously agreed not to leave this site until the entire province was quiet and peaceful. Also pleasing was a letter from Father Morán for the President, carried by my lieutenant, Pablo de Cales, requesting their just and necessary requests be conceded. In order to quickly get this result, and for the petitions of the settlers, he provided the following letter:[30]

Illustrious Lord: Now one should finish the work begun in the pacification of this province of Manché, reducing the apostate Indians, converting the heathen that await conversion in this land, and defending these new vassals of His Majesty against the pagan Indians of Ah Itza who continually attack, making notable trouble. Only a year ago, they carried off more than 100 captives, among them small and large, without counting another 20 that they had killed. This month of May on the 18th (as written by Don Martin Alfonso de la Tovilla, governor of these provinces and lieutenant of the Captain General), they came, as is well shown by the effects that they left behind—the many loads of supplies, bows, arrows, lances, thongs, and shields—and they returned more lightly leaving all, even the idols and musical instruments all brought to celebrate the sacrifices that they expected to make of these wretches *if the Spaniards had not come.*[31] Nor can those who are in this land, thanks to the good foresight of the Governor, leave and allow the sheep-eating wolves to destroy the new plants in our Holy Faith, to shed the blood of these young ewes now added to the flock of our good pastor Christ, to offer them to the common enemy that is always eager to drink the blood of his faithful.

I have said that 1,600 Ah Itza Indians from the interior came within two harquebus shots of Toro de Acuña, which wouldn't have discharged a great number of muskets the night that they arrived (except that the governor was vigilant in the service of His Majesty, and wanting to lecture his men on warfare, gave a false alarm to his soldiers at midnight). They made a great commotion, so much that when they [the Ah Itza] heard the noise of the harquebuses discharging unexpectedly, leaving behind what they had, they fled in fear. At the same time, I learned afterward, 400 Indians arrived at a town of heathens, even though already catechized, twelve leagues from this settlement and burned five houses and in them eleven Indians, removing twenty captives.

Each day, they say, come spies through the forests, waiting to see if the Spaniards have left in order to enter with great rage and a multitude of people to destroy the entire land. If this enterprise goes well, Indians who spoke to them said that they intend to raid the Verapaz. For which reason I supplicate that Your Illustrious Lordship ponders well all that I have written, for in this I have done what you have ordered, which is to advise repeatedly of what is necessary to place it in execution. Assuming this, from what I said, then the perseverance of the Spaniards in this land is obviously necessary. What Your Illustrious Lordship can do for the [Indian] settlers is to continue to have them offer labor, but excuse them for four or five years from the tribute assessed from 1632 to 1637. Very pleased and thankful to Your Illustrious Lordship for this favor, they would have strength for whatever work is necessary to help me in this reduction and conversion.

First, because they said it is important. They have told me many times that if Your Illustrious would concede this favor, they would be content. They are waiting for your consent because it is not possible for them to continue, for they don't have now a shirt to wear or even some shoes. Although the land is fruitful, it is a time of want, and they have neither the means for commerce nor trade. Even if they had it, it would not be good for them to leave the site until the land is more peaceful. Because today there is no security. Only ten have remained with me. The others left—when I went into the interior with four to discover and congregate the missing ones—with the story that they lacked supplies, and because a monk whom I had left with them was new in the land and not used to such actions.

Advised by the lieutenant of the Governor of what had happened, when I was pleasurably occupied finding new Indians with my four Spanish companions, I had to quickly return to inspire those who remained. Those with me continued for although dispirited by being so poor, they were people of honor and duty, and so continued forward with what we had begun. It would very much please them if Your Illustrious will assist so that they would not have to return. I am happy to advise you of the grant that you can make them, for it is without cost to Your Majesty since these Indians are not tributaries, but it will result in great service to the King, our lord, and augment your royal possessions. If [it had been] allowed over the past five years, there would be many tributaries in this province, whereas now there are no more than twenty inhabitants. Knowing of the fertility of the land and great convenience for the ships that go from Honduras to Yucatan, others would have come here.

The inhabitants say that having done their duty, they then are required to give ornaments to the church and pay for the cows that His Highness ordered given yearly. Also they are obligated to support a monk, with which they save the treasury of His Majesty the cost of one of the parishes abolished when all the Indian had fled. Now they have been ordered to return because we are congregating the towns even more. With the help of the settlers, they came together, even though some didn't leave to become rebels. The congregations are larger, even though from farther away, because I want to bring some Manché towns together to better administer and protect them from those of the Ah Itza, and to make a great town so the settlers have more service. They say most of the settlers will give up their slaves from Yol just as they will excuse them from tribute paying for five years. They will all be entered as tributaries to His Majesty, and these tributaries will gain because they will be secure in their lands. The Spaniards who stay with me wait for the resolution of all and in confidence of this favor. So that this important note arrives quickly into the hands of Your Illustrious, I asked Ensign Pablo de Cales to be the messenger, and confident in the favor that Your Illustrious will make, he went cheerfully.

I am sure [Your Illustrious] will consider supporting a work so important for there is no doubt that by these measures it is a great thing, and the most important that we have seen in our times. Also, I request Your Illustrious quickly responds because of its great urgency. Concerning it, could Your Illustrious suspend the expedition to the Ah Itza, which the Governor intends for the next dry season, until a better time? For we will need 600 or more settlers to reduce another nation.

These people are at peace, and I intend with the help of four or six Spaniards, who are here, to reduce them to our Holy Faith and add these Indians to this settlement. I think that with the help of God, we will have more than 400 settlers by joining here all the little

towns of the newly baptized and catechized, which I will have converted after five years. It will then be easier to make the expedition
[to the Ah Itza] with less cost to the royal income and less effort of
the Indians than as in the past, when it was very difficult for those of
the Verapaz to sustain the people brought for the conquest. This is
what seems best now for the good of this new conversion and its
increase. Your Illustrious, the assumption placed into execution
seems to me to be the best way to be of service to the Catholic king
and God, our Lord. May Your Illustrious have many happy years.
In this settlement of Toro de Acuña on the 28th of June of the year
1631. Fray Francisco Morán.

This letter, together with other dispatches and memorials, I sent with
Ensign Pablo de Cales, and I wrote to the Royal Tribunal as well as all
the Spaniards. I remained quite content with the hope of going the
following year to the Ah Itza. In this I contradicted the argument of
Father Morán, giving urgent reasons and offering to bring the case in
person to the Royal Tribunal on finishing my inspection of the provinces. Making these dispatches, I returned to Cobán and from there left
to begin the inspection of all my towns.

[The End of the Campaign]

Chapter 12, Book 2:
Of the Letters and Dispatches That I Sent to President
Don Diego Acuña, His Response, My Going to Guatemala,
the Memorial That I Gave, and What Was Ordered about
What I Had Requested

The following day, as I had received in the mail sent to Guatemala the
original letter of Father Friar Francisco Morán—which in essence requested help for the people because, as will be seen in the testimony
given here, it was very necessary—I wrote the President the following
letter:

Illustrious sir: Yesterday, I received again mail from the Manché
with testimony and a letter sent by Father Friar Francisco Morán.
Through it and by it, Your Illustrious can see the danger to all in
this land if one does not increase the number of Spaniards and
finish with this ghost of Ah Itza who so terrorizes these poor Christian Indians, and the land will gain and the Christian Indians will be
secure so that they will not need to flee.

I have inspected this province, although even if I hadn't, I would quickly agree with the indicated suggestion. In other words, now that we have begun this duty, it is not right to stop without finishing it as soon as possible. Although Friar Francisco Morán has little experience in the affairs of soldiers other than in aiding them, it is better, as the father says, to come in larger numbers. Without an increase in the number of Spaniards by at least another sixty, the Indians of the Manché could on some occasion secretly unite and betray us to the Ah Itza, thus killing us all like Mirones.

Thus Your Illustrious should see to it, as advised, that these reinforcements be sent without delay. This contradicts what I sent with Pablo de Cales, where I advised that one could delay before making new attacks. I always have been against this, for the Indians of the Manché will never be secure, nor pay those taxes supposed to begin next year, without the capture of the Ah Itza. They can't because there is no security for their fields, nor do they dare leave their town. Thus, it is necessary to act with all speed just like the order Your Illustrious sent to Pablo de Cales. Since these poor, distressed Spaniards await your response, you should not delay for speed is a thing of great importance.

I remain in these towns awaiting your response. Hoping that Your Illustrious will take care of this business as if I were there, for these are things of great service to His Majesty, as faithful vassal and servant, my person and resources are always at your disposal. I again implore Your Illustrious to send Pablo de Cales because it is very important for the solace of these Spaniards. May our Lord give Your Illustrious happy years so that your tenure ends with the pacification of the Manché, which is crucial for the augmentation of the Holy Catholic Faith and service of His Majesty. Done in Zacualpa of the Holy Spirit on the 10th day of September 1631. Don Martin Alfonso Tovilla.

With this letter also went the testimony that is repeated in the letter of Father Morán, and for this [reason] I do not provide the letter. The testimony is as follows:

At this time, I, Juan Alvarez Vegal, lieutenant of the governor in this province of the Manché, there being no notary at the present time, certify and swear it is true that on the 22nd day of this month of August of the year 1631 entered this town of San Miguel del Manché and stronghold of Toro de Acuña two Indians, one of fifty years of age and the other, her daughter, of an apparent age of twenty-four, and a boy of perhaps fourteen years. They said that they had been captives for a year and a half in the town of Ah Itza. As they were as slaves, guarding the fields of their masters, they fled and came to the site after having walked lost for forty days in the forests. They said that the Indians of Ah Itza were making bows and arrows to come to this land prepared to destroy, kill, and capture the inhabitants of it because they didn't want them to teach the Spaniards its roads, for they didn't want them to learn of their land. They said that more of them, 1,600 Indians, came to this site of Manché last May. At the same time, another 400 went to the towns of Noquichan, Çapeten, and Çiguana.[32] They killed some of them. Others who came with the Ah Itza to cause damage and kill were the apostates from the faith of the town of Mopan. They also were told that the Ah Itza were coming to attack this site (from where they thought the Spaniards had already left) in less than four days. Also, they said they would kill and eat the Indians that they captured this year in the Manché. They said they would treat the Spaniards just like those they had killed in the expedition of Mirones from Yucatan. They also said that when carried captive from the Manché, it took six days by land and one downstream by river until they reached the lake on whose island was the town of Ah Itza. In it, they say there are four rulers and eight houses of stone, where they have their idols and some young men who watch over them. Martin translated all of this, and the undersigned witnessed it. Done on the site of Toro de Acuña on the 23rd of August of the year 1631. Witnesses: Don Pedro de Avilés, Sebastian de Estrada, Blas de Escobar, and Juan Alvarez Vegal.

Within a few days after sending these papers, I had, as can be seen below, a letter from the President asking me to come see him:

What Your Honor wrote, the testimony, and What Father Friar Francisco Morán said on the same subject, I must study carefully. Therefore, to determine what to do, I agree that Your Honor should come to this place, and order sent here the two Indian women and the Indian man who have come from Ah Itza, and the report on the Indians in each town in this province and adjacent regions. Ensign Pablo de Cales is now ready to leave with some people, arms, gunpowder, and munitions. I have detained him until the arrival of Your Honor. Your Honor should advise Father Morán of this and that he should wait for a decision before writing. May our Lord guard Your Honor. Guatemala, September 21st of the year 1631. If the Indians are not there, Your Honor should send some person who can bring them here and come forthwith, because there is much interest in this enterprise. Don Diego de Acuña.

As soon as I received this letter, I left for Guatemala, which was no more than eighteen leagues from where I was, and after having met the President and Judges and conferred on this business, I gave the following petition:

Don Martin Alfonso de la Tovilla, governor of the province of Verapaz. They told me when I took possession of the office that the Indians of the province of Manché had some ago years fled to the forest to idolize, profaning the holy baptism that they had received and refusing obedience to His Majesty. Those of the town of Ah Itza had captured 150 Indians of those recently subdued in the province of the Manché. The Lacandon Indians took from the town of San Pedro Carcha another seven and sacrificed all of them. I took care to remedy this, lest these pains lead to others even worse. Then I came to this city to give an account to Your Illustrious, and the worthy head of this Royal Chancery and kingdom.

With your accustomed prudence and mature agreement, you ordered twenty soldiers with arms and munitions to go to the defense and pacification of these provinces. With the labor and solicitude for which Your Illustrious is notorious, these enlisted in this city. These and 100 Indians of war went on an expedition to the Indians of Yol, who had burned the town of Yaxha and killed six Indians of it, carrying off others as captives. In this expedition, they captured fourteen and burned the houses of the town, devastating the fields and taking away all the instruments that they could use to make others. Then they obtained, subdued, and congregated those of the towns of Yaxha, Noxoy, Ahixil, Manché, and Petena, many being Indians who had hidden in the forests for idolatry.[33] In the name of His Majesty, I took possession of all, counted them, issued laws, and settled them in the most comfortable part of the site called Toro de Acuña. This was not only to preserve all the subdued Indians but to serve as a restraint against the barbarous pagans of Ah Itza, so they can't invade as they have often done previously. This is what happened when, in this year, the intent of 1,600 [Indians] of war was blocked by an alarm that I gave my people on the night that they entered the town to kill us. Of the pursuit all the following day, in which they left many arms, supplies, and some idols, I have given an account to the Royal Tribunal with testimony and other, authentic messages. From the declarations of 2 of those 150 Indians taken a year and a half ago from the towns of the Manché, who subsequently fled from the town of Ah Itza and whom I have sent to Your Illustrious, clearly they are making great war preparations to return and molest these provinces.

For these reasons, I agree that we need many more Spanish soldiers to defend these provinces, punish the rebels who infest it, and subdue the land so that the monks can administer it in security and catechize others. Thus, not only will the just and holy zeal of Your Illustrious conserve the Holy Catholic Faith of these Christians but it will also augment the royal patrimony and monarchy. In order to pacify all these provinces with my own person and funds, I will need 80 more Spaniards with supplies, arms, and munitions, and permission to obtain from the towns of my jurisdiction 400 Indians of war. These Spanish soldiers can come from the four companies of soldiers that there are in this city or be conscripted as Your Illustrious feels is most convenient. The expenses that this will cost, it seems to me, if Your Illustrious agrees, could come from the tribute of currently unassigned vacant encomiendas, using them as a kind of reward for the persons who so come, thus paying for another year besides that which His Majesty had ordered obtained from the royal treasury. While augmenting the royal patrimony with new tributaries, the treasuries of adjacent towns (which are most interested in the pacification) can support the Indians of war, thus excusing the crown from further expenses.

I ask and humbly supplicate Your Illustrious that something so important be ordered, considering all the reasons, provided that it be done as most convenient but urgently, because tardiness has great risks and dangers. In keeping with my rights and those that were clear from the investigations that I have made and make, in compliance with my obligations and what His Majesty requires in the position given me, having provided exact testimony for this petition and from those who agree with it, it is with justice that I make this request.

This petition was answered with the following order:

Besides the commission and conduct given to Don Martin Alfonso de la Tovilla, lieutenant of the Captain General, for his territory, I also allow him to raise as many Indians of war as the occasion requires, leaving in the towns enough for their preservation and administration. Support for these Indians, as requested by the Governor, is to come from the funds of the adjacent towns. They shall pay the salary of the Spanish soldiers from the tribute and vacant encomiendas just as the persons entrusted with them; the yields of the first year being paid to the royal judicial officials of this court, it goes into a special account for paying the soldiers and other war supplies of this province of the Manché. The enlistment of the Spaniards should be done in the most convenient manner there is and with the speed that this instance requires. I have seen the testimony of this petition and so order. Don Diego de Acuña.

With this order, which as one can see follows to the letter what I requested, I departed very content from Guatemala to do all that was necessary, as will be seen in the chapter that follows.

Chapter 13, Book 2:
Of the Preparations That I Made for the Journey,
the Letter Asking for Spaniards, and the
Response of the President

As soon as I received the responses to my petition, I returned to my province and with all speed got ready the people, arms, munitions, and supplies. I advised the Spaniards in the Manché of the measures taken and that throughout the month of January would be coming Spaniards, Indians, and other equipment for the expedition against the town of Ah Itza. There was much pleasure on [hearing] this news because all greatly desired it. Because there was time before the people coming from Guatemala would be joining us, I gave an account to the president three months before the subsequent letter on their purpose, it being important for me to establish this in writing.

Illustrious Lord: Having come from this city to place in execution the order of Your Illustrious on the removal of the Indians and supply of this province, today I have begun it in the following manner. From the large towns of Cobán, San Cristóbal, San Juan [Chamelco], San Pedro [Carcha], Cahabón, and San Agustin [Lanquin], I have taken from each a company of fifty Indian archers, selecting the best among them, and providing each with cotton jackets and shields. Besides bows and arrows, each Indian carries a very strong machete on a spear shaft of a half vara.[34] Each of these six towns provides six companies with their captains, ensigns, and sergeants. All of these officials are trained to issue the appropriate orders to their soldiers. Each of these towns also gave fifty additional laborers to open the roads and assist the Spaniards.

For the sustenance of these Indians, I have obtained from the [Indian] communities 1,290 bushels of maize, 50 boxes of beans, 300 cheeses, all being paid for in such a way that it is at no expense to His Majesty, nor will it cost his royal treasury a real. For the Spaniards, I have collected in Cunén 516 bushels of wheat to make biscuits. So that there will be enough meat, besides the cattle already in the Manché, we will bring a herd of livestock and twenty animals to make into smoked meat. All of this, which is in my charge, is ready, and I wait for Your Illustrious to send me the eighty Spaniards. With them, and trust in His Divine Majesty, inside three months from leaving here, we will have the entire land pacified and under control, arriving in Yucatan through these forests, which ought to benefit, as Your Illustrious knows, the commerce by land from this province. Besides which His Majesty will obtain what he so desires, and all this glory will go to Your Illustrious, with which I remain very delighted and content in being able to do this service, for which when completed His Majesty will reward me as is customary for those who have served him faithfully. For complete success speed is extremely important, otherwise it will be necessary to renew some things, and because when the Spaniards come here it will already be January, and the summer, when this can be done, is March, April, and May.

If for the recruitment of the Spaniards you require my person in this city, I will go with good will. For in the service of His Majesty I don't refuse work.

Also I advise Your Illustrious that having all these Indians go is a very good gain for one interested in the quiet and security of these lands, and thus it promises a good end, just as in Flanders or other parts where I have been active in the service of His Majesty. On this occasion, I will increase the royal patrimony with as many tributaries as there are in all this province. In this you may be quite certain: that for my part, you will not lack support from me, in person or funds. Cobán, October 27th of the year 1631. Don Martin Alfonso Tovilla.

Pleased and, promised victory, I waited impatiently for the Spaniards offered to me. The feeling was only temporary because the Demon in his accustomed manner persuaded [others] that things were contrary to what they were and with many obstacles so that his idols would not go unworshiped and that these wretches would stay and remain in their old blindness, and all because the President did not fulfill his promise. As one will see below, after I said I awaited his response and gave thanks for what was done and asked that I be advised of the coming of the Spaniards, I received the following [letter from the President]:[35]

On receiving the letter of Your Honor, I conferred with these lords, and they and I believe that one ought to conserve and defend the state where one is without making any changes until His Majesty orders that this be done, and so I do inform you. In this we order that only for revenge in pursuit of raiders, as you did last year, and only on such occasions, may you make expeditions. Our Lord guard Your Honor as he can. Guatemala, the 11th of November of the year 1631. This should, Your Honor, be told to the soldiers so that they do what is necessary. Don Diego de Acuña.

Having received this letter, I sent another to those Spaniards who were in the Manché.[36] Their distress was such that they totally lost their hopes for good success, and from then on looked for an opportunity to flee or do some such thing. Although I issued a proclamation and made public the order that, on pain of death and treason to the King, none should leave the site without express orders from me, the demon, who as I said doesn't sleep, made them look for ways to leave. It was then that Father Friar Francisco Morán told them not to grieve over it, that he had the order of the President that he could request them, if necessary, to go with him to enter some towns they had discovered. He showed that he had this order in writing. After a few days he took them, saying that he wanted to obtain some sacks of maize from granaries near them. The twelve of them went to the town of Mopan, which was of apostate Indians.[37] When they arrived, the [male] inhabitants were absent, having gone to capture others from Noquichan, and as there were only the women with the ruler of the town, they killed the ruler and took up to forty women among them, young and old, others having fled, and returned with them. After three days on the road, having brought them back to the site of Toro de Acuña on the fourth day, the soldiers carelessly slept without any clothes.

Arrayed in two lines, one behind the other, the Indians attacked them a little after midnight. With much fury, they shot a great number of arrows at the Spaniards and took away the women who were near the opening. The Spaniards, hearing the commotion, awoke, and the first two who left their hut fell dead with two arrows in the heart, and the Indians wounded three others. Then they began to shoot the harquebuses. The Indians fled, leaving twenty women, for they didn't capture more than twenty. Then at daybreak, the Indians with the Spaniards, frightened at seeing the dead and wounded, all fled, leaving them alone with the father. Those at the site of Toro de Acuña burdened themselves with their women and children, and went to hide in the forest from fear of their enemies. This also took place among the Indians of the towns of Noxoy, Ahixil, Yaxha, and Petena, who fled again.[38] Within a day, they lost all that they had worked for so long. The father, being left alone with the Spaniards, went with them to the town of Cahabón, where I was, because as soon as I learned of the bad news I came there. Within three days, the father and Spaniards arrived there, the church remaining deserted with the ornaments and silver in great danger. I sent fifty Indians and six Spaniards to bring all from it. On reaching a hill a half league from the site more than 2,000 Indians appeared, taking all the ornaments and silver, and burning the church and all the houses of the town. I advised the President of all this, and he provided no more help other than to respond that he could not do anything until he had a decision from Spain.

This was the end of our conquest of the Manché and the measures undertaken to do it. The reason for its failure was a bad counselor who suggested to the President that since he could subdue all this land so cheaply, he should send a request to Spain for an agreement that if he would make the conquest at his cost, His Majesty would make him a marquess of the conquered land. As this seemed good to him, he did so and wouldn't send me the Spaniards, and it ended as we have seen, with all things done for private interests without looking out for the most important, which was the service of His Majesty and the common good. Those who read here should know well that the fundamental cause for the disappearance [of our conquest] was the absence of sufficient force. I trust in our Lord that in our time, someone will take up the aim of this conquest and subdue all the land so they will praise the Holy Name of God in it, and erase the memory of so many and so false idols as today they worship and the many errors taught to these wretches by the Devil.[39]

6

THE LIES OF FRIAR MORÁN, 1636

What follows is an intemperate discourse, filled with facts that can be proven untrue, on a ten-year effort to convert the Manché Chol Maya. Why publish it here? There are two reasons. Most important, Morán was there. Not only was he an eyewitness to these events but his actions (as indicated by Tovilla) significantly influenced them as well. Thereby, his opinion and interpretation are crucial to understanding what happened during the events that culminated in the expulsion of the Spaniards from the Manché. Second, not everything Morán says about native culture and his own experience is false. He does provide eyewitness information on life during those times.

Moran would survive for many years beyond the 1630s. Unfortunately for him, Spain tore itself apart in the 1640s, and thus, the Spanish government had neither the time, money, nor interest in conquering unknown lands.[1] It would be forty years before the next serious attempt to explore the lands of the Manché Chol was launched.

Report That Friar Francisco Morán, Friar of the Order of Preachers, Made to the Very Reverend Father Master of the Holy Palace Friar Nicholas Ricardí on the Conversion of the Province of the Manché and the Pagans of Ahitzas in the West Indies

Our Very Reverend Father: So that it be clear for the Very Reverend Father that the friars who come from Spain to the Indies are moved by zeal for the good of the souls, causing much benefit in them, winning many for heaven, especially those who live, for example, a religious life and more those who are the salt of the earth, etc.; understanding that our Very Reverend Father would be pleased to receive it, with all respect I made him this brief account of how, for the period of eighteen years while living in the Indies, I worked and acted in the service of God and the Order, doing what I did without any complaint.

In the year 1618, I came to the Indies, having been accustomed to it from my previous missions [for the] sons of Saint Dominic, and studied in Guatemala the two years of theology that I lacked. In obedience to two decrees, within six months I learned the language of the Indians [who lived] nine miles from Guatemala so that I could administer the Holy Sacraments to the Indians and preach to them in their mother tongue. Then [I was assigned] as priest of a *doctrina*, which is what they call a parish of Indians of up to 600 households, to be in charge for no more than ten months. Seeing how well the Indians understood my preaching, and how they followed it with care, the position gave me great pleasure. At the end of that time, I went to the head of this province of our order, then Friar Alonso Guirao, and was assigned to the convent of Cobán.[2] From there, I went to the pagans and helped in the reduction of the apostates of the Manché.

I don't know if it was due to my good health or the ease that I had in learning languages. I think that it was even more to good spirit, for in truth it was not a mission that I asked for but for which I felt much. This change increased even more my feeling on seeing how greatly the Indians in my district wore themselves out saying farewell, the church filled with weeping and bathed in tears, doing everything possible to prevent my departure. Even the youngest women went through the streets wearing out their voices and [raising] their hands to heaven, causing in me such feeling that I could not leave without also spilling many tears. Having these feelings, I wrote to the prior asking that he cancel my transfer. The Indians were also sending out their petitions asking that I return again to their town. The holy prior, feeling that I could serve more elsewhere, did not accept my requests or the petitions of my Indians. He gave them another minister, and I went on my trip.

Thus, I came to the land of the apostates of Manché having learned their language from the grammar and vocabulary written by Friar Juan Ezquerra and Friar Gonzalo Ximeno, who are both in heaven boasting the glory of their works. After two months alone and sixty leagues from my convent, without having any contact other than with these barbarians, and given my natural inclination to understand it, I began to learn their language. With the abuses and rites of these Indians, they were Christians in name only for like a land without water, lacking the irrigation of the evangelical word, the very new roots failed and dried without producing any fruit. Therefore, I dared them to do away with the thorns and spines of pagan life.

Not that I concerned myself if they kept natural law, such as having two wives who were sisters, but rather if they sinned by offering their own blood and that of their children to the Devil by cutting the ears and pricking the fleshy part of the arms, thighs, and legs. The dead they buried inside the house where they died, not in a grave but thereabouts curled up in a ball, and with them their bow and arrows with which they sleep, and the gourds and all that they had used in life. Then they fired the house, going far from it to other huts and waters. They told me that they did this to erase the memory of their dead father or mother, etc., for the great pain that it caused them. They agreed to end these abuses and many other absurd things, and that for better public order, they should live together in towns. To encourage this, I ordered them to make their orchards next to their houses and keep their animals close by, planting cacao trees, achiote, and vanilla, which are the fruits from which they make chocolate. Learning from Saint Paul, I instructed them to gain them for Christ. Nor was it difficult to use my own hands to obtain, when opportunities arose, my own sustenance.

By these means, I so gained their goodwill that some informed me of what passed among the others, giving me news of that hidden in the forests. Putting a sash on my skirt, taking my staff, and selecting eight or ten of the most helpful Indians, I went through the forests on foot looking for them, each time bringing back a hundred, perhaps eighty, perhaps sixty. I went on more than forty of these raids, many times through inaccessible mountains, passing turbulent rivers without taking heed even though they grew deeper with the many waters of these mountains and, at times, delayed me four, eight, ten, and more days. Content with [eating] palm tree tops and snails from the canyons, but continuing to search the forests, in the end I returned with my lost sheep. I reduced even the least of them, although hungry, tired, and covered with mud, with no less pleasure than the evangelical pastor of parable returning with the least of his sheep. In summary, from the apostates and the pagans that I discovered from the year 1625 to those of 1628 and 1629, I made five towns.[3] I and my two companions (who learned the language as I did) catechized and taught them, making with the governor of Verapaz an agreement for him to take possession of them in the name of His Majesty. As is obvious from the information I have already provided, I persuaded the Indians to pledge allegiance to His Majesty and, as they had for me as their father, obey him without reluctance.

As the number of people increased, with more each day being discovered, I now began to administer an Indian town of more than 1,000 households. Because our convent of Cobán was sixty leagues from us, it seemed necessary for better administration to establish a new convent. Therefore, I asked at the provincial meeting called by our Father Friar Jacinto de Oces (Supreme Vicar and Inspector of the provinces of New Spain) for permission to establish a new convent in the province of Manché separate from that of Cobán. By the acts of the meeting, celebrated in Ciudad Real, Chiapa, in January 1628, they approved my petition and I was appointed first vicar, but only after completion of my term of office as prior of Cobán.[4] From my convent of Cobán, with permission of my Reverend Father Supreme Vicar and the council of the fathers, I took for use at the new convent being established in the Manché [the following]: sixty cows, twelve recently pregnant mares, eight horses, two burdens carrying male mules, and five female mules. The new convent would have had new converts if the Demon—begrudging the good of the souls, and using as his tools the fierce Indians and warriors who with for many years he did notable havoc—had not placed an obstacle to it.

There is a town of Indian warriors called Tayasal and they, who they call Ahitzas and are so cruel that they eat human flesh, raided the towns of new Christians, capturing more than 300 persons, among them old and young, killing the men that they took and keeping the women to use as slaves.[5] They raised the children according to their pagan customs, which is what I am most sorry about and want to weep tears of blood for my children engendered for Christ with holy baptism. These Ahitzas in the year 1625, in the province of Yucatan, killed twenty-five Spaniards, impaling their captain called Mirones, and two Franciscan fathers. In part of Verapaz, they martyred forty years ago the Reverend Friar Domingo de Vico and his companion, Friar Andres.[6] For those who protest the date of martyrdom of the holy Friar Domingo, there is no doubt of what happened, they burning him after killing him with arrows next to the high altar along with two other children brought to help him say mass, and so blinding the church. From then until the year 1627, when I went to explore these lands, no one had dared to enter them.[7]

Employed in this considerable work and despite the danger of death that this journey required, in truth I can say that I succeeded like the Israelites, who after a long tiresome road in exile discovered that happy land that flowed with milk and honey. This is because I had discovered extremely delightful and pleasant woods, with much hunting, and much wax and honey from trees filled with beehives. There are two turbulent rivers. One is the Icbolay and the other Tuhalha.[8] Both are navigable and have a great number of fish, of which the Indians brought me many. The Tuhalha River has beautiful beaches. It is very temperate and healthy although somewhat on the warm side. I discovered some rich salt deposits. They came from a stream so dense and salty that its over-flow on the plain was turned naturally into salt by the sun.

These salt deposits were held tyrannically by the Ahitzas, who took them from those Christian Indians who, after being baptized by Father Friar Domingo de Vico, the fathers of Cobán of the province of Verapaz removed from the province.[9] Afterward, the enemy pagans took the salt deposits and kept the remaining lands very poor, for they had the cotton, cacao, achiote, chile, hunting, and fish harvested from this land when it was at peace as well as the salt deposits. Those of the Verapaz are in such need of the salt that for lack of it, they go fifty leagues distant from their houses to Guatemala.

This province of Verapaz had three bishops, the first whom His Catholic Majesty Philip the Second, paying much attention to those who had worked among these Indians, made bishop, being the very reverend Father Friar Juan Angulo; after him Bishop Cárdenas, both being friars of the order of our father, Saint Dominic. The third, Bishop Hervias, I think was the last.[10] The poverty of this province, caused by the pagans who took the best lands, ended the bishopric. The province of Cobán and Manché also lacked the sacrament of confirmation that no one had received there until thirty years after the start of discovery. Perhaps due to its absence, it has been so easy to leave the things of the faith.

The pagan Ahitzas are those who, in the year 1626, captured fifteen Christian Indians six leagues from the convent of Cobán, soon killing two and offering their hearts to their idols. These are those who, in the year 1630, attacked my new convent of Manché, burning my cell with all that it had: my private library, pictures of saints, and boxes holding the little owned by the convent. They set the church on fire. Breaking the altar, they carried off the reliquary (for the consecrated Host), chalices, silks, ornaments, a silver cross, and bells. These are the same who on another raid took captive some of my children, carrying off twelve Spaniards and some Christian Indians. They took captive forty-five people, among them pagans and Christians. We pursued them for a night in the forest [until] with a great shout they attacked us. Shooting together a great number of arrows, they killed two Spaniards. I quickly confessed them, and we buried there in the forest those killed by the Indians.

Although those returning had seen much resistance, I spoke to an Indian who came to the town and he died with all the sacraments.

Another, who died on the road, also confessed. Among those who fled due to these disturbances was an Indian who recently gave birth, leaving the infant to be baptized. Because of the danger, she spent a long time fleeing on the road, carrying a boy. As I had no one who could give milk, [the infant] died to live forever.

As for me, these barbarians intended to capture and tie me to post, cut off my living flesh, and eat me. I never heard of a tyrant so cruel as to invent such torture. The idea without doubt came from the information provided by those they had captured, since I have preached many times against their cruelty as being so much worse than the tigers who eat human flesh. In their opinion, killing me would remove one who knows their land for I am on the threshold of their houses.

I don't see the need to tire our Father in Rome by indulging in a long history of the ten years I spent in exploring these lands. [In summary,] there are up to 60,000 pagans, not counting 20,000 and more apostates who had fled from the province of Yucatan to live among them, who live in these lands. Each day, many flee from Yucatan to the province of the Ahitza. All recognize it as the Geneva of those who don't like the faith and desire its ruin because of the effect of the gentle influence of evangelical law.[11]

Reverend Father, I desire peace for this land so rich in many goods and so populated with Indians. Therefore, to avoid the indicated problems and many others, I have given a memorial to the Council of the Indies. It tells them of the rich salt deposits, and of this land that is so pleasant and fruitful. It is necessary to establish a town of armed Spaniards.[12] Taking control of the salt deposits will pacify the great town of the Ahitza [Tayasal], which has 10,000 households and is the cause of all the cited problems. There are no others in all this land for some hundred leagues long and more than eighty wide. They would have nowhere to retreat, for on the south is the province of Cobán, on the north Yucatan, on the west that of Chiapas, and on the east the North Sea. All known adjacent provinces are subject to this town [of Tayasal].

The Indians of Yucatan would not leave their lands knowing that Geneva is under our control. The Indians of the province of Manché stay hidden in the forests for fear of their cruelties. They would return to their towns and our administration. By these means, we would gain control of a great and rich province, obtaining an infinite number of souls for heaven, and by that our holy Order would obtain great honor and glory, expanding even more than its fame with more subjects. These lands would require three and even four convents in them. Of their subjection and pacification by the indicated method, from my knowledge and experience gained in the ten years in contact with these Indians, I have no doubt.

I beg Your Great Reverence to persuade the Congregation of Propaganda Fide to give me all authority necessary for the pacification of the indicated province, for the conversion of its pagans and reduction of the apostates.[13]

Having been one of those who had governed, through knowledge of the inhabitants and their languages, I have asked His Majesty, for its good effect on the creation of peace, to order the foundation of a Spanish settlement at the site of the salt deposits. I have little confidence in rule by soldiers, who would blindly covet, as happened on so many other occasions and expeditions, and so in the end would effect their results. Therefore, I want those who go to guard against it by providing the salary that His Majesty requires for the poor soldiers. Being, as I have seen over many years, that expeditions often lack supplies, it is for this reason bad results come from the conquests of the Indians.

Very Reverend Father, if the people who are here in Guatemala were placed under my orders, there is no doubt that peace can be given to all of this province of pagan and apostate rebels within two years. Having been offered the use of some faction to conquer the great town called Tayasal, to succeed it will be necessary to give me full authority to require, demand, and arrange all concerning this conversion without being accused of any irregularity, or some other criticism. Since the reason is good, there is no doubt of the heavenly reward for the conversion of these souls. May our Lord guide our Very Reverend Father, in good and honor, for long and happy years.

7

BETWEEN TWO WORLDS, 1653–1654

This is the story of some Acala Chol Indians, as told through the letters and edicts of Spanish friars and colonial officials. The Acala were brought by Friar Morán into the Manché Chol area to help him convert the Manche, and later, were left behind when the Spaniards returned to Verapaz. Ultimately, the Acala attempted to return to the Verapaz highlands without cutting off all contacts with their lowland friends. The Spaniards wanted to break those pagan ties. Finding a distant land with a similar climate, the Spaniards resettled these Indians on Guatemala's southern coast. The tale apparently ends here, with the Acala in their new town of Atiquipaque. Yet what was their fate afterward?

Atiquipaque seems to have remained exempt from paying tributes for 100 years for there is no record of taxpayers until well into the eighteenth century. But during this same period other Chol were also settled in this town. Thus, in 1676, Friar Francisco Gallego sent ninety Chol-speaking Ahxoyes from Cobán to Atiquipaque.[1] By the end of the seventeenth century, the parish had split into two—with Tacuilula being the parish capital for Atiquipaque and Tepeaco. In the last quarter of the eighteenth century, the inhabitants of Atiquipaque only spoke the Szinca language found elsewhere in this province (Cortés y Larraz 1958). There was no memory of the Chol language.

The town itself died early in the nineteenth century. The few remaining inhabitants moved to either Guanagazapa or Taxisco. Today, neither of these two towns possess any speakers of the Szinca or Chol languages. As is true throughout the former province of Guazacapan, inhabitants of these once-Indian towns speak only Spanish.

Letter of Friar Juan Ochoa, Parish Priest of Cahabón,
September 28, 1653

Don Bartolomé Flores. Wishing Your Mercy that your soul, and that of my lady Mariana whose hand I kiss, is in good health: [This letter is in] respect to Pedro Choco, who Your Mercy agreed, because of the unrest, to take from this town [Cahabón] along with those who not only came with him from the forests but many others, since it has been years now since he, Gaspar Xoy, and others were removed by Friar Francisco Morán from this town and taken by him to the Manché to teach the Chols, not only to teach them but to save them from perdition. Worse, those of the Manché fled from us twice and apostatized from the faith.

Now, in the two years since coming from the Manché and wanting them to make their houses in this town, go to church, and follow the law of God, they are in danger of fleeing as they already have four times apostatized, which suggests that they will do it again. Since this town is very close to their lands of San Marcos, it seemed to me, Your Mercy, better to send them elsewhere to Christians who know what ought to be done as this would be a great service to God.[2] This is what those who administer the waters [of baptism] think: that because they don't want to stay here, and since if they stay it will cause more grief, we can't advise otherwise.

Letter of Bartolomé Flores, Governor of the Verapaz,
October 9, 1653

Very powerful lord: It is my duty to obtain some remedy for the idolatry that, being used by both many pagan nations still not reduced to our sacred religion and apostates, spreads to this province. I had received notice in April of the year 1651 that an Indian known as Pedro Choco— who right now is in this city of Cobán, the capital of these provinces— had his entire family in the forest. Having moved to where, ultimately, all learn idolatry, and having made it my business to learn where his wife, oldsters, and most of the rest of his family were, I obtained fifty Indian archers, among them the best in this city. Because of the very difficult nature of the swamps and rivers, everyone found twenty-four leagues of these roads so bad that they were impossible for horses; nevertheless, the Indians undertook this business with all care, capturing the wife and some of the children of Pedro Choco.

Among the others, they found nine persons and many new arrows blackened as when they paint them to use in their idolatry. On hearing them, six Indians with long, painted hair escaped. Cornered against a large river that they couldn't cross, they forced Domingo and Juan Choco, the sons of Pedro Choco, and Agustin Xoy, the son of Gaspar Xoy, to return to this city. Learning of their crimes, the learned assessor sentenced Pedro Choco to 200 lashes while being led through the public streets. He also must serve eight years in one of the convents of Guatemala City [Antigua] and spend ten years in exile from this city where he had once lived. Finally, on pain of death, he should not break these orders. To prevent the rest of the family from escaping and make it impossible for them to return to their idolatry, they brought them to Los Esclavos, a town in the jurisdiction of the province of Guazacapan.[3] Also, they sent another 150 archers to their old refuge, said to be the home of other families, to break the idols in their fields and burn their huts. Having gone to execute the order, they carried it out.

Without knowing where the fugitives went or where they had taken their idols, and having gone to their huts and destroyed their fields, the archers returned to this city. By January of this year, the Indians taken to the town of Los Esclavos explained where they had gone and what they had done. Those captured then assured the authorities that they had no desire to leave this province to live [in their old homes], for they lacked any security there, but would like to go one more time to the forest [to speak with] their brothers and relatives. At this time there came from the forest two naked Indians, with long hair and holes in their ears, all being a mark of that idolatry in whose name they hid in their forest settlements.

They told me that all wanted to live as Christians, and be pardoned and provided with clothing. I promised to pardon them, treat them like the others of this province, and help them with all that they wanted so that they could come with the greatest of ease. I gave the children and women an ax to make a canoe to cross the rivers and be reduced to our Holy Mother Church, and I sent with them four Indians of this city for their safety, but not before they and another Indian from those who came from the forest promised to return. Again I assured them that if they returned within twenty days, neither the Indians of this city nor I would penalize them.

Being notified that a dead body, already eaten by dogs, was found in a field next to the town of Rabinal, I left to make an investigation and punish the guilty. Being advised while doing this that fifty-eight people, including nine babies needing baptism, had come to the city, I sent orders that they be treated well in the prepared houses, given lands to make their cornfields, and helped as if they were our children. Finishing my business, I returned to this city and at once went to see all who had come from the forests. Among them was Pedro Choco, who following his sentencing, was separated and sent to the royal hospital of Guatemala. I felt that he should not be treated so strictly for most of those who have come were his children and grandchildren.

Judging that since there were no more in the forest, none should be allowed to return to it, I ordered that none should leave this city without my permission. I had the nine infants baptized with a big party, I being the godfather of three of them. One of them, who had died [a male child], was brought to my house from where, with all ceremony and the participation of the entire town, we took him to the cemetery and so left these Indians content. I saw that they gave them [the newcomers] cotton so that they could make their cloaks. I took care that they be taught Christian doctrine to help them forget their bad customs. Thus turning their heart to God, I saw that they professed in our holy faith.

Not seeing Pedro Choco and the rest of his family in the church at the beginning of September, I learned that they had gone twenty-four leagues to the town of Cahabón, a place often visited by rebels of the Manché. Having made some inquiries, I learned that two children of Pedro Choco had asked Friar Juan Ochoa, who had administered these towns for more than twenty-four years, if they could speak to those at war so that if they found them in the forest they would not kill them. This I suspected to be a lie. I felt all was not well, that they wanted to go back to their old life and deception that they had hidden on coming from Cahabón. I knew that on going to the forest, these two children of Pedro Choco and Gaspar Xoy would return to the site of their farms and their old rites and idolatries.

I therefore arrested Pedro Choco, Gaspar Xoy, and their wives. I placed all those who had come with them (from the forest) in the houses of individual Indians. By pretending ignorance of their plans and welcoming them, they gave themselves away. By consulting in this instance Father Friar Juan de Ochoa, who as I said to Your Highness has been here more than twenty-four years, I have received the letter included here [see above]. From this Your Highness can see that for the service of God in this province, there is no part where I can safely send them because of their customs and the permissive example that it gives to others.

Masters of idolatry and superstitions, four times they have apostatized. Even when His Majesty orders that they should live as Christians, it does not seem good that these being such bad examples, they should live where they could contaminate others for it is impossible to prevent them from communicating with the others. Thus, they stir up those who are quiet and living as Christians. Also, it is impossible to prevent them from going to the forest whenever they want to consult the Devil. If they decided perhaps to go next to the salt deposits, I would lose all control over them.

Thus, Your Highness, it seems to me one should take all these who total up to sixty, including young and old, and bring them to this city, the infants divided among the convents where they could learn the Spanish language along with Christian doctrine and forgo such bad ways they would learn with a bad upbringing. The others should be taken to the town of Amatitlan where Father Friar Alonso de Triana, who knows the Chol language that is the mother tongue of these people, could teach them the Christian doctrine just as the children given to the convents. With the care of the officials of the town, in my judgment they would not return to it.[4] If you give them exemplary punishment, Your Highness could cure this great evil, and it would provide a great service to God, our Lord, and Your Majesty, and a very great good for the natives of this province. They would thus live quietly and, in the future, avoid doing it again to avoid being punished for it.

Your Highness would be best served if you order me to execute these orders, because of the poor security among them, as soon as possible. Although I will do what I can, I can't do much for I have neither the means nor Spaniards to guard them, and thus I beg Your Highness to quickly do whatever seems most convenient for the service of Your Majesty and the quiet and security of this province. May God give Your Highness many years. Cobán, on the 9th of October 1653.

Letter of Bartolomé Flores, Governor of the Verapaz,
and Friar Andres de la Tovilla,
Prior of Cobán, November 3, 1653

Very powerful lord: From the October 21 letter of Don Diego de Escobar, I learned that Your Highness had ordered me to consult with Father Friar Andres del Tovilla and Friar Alonso de Triana regarding the best policy for the Indians coming from the forest. Agreeing with both the difficulties coming from nonenforcement of this decision, and what should result from such a meeting for Your Highness, I followed your orders of October 9. Inasmuch as Father Friar Alonso de Triana was administering Amatitlan, to serve Your Highness I have only spoken of it with Father Friar Andres de la Tovilla, the prior of this convent. We both feel that the inconvenience of leaving these Indians in this jurisdiction is great because of the poor security there.

I have certain information on their intention to return to the forest; they don't want to live anymore among Christians and only wait for an opportune time to easily execute their intentions, such as this month when all the Indians of this city leave to work in their achiote orchards in the forest to pay their tribute, or when I inspect the province, or whatever other thing presents itself. I can't jail them in the time of planting to prevent them from becoming lost. Since they are used to the hot lands of the forest where they live a barbaric and brutal life, it is unnatural for them to live among Christians. Yet it is impossible to allow this.

Due to the difficulties of women, burdened with infants at the breast and many other young, yet needing to walk many leagues, three of the recently baptized infants have died. They [the women] need help for they lack a good supply of provisions, and the way they still would have to walk is extremely long and rough. As this has been voluntary and not forced, they can't go alone but require considerable attention, and we have not found any other way in our opinion, nor one more necessary, to save these souls.

If Your Highness should decide where to send them, ordering me to obtain what is necessary for their trip and providing funds for those who will carry it out, all will be done in conformity with the orders of Your Highness, as it would be most convenient for the service of God, our Lord, and His Majesty, who God guards.

Letter of Bartolomé Flores, Governor of the Verapaz, May 11, 1654

Very Powerful Lord: In the letter of April 13, I gave an account to Your Highness of certain information requested from the mayors of Cobán on the return and departure of the Chol Indians to the forest, and how it was impossible to detain them.[5]

Subsequently, I have received the orders of Your Highness to send Gaspar Xoy, his children, and those kept in the jail of Cobán to the town of Rabinal, and that the others be taken to the town of San Pedro Carcha. Being so divided, they would be held more securely. I gave these orders to Diego de Coto Mesquita, treasurer for stamped paper in these provinces, to assure that all is carried out in peace, security, and for the good of these people.

Having been advised by the officials of Cobán that as of the 8th, all the Chol Indians in this city had gone with their wives and children to the forest, I alerted two hundred archers, who immediately found in some fields and houses some seventeen persons, among them old and young, there being still missing twenty others of all ages. Searching for them, they asked those taken, and they responded that they neither knew where they fled nor where they could be found. Having been told that a youth named Sebastian Tzibalna could tell them more, they questioned him. Although at first he refused, he finally said that the children of Pedro Choco, who were among those who remained in this city [of Guatemala] in the hospital of San Alejo and convent of Santo Domingo, had gone to those of Cobán.

For one night, they stayed at the house of an Indian called Domingo Chojom, then they went to the forest. On that Holy Thursday, two Indians from the forest, hidden in this city of Cobán, told them that all in the forest hamlets would come one night and then there would be riots. Then, in fear, all would leave and go. They swore that there were four hamlets in the forest, one having one hundred and fifty Indians, another eighty, another sixty, and others at the site where they killed in past years the friars, but they didn't know the number of Indians there. The children of Pedro Choco had communication and dealings with the forest Indians in the house of Domingo Chojom. They know them from when they lived in the forest.

As I have advised Your Highness, there has always been poor security for these people. It is not convenient for them to remain here as many might follow their example. The land is very hilly, and it is impossible to prevent their idolatries. It would be a great service to God, our Lord, and a reduction in the load of His Majesty, if Your Highness will look favorably on this proposal. It will produce good results and, as I have said before, there is no other way to remedy it. As a service to Your Highness order me to rapidly execute it, although because of the few inhabitants in this large province, I can't enact it as rapidly as I would want. May God guard Your Highness. San Andres Sacabaja, on the 11th of May of the year 1654, Don Bartolomé Flores.

Edict of Fernando Altamirano y Velasco, President of the
Royal Court of Guatemala, August 12, 1654

In the city of Santiago of Guatemala, on the 12th day of August of the year 1654, His Lordship the Lord Don Fernando Altamirano y Velasco, knight of the order of Santiago, Count Santiago [de Calimaya], President of this Royal Court, governor and Captain General in its district, having seen the decrees issued regarding the reduction of the Chol

Indians who were living in the province of Verapaz in their forest hamlets and idolatry, and although ordered placed and divided in two different places, some of them have joined again. Because of the poor security, most have left this city and returned to their hamlets. His Lordship being informed by the governor of this province of this, he does say:

I order and request that the Indians of the towns of Guazacapan, Taxisco, Chiquimulilla, Nestiquipaque, Tacuilula, Tepeaco, Guanagazapa, and Gueymango go to the town of San Juan Atiquipaque, and in it make for the Lancandon Chols the houses necessary for them to live.[6] They shall clear a quarter league about them to make their fields of maize and cotton, and divide the lands where they can plant cacao, vanilla, and achiote. Regarding what is being done for the population of these Indians, everything done within the town of Atiquipaque shall be in consultation with the priest and vicar of the parish of Gueymango. No one can remove an Indian of the revived town from the lands of the settlement or deprive Indians of any plants cultivated up to the present time.

The current governor of Guazacapan province and those who follow him shall have special care to conserve the population, they being exempted from all personal service to travelers, dye workers, owners of ranches, and other persons. The residents there should not order them to help them, nor annoy them, but help and favor them as new plants in our holy Catholic faith. Don Fernando de Ribera is in charge of the education and teaching of the natives, and on hearing of any problems, is ordered to do what is necessary for the good conservation of the settlement and ease of the natives.

The mayors of the towns of Ciudad Vieja, Alotenango, San Diego, Escuintla, Guanagazapa, and Tepeaco shall provide beasts of burden to Lacandon Indians. Funding shall come from their town treasuries to pay for Indians to watch them and take them to the settlement, going from each town until they can be taken to and safeguarded in the settlement. These towns, as neighbors to the town of Atiquipaque, should watch the paths and roads of their towns to prevent their use by some of the Indians ordered to settle here.[7] Thus I do order this for His Highness: Don Diego de Escobar [royal scribe]

Letter of Fernando de Ribera, Chaplain of His Majesty,
April 20, 1655

Illustrious Lord: Sunday, on the 18th of the current month, God was served by the marriage of four Indians of Guazacapan. They married

Chols that Your Highness had ordered settled in Atiquipaque. With great pleasure from all sides, all were merry, and there was a feast made by their parents and dependents with whom they live happily and secure. I had my mind eased from the difficulties that I had expressed to Your Highness on other occasions.

In conclusion, lord, excluding three reserved only for tidying up and cleaning under the direction of the most important people, they used the city hall and houses for three days. To execute the orders of Your Highness, I have informed the governor of this province of the needs of these three women. Thus, those with the rods of judgment can in the time of inspection provide a good outcome in conformity with the good judgment and direction of Your Highness in the service of both Your Majesty and my desire.

The chapel master that Your Highness named for this town has two houses: one for his dwelling, and the other that serves as a school where he receives the boys.[8] Given his zeal in his brief time here, I must approve his courteous action, and have provided all that is necessary for his sustenance and needs. Finally, so that they would be settled, I have had cacao and achiote planted behind the houses of the Indians; it was their mothers who brought the vanilla. In this way, in these two months, I having fulfilled my obligation, if they do no more than adorn and conserve what Your Highness has given, all should be well.

May God guard Your Highness in the duties in the lordships that have so illustrious a prince. In Atiquipaque on April 20th of the year 1655, from the humble chaplain of Your Highness who kisses your hand. Don Fernando de Ribera [priest of this parish of Gueymango].

Letter of Alonso Paez de Grajeda, Public Scribe and Scribe of Inspections of the Town of Guazacapan, December 4, 1655

Alonso Paez de Grajeda, public scribe of Guazacapan and scribe of inspections for His Majesty, at the request of Don Fernando de Ribera, priest appointed by royal patronage to the town of Gueymango and others of its parish, vicar of the province, ecclesiastical judge of its jurisdiction, do swear that this is true testimony to the lords who have requested it.

As required in the edict of His Lordship, the Lord Don Fernando Altamirano y Velasco, count of Santiago, knight of its order, president of the Royal Court of Guatemala, governor and captain general of its district, ordered the priest to go to this town of Atiquipaque in his parish to supervise and arrange the settlement of the Indians called Chols, who Captain Don Bartolomé Flores, governor of the Verapaz, had removed from the borders of Manché and Lacandon, where they were living, and sent them to settle in this uninhabited town of Atiquipaque. His Lordship having sent an order that Captain Don Miguel de Esquivel y Ylariasa, governor in this jurisdiction, should help in the settlement of the Indians, it was done under the care of Don Fernando de Ribera, and the governor issued his orders so that the Indians should bring all that was necessary.

The governor of this province, being helped by Don Fernando de Ribera by his good arrangements, thought on providing lodging for the Chol Indians in this town while preparing the houses and charging the cost to the account of the city of Guatemala. With his assistance and help, he made twenty-eight new houses each with fired-clay kitchens, placing them in streets separate from each other and apart from the habitations of the Hispanic people.[9] After, with the help of the vicar, he prepared forty-six houses where before there were six poorly used by the five mulattoes and two Indians who were the previous inhabitants of this town.

These were devoted to our Miraculous Image dedicated to our Lady of Christmas, and strangely her miracles are well known, with people coming every day on pilgrimages from many places to ask for her aid. The mulattoes have assisted and served as best they can, with all veneration and reverence in a tiled hermitage that they slowly built, with their altarpiece of very good pictures. Today, it is renovated by the order and plan of the vicar, who ordered it expanded into a church and placed in the passage to the door a pulpit and baptismal font that they had lacked before.

He assisted and sustained them for eight months, giving them meals, cotton to weave and prepare blouses and skirts, chickens for their people, axes, machetes, and knives for their farming, and paying for other metal goods. Don Fernando de Ribera, desiring their increase and conservation, had them plant many feet of cacao groves. In the space of a year to six months, the planting has already produced more than eight feet of cacao seeds.[10] It is fortunate that the vicar gave out all that was necessary, because thanks to their irrigation ditches, which brought in water, they had plants and could sow more than enough fields of maize, cotton, and achiote plants. The transplanting and cacao seeds for their support were all paid for by the vicar, because they came poor and naked.

I, the present scribe, saw during a survey made today with the Chol

Indians the sowing, cacao seeds, and provisions in their houses of maize and fruits to sustain them. By the zeal that the vicar had to increase and conserve them, the Indians became acquainted with the love and kindness that the vicar had shown to the Indians who had come freely to settle in this town. The inhabitants, 160 persons young and old, among them 107 Indians (43 of whom are Chol) and 53 Hispanic people, not counting those who sell goods and do not live here, thanked Don Fernando de Ribera for their pleasure and happiness.

What is more, this said settlement is very useful and necessary thanks to the miraculous lady, because the inhabitants of this coast, recognizing her as exceptional, pass the night here. Some come and go from the city of Guatemala to this jurisdiction. The Villa de Trinidad and its port, that treasury of the kingdoms of Peru through which comes the tribute and income of His Majesty, is the origin of others.[11] Because previously their travels here required much work and discomfort, it was necessary to obtain Indians from other towns.

Moreover, irrigated as they all are with abundant water that can be brought wherever one wants (for no ravines prevent it), these lands are of the best in the jurisdiction for cacao orchards. The boys of the school own the flat and shady lands irrigated with the new canals for the cacao orchards. It is a place and site where one can create in time of need the means to assist others of this coast; thanks to the abundant plants of the land and the good fortune derived from them, they can expect success in commerce.

I have seen that they shield the church with care and love. I wrote of the Christian doctrine being taught, having for master and scribe one of those called Tlascaltecas of Ciudad Vieja, who His Lordship, the lord President, with his zeal for service to His Majesty in conserving its population and in exultation of our holy faith, sent with a certificate of trust given by His Lordship so that he would assist this town.[12] The vicar has provided for him clothing at his cost, thereby allowing him to go today to his wife with all necessary woven blouses and skirts for his children, making them as welcome as all of those most newly settled.

The Chol Indians have two mayors, aldermen, constables, deputies, and a church steward. I have heard the vicar speak in their language, to which they respond and obey his orders. As being exempt, for their good conservation, by Your Lordship from personal services and attending to travelers, they understand the pleasure with which they live and the good treatment given them. Although they would want to be in the forest, they are grateful for the education of the vicar. They are taught, and are taught by him alone at his own cost, with such care, love, and profit that they pray every Wednesday and Saturday of every week the rosary of our Lady.

Today, they and the schoolboys assisted, with all solemnity, in the prayer to the Virgin Mary [the salve] and the litany. Already they are as advanced as the sexton that officiates over the masses in the choir. This work has gained such good fruit owing to the direction and guidance of His Lordship and the efforts of a minister having so much zeal for the service of God. His vigilant care, love, and kindness, and his concern and assistance, have continued without halting. This is evident from the petition given today in Atiquipaque on the 4th day of the month of December, being witnessed by Francisco de Gaviria, Juan de Castillo, and Cristóbal Marroquín.[13]

8

THE REDISCOVERY OF THE
MANCHÉ CHOL, 1676

Spanish emissaries again entered the world of the Manché Chol in the last quarter of the seventeenth century. Prior to that, the Indians were free of Spanish control for forty years. This does not mean, however, that they lacked for outside influences. The great annual highland achiote fair on the banks of the Chixoy River attracted merchants from throughout the lowlands, even from as far away as Lake Peten.

As Friar Francisco Gallego notes here, this was the "Indies" of the highland Verapaz Indians. Even more, these lowlands were the "Indies" of the Kekchi Maya, and in their economic enterprises they acted like conquistadores in these territories. They came to exploit the resources of these lands and intended to use the local population to gather wealth for them. Kekchi settlers from Cobán and Cahabón began to appear in lowland towns in the last quarter of the seventeenth century.

It was these Kekchi who provided the main resistance to the missionaries' return, inciting the Chol to attack them and providing the Spaniards with misleading information. Nevertheless, according to Gallego, the native Chol retained a certain amount of respect for the friars and elements of the Christian religion, which made it easy to reestablish a Spanish presence in the area. We do not possess a Chol chronicle to confirm, or correct, this impression but it certainly seems that the Chol had again invited missionaries to come to their homeland. The Indians, it appears, desired the artifacts of Spanish culture, yet the Spaniards were seeking more than just a favorable trade balance.

Memorial on the Works and Progress of the Chol and Manche [January 27, 1676]

Presented to His Lordship, Lord Don Fernando Francisco de Escobedo, president, governor, and captain general of these provinces, by the very reverend Father Master Friar Francisco Gallego, father of the province of San Vicente, Chiapa, and Guatemala, and the Order of Preachers, in the name of his religion. With license, in Guatemala, printed by Joseph de Pineda Ibarra.

Lord: Your Lordship strongly ordered me to give an account of the state, and the progress of the things of the Chol and Manche, and although excused again from not speaking of matters happening so far away, and since it is supported with only the testimony of a companion and four or six Indians, who have gone with us as assistants and servants, the supporting affidavit is weak. So, if His Majesty did not urge us to speak of the matter, we would be risking our credibility to do so without authority. I also ask pardon because speaking of one's own activities is to risk a fall from pride. In this work, I didn't have any part other than to be the companion to Father Friar Joseph Delgado, who is the one who did it all. Thus declaring that all the action mentioned in this paper was his, and asking that I be excused from speaking of matters that I don't know from personal experience, I have hidden many things and left their payment only to God.

Going north from this city to that of Cobán, commonly called the Verapaz, and in the same direction going from Cobán to Cahabón, is a distance of twenty-three leagues.[1] From Cahabón to the first locality of the Chol, there is another twenty-three, with twenty-nine rivers on the way; although twenty-six are dry, when they do receive water, they are more rapid than the most famous waterfalls. On this difficult expedition, although we went by horse, if there was a storm, we thanked God that we could leave them to go by foot. We, Father Friar Joseph Delgado and I, arrived at this site between the northeast and east. The Indians who went to this city to ask for ministers originally came from here.[2] This His Highness ordered me, I being prior of this province, to provide. Here, the previous year, Delgado had brought together these Indians and catechized them, and they understood most of the fundamentals of Catholicism. Delgado, having learned enough of their language, was able to be a minister for them. He placed them at the sites; the first one's patron was the glorious Evangelist Saint Luke [San Lucas]. Two leagues away was another tiny town, with the patroness of our Lady of the Rosary [Rosario]. Between these two, but five leagues away, was another called Saint James [Santiago]. These were bad sites, better for wild beasts than a settlement of Christians.

We were with them for some time, and although they came to us asking for Christianity, they had so little grasp of the fundamentals that we needed to teach them. Having finished catechizing, since the baptized seemed well disposed, we suggested that all three towns join at a larger site. To us it seemed to be dull to fish, so we decided to be hunters. Thus, it seemed to Father Friar Joseph that 300 souls was a small number, and wanting to obtain enough profit from his work, he inquired about entering the land north and east, but more to the north of here, at a distance of twenty to twenty-two leagues.

This met with great opposition from our recently baptized Indians, and with no less resistance from the pagans, all saying instantly that we should not make this trip because, they said, a peak that was the God of the Forests would not let either us or our beasts of burden pass. None being willing to prevent our trip, though, they agreed to our requests.

They gave us three Indians, who carried a sack of beans, two hammocks, a little chocolate and biscuits, and a basket of vestments. Having forgotten to cook the beans, they could not serve them so quickly. We had the duty of teaching the boys of the towns and putting God in the hearts of the two boys of eighteen years that were our porters. Also going with us was a judge. Our Lord knows that in the towns that we formed, we had always appointed judges, in the name of His Majesty, feeling that they would be useful to us. Your Lordship, in giving us our orders, noted that we should take care that they [the Indians] don't go back to sinning. The aforementioned judge opened a path for us with a machete, and if he had not done so, we would have done so with our bodies. We slept that night in a house, on the banks of a large river, owned by one of those who had left the Indians of San Lucas. Farther downstream of this river, known here as the Tiyu, is the famous Maytol.

On the second day on the road, we soon found ourselves near the God of the Hills, which is a quite high and very beautiful hill. Our companions began to speak among themselves, and the little porters, as the closest to us, said: "Fathers, if you want to pass and don't want to die, we should burn a little incense to this hill; that is what is done by those who climb it." Father Joseph responded: "We are servants of the God who created these hills and thus we have no fear of them; besides children, the fine storax incense carried with us from Castile is for when we say mass." Then, walking like monkeys, and with us behind urging the mules forward, they climbed without any difficulty. We found on the top of the hill a small plaza, seemingly swept clean, and in the middle of it a little fence of sticks, and within that a burning fire.

Telling them to rest, we spoke with the porters, who told us that due to the diligence of travelers, this fire was always burning here for no one would fail to offer worship to this hill. We asked if the Christian Indians coming from the Verapaz would worship this hill when they pass by here. Hearing that this was so, our companions prayed that God would grant what we heard is not the truth. Told that now that we had climbed the hill we should offer copal, we replied: "Sons, we have not yet descended the hill, but on our return we pledge our word, that we will burn copal." We found ourselves now with strength to descend the hill on horseback, for the way down was not as difficult as that going up. The Indians who guided us went a short distance more and then set down their burdens, saying that they had no obligation to go farther.

We remained like monkeys in the forest, and as a consolation, our porters stayed to serve us. Finally persuaded that the hill would not stop us from passing, the Indian owners of this land placed there a spy to advise them of what we did. We tied our hammocks in the middle of a forest neither horrible nor harsh. There I struggled with various thoughts, and among them, the one that bothered me most was that my boldness and the innocence of my companion would kill us without producing any result. At that moment, I heard a conversation going on with one of the boys. "Father Joseph," I said, "what is Little John telling Your Reverence?" Our father said to me that among them the word "father" has the meaning of awesome, pleasing, and formidable. This greatly consoled me, so much so that from thenceforth I no longer had fearful thoughts, being certain that no matter what would happen we would win against adversity, and I stopped being sad.

It was the neighboring Catholic Indians who made this the most difficult conquest of all. This was because the surrounding Christians had this forest as their Indies from where they obtained much wealth, some as cacao and others as achiote, more than 36,000 pounds of which left each year for the Verapaz and the castle, with very little of this crop coming from the Verapaz itself.[3] A machete that was worth four reals in this city exchanged for twelve *zontles* of cacao in the forest.[4] Therefore, they advised the Chol to hide, telling them that the Spaniards would look for them in every way possible. They defamed the priests by saying that they were avaricious to support themselves, that the King's officials were tyrants who ordered people whipped and chained, and other things that horrified the Indians. An Indian of Cahabón going to the forest, when asked why he was there, would reply: "I came here because in my village, chains, jails, stocks, and the whip are waiting for me if I fail to pay the tribute."[5] The forest Indians, out of pity, would give him a zontle of cacao or something else, and he would pack his bundle and return to his town.

Other times, these Christian Indians entered the forest and seized the cacao, negotiating for it more often by force. They would frequently tie up and whip the Indians in their own villages, taking everything they had as if, Your Lordship, they could do what they wanted having discovered this land. Nor could these others, being naked Indians, make resistance (be they 100 or 200 in their town).

After dusk, the Indians came who lived on the other side of the hill, and we spoke briefly to them in their language. Asked what we were doing in their land, we said that we were servants of two great lords, one of heaven and one of the earth; that of the earth had sent us to teach them the road to heaven, to make them Christians and pour on them the water of the Holy Spirit.

To that they replied that they were poor and had nothing to give us to eat. As for changing religions, they were like horses, or beasts or stones, and didn't know what they wanted to do. To that we responded that it was true, they were horses, stones, and sticks, for they lived like brutes in the forest, not knowing God. As for giving them something to eat, we could take care of them, and our King had not sent us here out of avarice for tribute since in his palaces pearls were like trash, and it would be many years before they would have to pay tribute. God, since they did not know what they wanted, had sent us so that they might desire what they did not yet know.

With that, very content, they embraced us, saying: "You are welcome to our land in that you come like the sun, moon, and fire to banish our ignorance; and for lack of your light, our fathers and mothers are like burning coals at the feet of demons in hell forever." At this point, a quarrel broke out among the Indians as to what settlement we should go to first. Immediately, they began to open a road as wide as the one that goes from Jocotenango to this city.[6] They spent an entire day, with great pleasure, in clearing it. If they came to some ravine that could not be passed on horseback, they carried us. If we went down some slope where we could slide, two Indians held us each by the belts we wore, grasping us so strongly that it sometimes seemed they tied us to two poles. They assured us that they intended to descend very slowly so that we would not die, so that the Spaniards would have no cause for retaliation. We reached this day the bank of a beautiful river, which they call

Yaxha, the best waterway in this province (one that has few good ones in it), and by it began to eat.

We also were hungry, and had but to ask for something to eat and from the river they obtained some little fish as small as those of Lake Atitlán that they call in their language *chilan*. Wrapping them in some palm leaves, they placed them in the embers for a little while; then they gave each of us a tamale and three of these little fish. We knew that they felt sad that they had nothing else to give us at that moment. The next day, we arrived at the house of a headman, who we called Don Martin Matzin, who gave us eggs, fish, and very good tortillas. He saw that the priests ate, but with all the Indians around them, the priests felt it necessary to give a little to each one. Annoyed by this, he said: "Eat, don't starve yourselves, you are in my house."

They all agreed with us to establish a town at this site. Because we knew that near here had been the town of San Jacinto, we said that this town should also be called San Jacinto. Father Friar Joseph preached to them, and they said they wanted with all their hearts to be Christians, that they had been lost since the fathers left them. They begged us to baptize their children so as to give them a foothold in our Catholic religion. We baptized some children of the principal men. We took with us from here an Indian, who we made a fiscal, and taught him the doctrine, which he learned in five days, and sent him back to their town to teach them there.

Four leagues from here was another headman, who we called Don Pablo Ilxil. Matzin didn't want us to go there because he said that they lacked food (and it was so). Nevertheless we went, and God inspired Don Martin to send some plantains, eggs, and tortillas every two or three days. He sent someone to check to find out if we had died. We would have been extremely bad off without this help. Previously at this site was the town of San Pedro y San Pablo. Thus, following the previous procedure, the settlement here we called San Pedro y San Pablo.

Showing them the same compassion as elsewhere, we baptized some children. They asked for an Indian who would be fiscal, and although we did not give them one then, we did afterward. Then we went to a site four leagues away called May and today called San Joseph. Here, some Indians wanted to kill us with bows and arrows. We were in an abandoned house when we were advised that they were coming to kill us. We suspected that our guides had influenced them to frighten us so that we should not continue forward (we had found out in San Pedro y San Pablo that these guides were from Cahabón).

We went out to meet them, and they made known that they were too afraid to kill us. Taking one by the hand, Joseph asked if he had come to kill us. They stood trembling like mercury. To calm them, I gave each a little salt and some tiny beads of a rosary. I asked them to search for the people of these houses. Two hours afterward a family came, whose head was a son of an Indian of Cobán who had settled in these forests called Don Juan Pot, and an old woman more than 100 years old. Having spoken to her about our holy Catholic faith and the precious water of holy baptism, with tears in her eyes, she repeatedly asked for the water of the Holy Spirit. Judging her near death and sure (as it so happened) that I would not find her alive when we returned there, I baptized her along with some children that the Indians had brought for that purpose. The Indians agreed with us to establish a settlement here, as we did with those in the first town.

Our guides, even though quite well paid, gave us a thousand reasons to refuse us and hide the Indians, not wanting us to teach those only four leagues away at San Miguel Manché.[7] Although we would have gone farther to discover another settlement, they succeeded in their ends. Now it began to rain, and because of the floods, we agreed to return to the town of Cahabón in order not to die of hunger since here there were no ranches or towns where one could obtain help in case of need. Here, we learned that near Cobán there were others, those they call the Axoyes, similar to those we had seen on this trip.

We left by the same road that we entered, for there was yet no other road. We placed crosses in all the towns, at the banks of the rivers, on the roads and on Escurruchan [or Esqurruchani], which is what the Indians call the hill that they call the God of the Hills. As we said, on this hill we placed a large cross, venerated it on our knees, and in front of it burned storax gum, thus fulfilling my word to the Indians. We gave them to understand that our action was neither idolatry nor sin. Now today all these roads are open, filled with hamlets, and when we see our crosses, we feel great comfort. I imagine that if some stick of them falls, they would be happy here to raise it, for the Indians take much care with them. Asked why we worship them, they respond as we had taught them: "*Chamay tzambuna cahaguavil Jesús Cristo, Tuvt Santa Cruz ucaba vmene catanal,*" which means, "Our Lord Jesus Christ died, extended on the face of this stick, which they call the holy cross, for our sins."

In Cobán, inquiring about the Axoyes, we found 180 persons who appeared to be as Christian as us, all the older males having been baptized in the baptismal font of Cobán. They came at my request, as they were Indians of the forest. On asking them to cut their hair, something that took great effort with others, they said to me: "Don't dirty your hands, Father. We will cut it ourselves." I told them that they should wear clothes, and in a short time, their appearance altered to the point where you could not distinguish them from those of the Verapaz. They knew the Christian doctrine in two languages, and saying that I wanted to baptize them, they responded, "No father, we are already baptized. What we want is confession." I told Father Friar Joseph and Father Friar Domingo Gamarra that they were baptized in the baptismal font of Cobán, wanted to confess, and that they should hear their sins. They did so, and it surprised them how much the Indians knew about our Holy Catholic Faith.

Wishing to verify this, I called them and said, "Come here, my sons. What is the Christian doctrine?" They told him, "Father, we have the saints and crosses; on Sundays we recite the doctrine together, and during Lent we scourge ourselves. Now that you are interested in us, we want to confess because we know that when there are priests, we have the obligation to tell them our sins, and when not, we ask God's pardon for them. Grant that we be given the body of Jesus Christ, which we desire. Go to our town, and we will bring everyone together and you can marry us, as God commands, and baptize our women and children who are not baptized, so we may live in the law and grace of God."

This trip was not possible, for the Reverend Father Inspector of this province sent for me. Although afterward they wanted our visit, we not being able to do it, every day they came to see us in Cobán, bringing us little gifts. They came from the northeast, two days by road from the hills of Sacapulas.[8] Here, near the banks of the river of Sacapulas, are forty houses and a river filled with canoes. Using them, the Lacandons go to the lands of the Verapaz and those of the Verapaz go to the lands of the Lacandon. It is here that they make the achiote fair of Verapaz, and to it come the Lacandon, Ahitza, and many other nations of Indians.

The second year, having been called to this city by Your Lordship to provide an account of this business for the Reverend Father Vicar General, Your Lordship approved my request, and gave Don Bartolomé Coco the title of governor of Cahabón for helping in the preparation of the road used by the fathers. Also, he discovered for me some pagan Indians, although this with much fear, and persuaded the pagans to be obedient. They opened wide, good roads and created settlements, although not very large.

As a result, although with difficulty, we made three settlements. Their houses are one, two, four, five, six, and seven leagues from each other. In response to our requests to leave the forest, they have made tiny towns, beautiful churches, and little houses for us, and they live together here.

When it is necessary for them to go to their old fields, they don't ask permission for two or three days. On completion of their duties, they return and present themselves, telling us that they have returned. At the shout of a constable, they join for mass and, most days, hear the doctrine, which they have learned very well. They bring us a little palm leaf for our beasts of burden, as they carry our loads from hamlet to hamlet. In this way, the loads are light.

Some days, they bring us many tortillas; there isn't a person in the town who doesn't bring them. Although they agree to divide this duty among them over all the days of the week, they don't do this. They are accustomed, nevertheless, to feed us six or seven days. Sometimes, they give us a piece of wild goat, peccary, armadillo, or *tepezcuinte*.[9] A few times, it was some snails and little palms.[10] This is if it doesn't rain, because when it is raining there is nothing, and there is always some rain. Some Indians there have given a plot of land for a church and our house. Living near us, they go to the kitchen, and if they see nothing to eat, go to the forest or the river with their children and search for something that we can eat. They survive on a kind of half-cooked *pozol*.[11] They eat little, and this is how we sustain ourselves, for otherwise we would die of hunger. Until now we haven't had fruit, because it seems that the Devil taught them nothing about how to support themselves in this forest, although they tell me that this is not so farther into the interior.[12]

On the way back to the town of Cahabón, with the permission of our prior, I have dressed the women and given them banners, silver vessels for serving liquids at mass, images, saints, rosaries, and occasionally bells. There is no Indian, without four or five pesos from us, that does not have a bit to eat, salt, and other little things. As of today there are eleven towns, and in these towns, baptized with all the solemnity ordered by our Holy Mother Church, are 2,346 souls. This does not count many others who each day come, as is evident from the books of baptism.[13] The names of the towns of the Indians [and number of souls baptized] are as follows:[14]

San Lucas 190	Santiago 194
San Miguel Manché 242	San Francisco Socomo 185
San Jacinto Matzin 198	San Fernando Axoy 180
San Pedro, y San Pablo 240	San Sebastian Uchin 43
Asuncion Chocahau 150	San Joseph May 300
Rosario 200	

This is the number of people baptized in these towns, not counting the others, who live in some hamlets in the forest. Also, the father priest of the castle has removed more than 600 souls from the following sites: Niha, Tuilha, Petenha, Tzatum, Vlpop, Pululat. He [the priest of the castle] said that they had been their dependencies and, thus, belong to the castle. Those of the castle advised these Indians that we went with Indians of Cahabón, tying up the Chols and sending them so tied to Guatemala. What's more, that we carried matchlocks although only six people, and two ten or twelve years old, went with us. Therefore, they abandoned their hamlets, fled from us, and gathered near the castle.

Despite all this, we had begun this business before the father. We were the first to speak with them on the matter of religion. We cut their hair, giving them rosaries. The crosses placed in their little towns were quickly given little houses of sticks to protect them and show the disposition of their inhabitants. Those in the castle said that these [houses] were only a convenience for those who had to sleep overnight in the forest.

The father alleged that we had gone to his dependencies. As we did not search for Indians for us but for God and His Majesty, he should thank us for our help. He acted as if the English had provided the maize and stolen the Indians of the settlements so that they could serve them and give them whatever they want. Forgive us, Your Lordship, but loyalty to our King and Lord obligates us to go to speak to all, even though we have sore feet. With this, he closed to us the way through this mountain range as far as the borders of the Rio Maytol, there in the castle they call Factum, that being a greater river than the river of Seville, and prevented us from going to the following sites:[15]

Yaxtihal	Vacan	Tzucah
Temax	Tzibac	Tzetum
Yaxtxal	Guayn	Beycuha
Paliac	Tute	Campin
Tzisibin	Hutoco	Tite
Vchapan	Culamay	Chibul

All these settlements, going from the west to the northeast, have 150 persons.

From San Miguel Manché, going to the northeast, we have noticed the following settlements and have spoken with some of their headmen:

Putzilha	Tzequischan	Tzibalna
Yaxapeten	Noquixchan	Tinocacao
Tipata		

All these settlements have less than the above number. But experience teaches us that there isn't a headman in the forest who doesn't have 190 or 200 persons. The last town of Tinocacao—meaning in their language "large town," whose name they say comes from Chabac, which in their language means "two zontles," or in Spanish "eight hundred"—is twenty leagues from Bacalar. San Miguel Manché is thirty-two leagues from Cahabón. Pusilha [Putzilha] is two leagues from San Miguel Manché, Yaxapeten another two, Sibalna [Tzibalna] two, Tipata four, Noquixchan three, Tzequixchan [Tzequischan] two, and Tinocacao four. Although this is not the legal road it offers much. This, Lord, is the beginning described here. I wait for the power and help of His Majesty, and of Your Lordship, to help us do what is necessary, and without that nothing can have permanence.

We want always to pay God back for the little that we have done. The prize of such small effort is bringing to God more than 200 children with the water of holy baptism. If His Majesty (whom God guard) supports this enterprise, there is the glory of gaining for God the 30,000 souls and more who are in this forest. This will hinder such idolatry as his Catholic vassals of the Verapaz commit on entering these forests (because to halt the commerce is impossible).

Also, it seems His Majesty should do this for God, and even more for these wretches, in payment of which his vassals of the Verapaz, Sacapulas, Ocosingo, those of the castle, and others would gain all the fruits of this forest. Those of the Verapaz would gain its achiote from the castle, and Amatique its cacao and achiote; those of Cahabón the cacao, and the same for Sacapulas and Ocosingo. It would also open the commerce of this province with Yucatan. This would easily and quickly remove the demon, whose slaves are his visible symbol, from it.

Your Lordship ought to move to encourage us in this enterprise, which would only do what Your Lordship so desires, as Your Lordship knows, having put me in charge of it. Without doubt, the encouragement of Your Lordship would be effective in so Christian and Catholic desires. The Royal Court also, for so has your Highness spoken on the arrival in this city of six Indians, who came from Cahabón to ask for Christianity. Instructed by Catholic zeal and your native Christianity, you ordered that town dwellers be given tested and approved ministers, and this is the foundation of the situation existing today. There is no other business that we urge more, Your Highness, than [for you to] order us to so serve you. The land has much cacao, achiote, balsam, wax, and brazilwood, which produces a kind of dye called *chocho* that, if I am not mistaken, is *xocuque*. All is easy to take by ship coming from Spain by the river mentioned previously.[16]

I sign it in this convent of Santo Domingo of Guatemala.

9

THE ITINERARY OF

FRIAR JOSEPH DELGADO, 1677

Having been published and translated into English three times before this edition, the adventures of Friar Delgado among the Chol and with the English pirates (where he lost his shirt) may be the best-known document on the Chol in the literature; its wealth of detail has allowed experts to carefully, and wrongly, define the Manché Chol area. The Manche didn't live in just a portion of southern Belize and the southeast corner of the Peten department.[1] In reality, the document only marginally discusses the Manche. It is really about other Chol: the Mopan- and Yucatec-speaking inhabitants of Belize and the Peten. It hardly mentions the western portion of the Manché territory, which lies on the Rio Manché (the modern Rio de la Pasion).

Nonetheless, Delgado's text is useful for the Chol-speaking settlements, other than those of the Manché, along the Yaxal River and following the coast to Campin. The numbers of people reported in the indigenous houses remind us that this was a region still largely unaffected by Spanish attempts to concentrate Indians in European-style settlements composed of nuclear families. The definition of a region in the Ahitza political sphere helps to define the boundaries of that state. Finally, the reference to the English attack, and the kidnapping of a servant of Friar Delgado, is the first appearance of a process that will greatly contribute to depopulating these lowlands: the raiding of these lands by the English and their allies for slaves to sell abroad.

Hamlets and Rivers from the Town of Cahabón
to San Miguel Manché

From the town of Cahabón to Cerro Tituz it is eight leagues.

From Tituz Hill to the Canquén River it is eighteen leagues.

From Canquén to the town of San Jacinto Matzin it is two leagues.

From San Jacinto to the town of Noxoy there are five leagues.

From Noxoy to the town of San Francisco Xocmo it is four leagues.[2]

From Xocmo to the town of Asuncion Chocahau it is five leagues.[3]

From Chocahau to the town of San Joseph May it is five leagues.

From May to the town of Asuncion Chocahau, called the town of the mulattoes for the inhabitants' curly hair, flat noses, and thick lips, it is five leagues.

From the town of the mulattoes to San Miguel Manché it is five leagues.

By another road to the towns of San Lucas, Santiago, and Rosario from Cahabón it is thirty leagues.

From San Lucas to the Canquén River it is twenty leagues, more or less, crossing many rivers, among which, after a half-day's travel, is another large river that one can't ford any time of the year, called the Tuy.

From the Tuy River to a hill called Esqurruchani [or *Escurruchan*], which the Indians call God of the Hills, it is a half day of travel until one arrives at another great river, called the Yaxha.

From the Yaxha, it is a half-day's travel to the Canquén River.

From here, they go to the town of San Jacinto Matzin and take the road of the Manché.[4]

Hamlets of the Province of Chol and
the Distances between Them

It does not seem out place to give here the list of the hamlets of the province of El Chol, as seen by Father Friar José Delgado in the year of 1677. Although we have seen all of them, I know that the people in them have moved, for we used this information to reduce many barbarians scattered in these forests; this list (and the travels described) ends at Salamanca de Bacalar:

From Manché to the settlement of an Indian called Bol it is four leagues. From here to a settlement of an Indian called Marcos Tzibac it is four leagues. From here to another called Juan Petz it is five leagues; and to come to this settlement one crosses twice the dangerous and large

Yaxal River.[5] The first time I went this way by means of a wooden bridge, and the second time I used fords (helped by some stepping stones) through the river. There were also many falls and rapid currents, but with care and high water one can pass and go by canoe.[6]

Leaving the house of Juan Petz, I went to sleep in the forest next to a stream called Conconha that was seven or eight leagues away. From here, I left and went to eat by another river, called Latetun [or Latentun], that was four leagues away. From here, I came to a large settlement four leagues away where there were many Indians known as Pachs. The headman was Vicente Pach. This Indian is a priest of these pagans.

From here, I left and went to eat by the bank of the Yaxal River that was five leagues away. To come to the site, on leaving Vicente Pach, I crossed the Yaxal River on a bridge of wood. From here, I left and came to another settlement five leagues away of an Indian called Martín Petz. [In all these settlements there were in each house twenty or thirty individuals, and in many others, a half to two leagues away, many people who I did not see for the Indians who accompanied me were sick.]

I walked this entire road, from Manché to the site of Martín Petz, in four days. In all these settlements, in each house, there are twenty or thirty souls. [And there are] so many more in many houses within a league or two that they could [together] make a famous and large town because even the smaller houses have twenty, thirty, or forty souls. Other houses are closer, within a quarter or half league, others three quarters, and others less. In this way, there are many people. May God bring them to knowledge of himself! I didn't go to any of these close-by hamlets because the Indians who came with me from Cahabón were ill.

Now I will say that from this settlement of Martín Petz there was, according to the account of this Indian Martín Petz and the merchants among them, the following road to the settlements of the Mopans and Ahitzas. The Ahitza Indians were on an islet in the middle of a lake, but also had settled the mainland. All is savanna, except that intermittently there are a few tracts of forest.

From this house of Martín [Petz], it was a half day [six leagues] to the house of Miguel Batena, which is on the bank of the Oxtum [Ochtun] River, and thirty persons [live there].

[From here it was four leagues to] the settlement of Cantelac, whose Chicayes [or Chucui] Indians speak another language, called Omon [which perhaps is the same Chol language].[7] In this settlement of Chicuy there were forty persons.

From Cantelac it is a ten league walk, one day of travel, to the settlement of Tixayab. Here there were 100 Indians, and many more with wives and children. These are the Ah Mopans who lived at Tixayab. Many who were in Tixonte [see below] had been moved by the Ahitza Indians, and nearby there were many more who had hidden.

From here, one went a day and a half by road [fifteen leagues] to Tixonte, that is, to where lived the Ah Mopans. In all these settlements from Tixonte [Tizente or Tizonte] to the lake of the Ahitza Indians, Martín Petz told me that people went four days by road, entirely through savanna, crossing the lake to a large island in the middle of it where the Ahitza lived with their king.[8] All the Indians of the forest recognized him and paid him tributes, for the Ahitzas not only were in the island but left for the mainland to people it. Martín Petz told me that there could be 1,000 Indians. . . . These Indians say that one does not go east.

In this hamlet [of Martín Petz], I found three Spaniards, which the English had robbed, from Bacalar or Tiozuco near the Bay of Ascension. These, called Alonso Moreno, Luis Gonzalez, and Antonio Mendoza, came to these forests with others from their province who know this land [to collect cacao from the forest Indians]. They said that at Lake Izabal, there is a boy called Juan Alonso de Arias who was a servant of Captain Don Francisco Santos. The boy is familiar with the forest, knows the language, and had gone with them as far as the Ah Mopan Indians. There are others in Bacalar who know it and its languages that are in Tiozuco or near it. I stayed in the house of Martín Petz with these Spaniards, who said they had gone to the following settlements going northeast toward Bacalar and from that of Cacique Martín Petz and the Yaxal River to the settlement of Timilahau, which is seven leagues away:

From here to Yocab, the settlement of the headman Juan Quiminche [Quimenche] it is eight leagues.

From here to the settlement of Pococ, which lacks a headman, it is six leagues.

From here to Saca [Xaca], where there is the house of the headman Joseph Ahcahcay, it is five leagues.

From here to the town of Campin, which previously was of the province of Yucatan and whose headman is Juan Chocoh Yancab, it is two leagues.

From Xaca to Anax, a settlement of the Chanes, is seven leagues.

From here to Techtutz, where the headman is Fulano Ziquen, there are four leagues.[9]

From here to the settlement of Mopan, whose headman is Juan Tziquen, there are eight leagues.

From here to a large town called Zaqui, whose headman is Juan Muzul, there are eight leagues.

From here to the Yucatec Indian town of Tipu there is a day and a half travel by easy road [to] where the enemy robbed me, but the Spaniards of Bacalar say that it is no more than twenty-five or thirty leagues from Tipu to Bacalar. I did not see the forest because I went by canoe.[10]

[These three Spaniards said that] leaving the settlement of Martín Petz, the Indians going north to the other side of the Yaxal River, were the Batenas. A league from here there were three houses with thirty or forty souls. Another house there, a half league away, called Tzunum-chan, had ten or twelve souls.

From here to another settlement called Yahcab was three leagues, and there were forty or fifty souls divided among six or eight houses.

Continuing toward the north, the headman known as Huizquin [Guy-quin] had, a league away, five houses with thirty or forty souls.

From here one could go to the Pots, two leagues away, whose three houses had twenty souls.[11]

From here, we went to another called Tzac, one league away, that had ten souls.

From here to the house of José Tzac was only a league, but there were six houses, and in them, forty or fifty souls. It was two leagues to another settlement called Tchax, whose two houses held ten souls.

From here going two leagues to another settlement, one came to Chuticol, where there were many houses, and in them, many people, being more than eighty with many children and women.

From here, there were many settlements that they didn't go to.

The Spaniards returned to the west and the settlement called Cache, two leagues away with thirty or forty souls.

From here, they went to another settlement, called Chicni, four leagues away that had in and about it two or three headmen, called Chicayes, Quines, and Tzaques. It had more than 100 persons.

They returned to the house of Martín Petz and went toward the south. From here to Timizique was eight leagues. Arriving at Timizi-que, they found many people. The English attacked us the next day, and coming by way of the Tutuilha [Tutuila] River, they captured the Span-iards and some Indians. The others fled. They released the Spaniards after many days on the banks of the Yaxal River and came to this house of Martín Petz again.

Up to forty people, in two houses a half-league away as well as three other huts, were near them. We stayed here to make a canoe to go to Bacalar. Having made it, we put it in the water of the Yaxal River, tying it up at high tide with strong cords. That first night, the river fell and the canoe was left hanging in the air. With the great weight the ropes broke, and the canoe went downstream seven leagues to the ocean. We spent another day looking for a tree to make another canoe and God allowed us to discover a ceiba, which in ten days we turned into another beautiful canoe. [In order] to become acquainted with the rivers and their mouths, I intended to go with the Spaniards to Bacalar.

The road and names of the sites from Tipu to Bacalar are the same as that of the rivers. There are twenty-five or thirty leagues by land to Bacalar. By sea, one passes the following rivers on the way to Bacalar:

From the Yaxal to the Zimin Rivers there is a half league.

From here to the Yechupan [Uchupán] River it is a half league.

From here to the Paliac River there are seven leagues.[12]

From here to the Puletan [Pulettán] River there are three leagues.

From here to the Vacon [Guacan] River there is a league. From here to the Vain [Goain] River it is two leagues.

From here to the Campin River it is nine leagues.

From here to the Puhuy [Pujuy] River it is five leagues.

From here to the Soyte [Zoite] River it is five leagues.[13]

From here to the Texach [Texoch] River it is two leagues.

From here to the Tahach River it is three leagues.

From here to the Xibun [Xibum] River it is ten leagues.

From here to the Balix River it is two leagues. Two leagues after, one enters the Tipu River.[14]

From here to the port of Bacalar there would be twenty-five or thirty leagues. One can ford all these rivers on the land side since although they seem very large and wide, they have in their mouths banks of sand.

On the Texach River, Saturday the 20th of August, God allowed me to be captured by the enemy, and they stripped me, leaving me without a shirt and in torn shorts.[15] They took my shoes and a boy called Juan Valut, who served me and who I knew as Juan Delgado. I am writing this a little after this event. Dated in Bacalar on the 26th of September 1677, that being the day that I entered this town after twenty-five days without eating anything other than wild grapes and being very hungry, cold and feverish, naked and distressed, etc.

For the truth of that I sign my name, Friar Joseph Delgado.

10

COLLECTION AND REMOVAL,

1685–1700

Expeditions into the northern lands multiplied as the seventeenth century ended. Cano in 1685, Ximénez and Prada in 1695, Pacheco in 1697, and Camilo in 1698, 1699, and 1700, as we will see here, were some of the friars and officials who entered the Manché lands during those years. The invaders were not greeted with shouts of joy. Ximénez tells here of Chols with "cigars in their mouths and bows and arrows in their hands" whose two-part greeting was "welcome" and "when will you leave."

The Spaniard Prada found people inclined "neither to God nor the Devil since, despite all their idolatry, they will not do anything for even a stick or stone. . . . Asked if they want to go to the Devil or hell, they say that they don't want anything. . . . What is certain is that they only worship their liberty." Certainly they didn't want anyone, neither their own leaders nor alien intruders, to tell them what to do.

The invaders thought, as Friar Prada phrases it, that "subjugation and fear are necessary," and used torture on recalcitrant natives. Friar Ximénez speaks of the "fitting sacrifice" of the Indians' "dirty and foul spirit," and Prada swears that "even if Chols changed into angels, they would in the end turn to witchcraft, heresy, and rebellion." Under increasing pressure from the Mopan—who were expanding into Chol territory, slaughtering their neighbors—it became impossible for the Chols to flee to more distant localities. In the end, caught between the Spaniards to the south and the Mopan to the north, the Chols were forced to accept a policy of tightly controlled resettlement on the shores of Lake Izabal and in the Verapaz highlands.[1]

Some Chols would survive at Belem in the Urran Valley, today's El Chol Baja Verapaz, until at least the mid–eighteenth century.[2] In Cobán, a few Indians used the Chol language as late as the early part of the nineteenth century.[3] The settlements in what is now Belize and in the Caribbean lowlands of Guatemala succumbed in the eighteenth century to a new, and completely unexpected, invader (see chapter 11).

When captured by a British warship and brought to the port of Hampton, Virginia, as a prisoner of war in 1733, the Spanish Captain Rodrigo de Torres did not expect to find Mayan slaves. Nor, on transfer to Jamaica, did he anticipate seeing many Maya on the streets of its capital. It was the Mosquito Zambo, a people of mixed Indian and African descent still living on what are today the coasts of Honduras and Nicaragua, who were responsible for the Mayan presence in the British colonies (Lopez Marchan 1733).

This population of Chibchan speakers seized the opportunity created by the War of Spanish Succession to attack the Hispanic-controlled Guatemalan coast in 1704, raiding the town of Amatique and capturing "many natives . . . and killing others" (Duardo 1704; Laylaya 1718). In 1707, the Zambos penetrated Lake Izabal, "where they carried off the women and children" (Lozada y Quiroga 1712; Laylaya 1718). In 1708, 400 Mopan Maya archers assembled to assist the Spaniards in defending the Peten when the Zambos came to within four leagues of Cahabón (Pereira 1708).[4]

The Mosquito Zambo threat caused the surviving Indians of San Antonio de las Bodegas to flee to the town of Gualan, a settlement where most of the inhabitants soon were Chol refugees from the lowlands (Galves Corral et al. 1707).[5] In the early years of the century, the attacks of the Zambos emptied a large portion of the coast. The British dyewood cutters came afterward to exploit a territory that their allies had depopulated, and in doing so, laid the foundations for modern Belize. In this way, the Mosquito Zambos and the resettlement policies of the Spanish spelled a definitive end to Hispanic Mayan conflict in the lands that were once of the Manché Chol Maya.

Friar Agustin Cano in 1685

After these two trips, when the friars brought the families of the two brothers Juan and Miguel Chen and those who were with the headman Juan Matzin, they quickly left for other parts of this forest, but not with such happy results because they couldn't find Indian houses or, if they did, it was difficult to persuade them to settle at the site of San Lucas. The route east to where the four messengers of the Lord Bishop died was the most difficult because of the need to cross the Zactun River immediately next to the site of San Lucas Tzalac.

The river here is rapid and deep, going between the great rocks needed to make a bridge. Lacking any trees on this side of the river useful for this purpose, we discovered on the other bank a tree of a kind famous for using as a bridge. Called in this land *guachipilin* and in Nahua *conacaste,* it was so near the river that on cutting it so that it fell properly, it could serve for many years; for the wood is incorruptible and strong, so much so that it is better than iron for nails. We made the Indians swim to the other side of the river to cut it with axes. We could not assist in this work, and after they had broken it with many blows of the ax, it fell in the forest, pulling down so many trees that the noise was as if two armies were fighting with rifles, shotguns, and cannon. The noise of the trees breaking and falling caused the entire forest to tremble. After all this, we found we still didn't have a bridge because it took much work to move it to where it could serve as a bridge for the Preaching Friars.[6]

Then, having gone in this direction for ten leagues, we arrived at farms where the Indians of Cahabón had died. With all the houses burned, we didn't find any people. It was a desert without any other sign that they had once been here than some fields of sugarcane, sweet potatoes, and other fruits of the land. It was depopulated since the deaths, two months previous, of the Indians of Cahabón. Continuing forward, the Preaching Friars followed ten or twelve leagues beyond some traces of what appeared to be the trail of the Indians, but they found no farms. Instead, they found themselves in swamps so vast that their borders were invisible. Because of this, and the lack of supplies, they returned to the site of San Lucas even quicker than they wanted since the Indians, their companions, were eager to go back. The tired Preaching Friars were glad to return for they were sick from the bruises inflicted by these forests and the lack of any Chols. Nor did they any longer believe that they had been there, for this part of the east was near the garrison of the castle of San Felipe.

With the same luck, they made several trips with the same aim in mind, walking on foot through these brambles and forests with neither road nor path. Without any food other than a little biscuit, chocolate, and maize tortillas; without more shelter than the habit, and even this such a hindrance that they walked only with a scapular and the warmth of a gown in the night.[7] In a land so rainy and filled with bogs, streams, rocks, logs, and spines, for they did not see any other thing in these forests but trees and spiny plants, the trees gave the best shelter. Huts of the Chols are difficult to find. When found, they are extremely dirty, filled with smoke and domestic insects like fleas, jiggers, and bedbugs, without being free of the innumerable kinds of mosquitoes, snakes, scorpions, and other poisonous animals of the forest. Despite all these dangers and annoyances, the Preaching Friars continued to walk through these forests looking for Chols.

From these travels, we learned that many Indian farms were next to a powerful river of this forest called here the Maytol and near the ocean known as the Zactum River, which means "white stone." Joining this river is the Tiyú, which we spoke of previously, and many others, to make a river larger than the Guadalquivir.[8] With this information, we went forth on another trip northeast of the site of San Lucas. By sunset of the second day, we discovered ten to twelve houses and the cornfields of the Chol Indians. Going to them, we found in the largest many people of all ages and sexes; in this house lived the head Indian of this hamlet. As he was a Christian baptized in the time of Father Master Friar Francisco Gallego and had been an agent of the friars in the town of San Felipe and Santiago, his name was Agustin Cucul.

Enraged by their manner without being calmed, nor hearing what they said, this Indian picked up his bow and arrows and approached the Indians of Cahabón and the Preaching Friars. Seeing his wicked lack of attention, the Indians of Cahabón prevented him from using the bow. He acted so disrespectfully that it was difficult for the Preaching Friars and Indians to hold back his fury. Indeed, they could do so by no other method than tying him up. Although bound, he did not cease to cry out, making a thousand curses for them to untie him; seeing him, the Indians of Cahabón had a great desire to kill him and would have done it if not prevented by the Preaching Friars.

They spent the entire night watching over this Indian. Hearing their voices, all the Indians of the other houses fled, reason enough being the fear that all the Chols of these hamlets had for the Preaching Friars. This is why the Indians of Cahabón had attempted to take them by surprise. Thus, they stayed awake all night attempting to pacify the Indian Cucul. They did pacify twenty or thirty Indians, both men and women of this house as well as in the two others closest to it. From the other houses, they couldn't catch anyone for they were far away and only twenty Cahabón Indians had come with the friars.

Above all, they fled on hearing the shouts of the Indian Agustin Cucul, who told them several times that these Preaching Friars had come to kill them. The others fled because the Preaching Friars could not capture them. This Indian, besides being an apostate, had a special mark on his skin to show what was in his heart. He, the Indian most well disposed and the most Spanish of his nation, was branded with lines, and on his breast was painted a chain in the manner that they painted the Toisón.[9] Moreover, in the middle of his stomach, in the place of the lamb was painted a very ugly devil that, as a symbol of God, should only be the immaculate lamb.

The next day, we checked all these houses and, although we saw traces of many others who had been here, could not find more Indians. Without trying to obtain more Chols, we returned in a day and a half with the pacified Chol Indians to the site of San Lucas. There were thirty Chols, and among them the Indian Agustin Cucul, who even outside his hamlet, continued in an arrogance and ferocity undiminished neither by affection, threats, nor gifts. Seeing his fierceness, we had no way of assuring that if we left him there, he would not flee. Therefore, certain that it was he who caused other Chols to riot and kill the Indians of Cahabón, to prevent other disturbances and require him to live as a Christian, I ordered that he be taken from the forest and brought to the town of Cahabón. I sent a report of all that had happened to Lord President Don Enrique Enríquez de Guzman so that he could approve it. After this they resettled other Chol Indians, some baptized and some heathen, of the hamlet of Agustin Cucul, and in this manner the town of San Lucas grew until it had more than 300 souls.

Friar Francisco Ximénez in 1695

I found in Cahabón Captain Juan Díaz, Lieutenant Don Juan de Alarcon, Sergeant Antonio Díaz, and other corporals with a company of 70 soldiers carrying firearms. There were 100 Indian archers, 50 from Cobán and 50 from Salama, 70 path makers from the town of Cahabón, and 50 burden bearers from the town of San Agustin [Lanquin], together with others making a total of 400 persons. We received a letter from the Lord President giving us orders to enter the forests on the day indicated, but neither open roads nor make settlements until Saturday, the 5th of March, when we could do, given the weather, what was possible.[10]

Coming with me were six friar priests: Preacher Jose Delgado, Lorenzo Rodríguez, Jose Guerra, Diego de Santa Maria, Jose de Bascuñana, and Juan Gómez. Among other things, we could confess and administer communion to all the soldiers. Well armed with these arrangements, we gave many sermons so that no member of the expedition, from the captain to the least of the Indians, could forget to pray. Those with duties as guards or sentinels prayed there and did not forget to say mass every day. All the Father Preachers said what we decided to say, and none of the festive days lacked their words or small sermon as required by the occasion. These are things required from any Christian, even if in their house and not in any danger like us who went on the expedition.

We all left from Cahabón on Saturday the 5th of March . . . to the first hamlet called Tipachché.[11] The clay road with its thick mud, filled with holes and across steep hills, was bad. Being six hours behind schedule, we needed to cross some streams flowing east and so forded the river of Cahabón, which goes to Lake Izabal. On the 6th, we left this hamlet, and walking five leagues north, arrived at the ranch of Timuchuch where we made camp. The road was bad, worse than previously, for it had steep slopes and was mountainous, with many rocks and swamps. This day, Sergeant Antonio Díaz, while cutting a stick to make a cross, was blinded by sap going into his eyes. The Indians call this wood *ixte,* chili wood, and say that the sap causes blisters on the skin.

In this camp on the day of our father, Saint Thomas, we all said mass because the road wasn't open. On this 7th day of March, Friar Jose Guerra and Friar Diego de Santa Maria left with twelve soldiers, fifty archers, and others for Tampamac to search for Chols. The friars would go on ahead and advise us of what they found there. The Chols received them well and promised the friars that they would welcome us. This site [Timuchuch] seems large enough for a settlement for it is the right distance from Cahabón, being only nine leagues away. The climate is hot, and the water from a stream is quite good and permanent, it being the headwaters of a river farther on called Tiyú and more to the east called the Maytol River, known as the Zactum on entering the sea, where it is then large and navigable.[12] Its land is fertile and has cacao orchards.

On the 8th of March, we left and went four leagues north by northeast, arriving at the camp of Tampamac. Here, we found the Father Preachers explaining to some Chols the reason for our coming. Some of them agreed to accompany us in opening the road toward Cancuén. It is a road that naturally opens between some high peaks with a steep slope, and after that there are flat lands, swampy, muddy, and flooded. In the entire road there was as much water as in a swamp, and thus it seemed to me a bad site for a settlement. Nevertheless, it was here that the Chols of Tampamac had their first huts. Fulfilling their word, waiting for us on the road to receive us were six Chol Indians with their cigars in their mouths and bows and arrows in their hands. Being without more adornment than given by nature, but not as good because they were very dirty, their speech was brief and succinct. It was reduced to two words, meaning "welcome" and "when will you leave?"

Responding, we thanked them for their welcome and promised to reply to their question at the hamlet where we were going. We spoke with them for the rest of the way without them saying anything of value. Baptized was the headman, Tomás Chiquiz, and mayor, Agustin Cavatzin, as were four others who couldn't recall their [baptismal] names.

Arriving at the ranch of Tampamac, we found with the Father Preachers some twenty Indian Chols, among them men, women, and children. We told them that the King, our Lord, sent these captains and soldiers to their lands; they had come, and the Father Preachers as well, not to do something bad but to save their souls. We told them that it was necessary that those not baptized be baptized and live as Christians guarding the law of God. We told them that baptism didn't matter much if they didn't keep the law of God. For this we would remain with them for a time, for we didn't come to leave but to gather them in towns, and thus, teach them jointly and live with them. The Chols were not pleased by what we said about gathering them in towns and needing to remain with them. But seeing with their eyes the soldiers who were going to carry out our orders, they said that, yes, they would come together in towns.

On the 9th, we passed an arm of the Boloncot River, its name meaning "nine eagles."[13] We walked four leagues to the north. On all these roads there were some Chol houses from the town of Tampumac [Tampamac]. On these first stages of our journey, we passed three or four peaks smaller than the volcano of Agua of Guatemala.[14] The other roads are flat. Some bad passes had curses as names.[15]

We left on the 10th, walking two leagues for there was no road; going north, we made many turns and arrived at a stream called Tichahac. This means "lightning." Here, there is a type of large tree that on being cut, gives a blood-colored sap like that of the dragon, and they call it in the language of Cahabón *pilix* and in Chol *cancanté*.[16] Everywhere, there is an herb similar to the doradilla that they say, when made into a drink, is good against worms.[17] They call it in Cacchi *pizih* and in Chol *zikh*.[18] Also, there are many *palos de María*, and its milk is medicinal.[19] They call it in Chol *zachahlanté*, which means "white pataxte."

On the 11th of March, we left the camp of Tichahac, walking three leagues to the east and seeing little difference, the road following the banks of a dry river that they call Tanquinhá, meaning "dry river." We arrived at the hamlet of Bictehum, or Amate Bridge. We found here a Chol headman called Domingo Canté. Father Preacher General Delgado brought him, along with others from these forests, to [Antigua,] Guatemala, twenty-two years ago.

On the 12th, we left Bictehum for the north, and walking five leagues— three by paths, two by ways newly opened by the Chols—we arrived at a canyon called Tuilhá, meaning "smelly water." We passed the Yaxha River, meaning "blue Water."[20] A branch of it came from underground, and after a short distance, returned into the earth and vanished from sight. In Tuilhá, a snake bit an Indian of Cahabón in a finger, giving him two perforations. They gave him a drink made from the "little bean of Nicaragua," with a little of the same potion being placed on the bite.[21] The Indian recovered and continued with his load.

On the 13th, we searched in many directions until we found a road opened by the Chols. Going past the Yaxhá River, we now followed the bank of the Cancuén River for a half league and then returned to the north. We walked six leagues, dying of hunger on the same bank of the Cancuén, when we found thirty or forty Chols of the site of San Francisco Zaczaclum, this meaning "white earth." Previously called San Pedro y San Pablo Nohxoy [Noxoy], the old names have changed and thus confused us because the Chols didn't recognize the old names. The headman Agustin Xiquin was the constable in Nohxoy in the time of Father Friar Jose Delgado. These Chols tell millions of lies, and one can't learn what is true. Here we rested two days, washing clothing and resting the animals. We arrived with few supplies, and very annoyed from hunger, mud, exhaustion, and sleeping on beds of green leaves.

On the 14th of March, we decided to send the captain to the headman of this site with a paper telling him to open the road and pass the message from hand to hand to the headmen farther on. Seeing the paper, the headman obeyed, trembling with fear. On the 16th, we left the site of Zaczaclum and went to the Cancuén River, camping on its bank. Then, we walked three leagues to the northeast to the huts of Pablo Tzuncal. From here, we summoned the headman of San Jose May. The stream of Pablo Tzuncal is the Cancanhá. It is not anything special, but we did find here more than 100 persons. At this site the soldiers found sugarcane.

We summoned the headman Matías May of San Jose May, but did not advise the sentinels. Therefore, when a little after prayers he came with others of his entourage, the first sentinel fired his gun, warning the second and alarming all of us. It was a pleasure to hear and see how everyone armed themselves. How quickly the soldiers assembled with their weapons. Quickly, the captain, lieutenant, soldiers, and Indians came at the sound of the alarm. The headman of May arrived with the response of that of Mopan and brought the same paper that we had given him. He said that the Mopan headman of Taximchan did not want to receive them because he couldn't open the roads, being ill and in fear of the soldiers; that little by little he would become Christian; and that he wanted many machetes, axes, glass beads, and salt. We sent him another message and will tell what happened [later].

On the 17th, we left Tzuncal for San Jose May, walking east six leagues. The road is bad, there being some horrible crags, and in them some caves, many small gullies, and mire. Many fell down and got stuck in the mud. Friar Lorenzo Rodríguez fell here and his mule got stuck; also the lieutenant, Friar Jose Delgado, and many other soldiers fell here. We found the huts of May on the bank of the Ixpoctum.

Living next to the stream Acté or May, we found 150 persons. This day and others, many ate at four in the afternoon. For lack of supplies some ate little, since the Indian bearers of Cahabón abandoned their loads and, we being angry, fled from us. At five in the afternoon arrived the headman Simon Cocahan of that Chocahau called Asuncion. He came to say that now the road was open.

On the 18th of March, we left May and, going from east to northeast, walked two leagues to the hamlet of Asuncion Chocahau, where we came to the stream Zacchay or White Fish. At this site we found an old dying headman. Father Friar Diego confessed him, and Friar Jose judged and anointed him. This day in the afternoon, two soldiers, Antonio de la Cruz and Salvador de Miranda, entered the forest and found some Mopans and their headman, Tezecum.[22] They brought these spies to us. They didn't want to say anything; only torture made them confess that they had come to see if there was merchandise. But they didn't bring anything to buy it with, not even arrows, nor any arms that they had hidden. At five in the afternoon arrived the Ahtzen Yahcab and Zuzben with some thirty Indians, and they said that the principal headman was Taximchan. This night, some of their guards told us that we were two leagues from their town, and that from Mopan to the savannas was two days by road and five to the Ahitza or Peten where there were many Indians who had canoes to go to the island where they lived.

On the 19th, we left from Chocahau for Mopan. The Mopans watched from their paths and, advising their companions, all fled, leaving the houses empty. We found many large cornfields and empty hamlets, and thus we saw and confirmed that they had fled. We brought our five Mopan prisoners in the middle of the army. We walked close to six leagues to the northeast for they had deceived us, saying that it was only two leagues, and all the Indians had disappeared from the route. This afternoon, the soldiers found two Indians. The one sent to bring the women didn't return. They kept the other in shackles. We found there a seated idol made of pieces of red wood, on an obvious path, very vulgar and ugly with eyes of mother-of-pearl with black pupils and ears with pieces of mother-of-pearl, all quite horrid. Brought to Friar Diego de Santa Maria, afterward an unknown person stole it.

The land is beautiful and, although hot, refreshed by the sea breezes that reach it. There are many hot land fruits such as lemons and the coastal anonas, which are red inside. There are maniocs, large sweet potatoes, and other edible roots. The water is fresh but little and smelly. The horizon is visible and [the climate] very mild. There are some wild turkeys.[23]

On the 20th day of the month, two Mopan Indians asked permission to call their people. They went with two soldiers and three or four Indians of Salama, but when on the road, attempted to flee like the others. Those of Salama tried to forcibly detain one of them and gave him three wounds when he fled. A soldier with a harquebus shot the other in the cartilage of the left shoulder so that he fell and they could catch him. They cured him even though he was in a very bad way. He didn't die because it was not a ball that entered but only the wadding.

The Spanish guard caught the other Mopan. Such was his strength that ten or twelve men could not subjugate him. Bellowing in anger and defending himself with teeth, feet, and hands, they needed to tie him up. The soldiers had wanted to kill him, but on the request of the friars, they left him. While lying on the ground, he grabbed a cutlass of a corporal of a squad and, if others had not taken it away, would have killed the corporal. The soldiers who discovered his attempt admired his virility for he seemed like a bat with two wings, one that they could and should sacrifice to the Devil. A fitting sacrifice of this dirty and foul spirit!

These Mopans are barbarous and a different nation from the Chols. The language is a mixture of Yucatec and Chol that few Chol understand. On the 21st, we began a trench around the entire site, thus making a large fort for protection against any attack. Although it was not strong, it was something of an obstacle.

On this day, the headman Juan Zibac [Tzibac] came with ten or twelve Manche Indians. We told them that the fort was important for their Christianity, and they helped construct it. On the 22nd, . . . some smoke came from the north, and the Indians said that the savannas were burning. Other smoke was from a maize granary that an Indian of Cahabón burned near our fortifications. This day, we spoke to a Mopan Indian who said that from here to the savannas took only a day by an open, wide, flat road with only some small hills. He said that if one walked quickly, one could arrive at the Peten in four days, and if one went slowly in five. On the way there were four savannas, each separated by some thickets of brush and some water-filled ravines and swamps with fish in them.[24]

The lake and island are large, and [the island] has a vast number of Indians on it, as did the mainland. Those of the island they call Petenes and the others Ahitzas, but they are all of the same nation and language. This nation of Ahitza extends to those of Xocmo and they travel on some canoes they have, using a large river that goes from Xocmo to the Peten. They travel on these from the east toward the west or northwest. On the edge of the savanna there is a ravine. In the savannas are two large rivers: one of Xocmo, and another that they don't know the name of. The Lacandons are those of Xocmo, who perhaps are the Ahitzas.[25] The hills of Bolomtevitz, which means "nine hills," are near the ocean on the east, after the savannas, far from here.

This day, the captain notified all the soldiers, Spaniards as well as Indians, that they should touch neither the fields nor the houses belonging to these Mopans because they did not come to cause evil but to preach the law of God. Henceforth, they should not annoy them by eating the crops of the fields of those that had fled, nor should they eat meat for it was Holy Week. They said this to the Mopans to pacify them and so they would understand that they didn't come to do evil. This is what he said to the prisoners. He severely punished Tucah, the Indian of Cahabón who had burned the granary.

At three in the afternoon on March 23rd, the headmen of Chocahau and Mopan (known as Tezecum) entered the fortification with four or six of their entourage. They came to submit. He told us that his hamlet is next to that of Chocahau and that the soldiers discovered it on the 18th day. They had come for the six prisoners and two wives. They released and fed them all. In less than an hour arrived another Mopan headman called Tzuc with all his chin, chest, and belly branded with an iron to show pictures, and his short coat of black cloth. He was an important man and very smart. He entered with three or four Indian women and gave me a gift of fifty cacao beans. We treated him well and went in search of the Taximchan said to be near here. He was sick from a gunshot wound, and we sent word that if he didn't come he would be sorry. They greatly feared the mules who they called the tapir of Castile.

We told these well-built and strong Indians that the mules would not kill or eat the Mopans because now they were our children, and they believed this.

At this settlement arrived two Indians from Cahabón, who took four months to get here, called Matías Bolom and Diego Can with a message for the missionaries and an intent to trade. These of Cahabón had hanging from the neck some crucifixes of brass. At every hamlet they mocked the holy cross, spitting on it by saying that it was no God but the idol of the Christians. The infidel dogs paid for their crime, but they had destroyed cornfields, hurt two, and maltreated another who they imprisoned for being fat and heavily built, this being the same day we arrived here and found the idol mentioned above. All of us spit on the idol and reviled it in the same hamlet where they had blasphemed our Lord Jesus Christ. We told these barbarians that we came to preach the law of God and make them Christians, not to kill or do evil. They said, shaking with fear, that this is what they wanted and that they wanted salt, machetes, and glass beads. These were Christians if they gave them something, and thus they were make-believe Christians. Some from Bacalar killed them [the Indians from Cahabón] here, to steal their merchandise.

On the 24th, twelve soldiers, Corporal Antonio de la Cruz, and twenty-five archers of Salama left to discover the road and savannas. They brought three guides: the headman Tzac, a Mopan, and a Chol.[26] These are the savannas that go to the Ahitza. On this day, the headman of Chocahau together with Tezecum and the prisoners returned to their houses. They said that they would settle in Chocahau and remain there. Shortly after, six or seven other Mopans arrived who we had seen in Chocahau. They had refused to admit that they were Mopans and the simpletons did not know that they spoke Yucatec.[27] All lied to escape. Afterward appeared the wife of that one hurt by the harquebus; neither she nor the five other women and three men who arrived with her showed any emotion. We gave them something to eat and they were content.

On the 25th, those who had gone to search for the headman Taximchan came with a thousand lies and said they couldn't find him.[28] On the same day, some Indians came to buy axes and machetes. They brought a little cacao, some painted cloth, and some of the very short coats without sleeves that they used. We examined them, determined that they were spies or fake merchants, and so would not sell them anything. Up to this point we sold axes and machetes to all. We warned the soldiers, and Indians under them, of certain punishment if they sold either ax or machete to these barbarians who had come as spies. Six Mopans with bows and arrows, intending to take their machetes, attacked three Indians from Cahabón collecting fodder for the mules. They defended themselves, and came to the fort and said that there were many in ambush. Fifty archers and four soldiers went out, but they couldn't find anyone. One night, a soldier from the valley of Urran went to cut fodder for his mule and a Mopan Indian chased him until he arrived gasping at the fort.[29] Because he left the fort without arms, the captain demoted him by taking his shotgun and giving him a lance.

On the 26th, four soldiers with the archers of Cobán went looking for the headman Taximchan and, on the same day, the explorers returned from the savannas. They said that three leagues from here was a stream that they called the Camarones where there was a large crag made up of pieces of stone. For the twelve or thirteen leagues to the savannas, from the Camarones to the savannas, there was no water and the fields were so large that one couldn't see their end. They found many pine trees and teosinte as well as twenty-two little settlements of the Ahitzas, plus traces of more than a hundred that had been there previously.[30]

This day, several trips made in the area didn't find Indians, but only [discovered] that they had cut down all the maize fields, removed the maize from their huts, and burned it all because they didn't want us to use it. According to the tracks, the Mopans went west to Xocmo. This night, headman Tzac brought eight Indians and five women. Among them was the headman Yahcab who had been in Chocahau with us. The reason that they gave for fleeing was that we were many. They gave us a gift of some tortillas, which we didn't eat because they were in the habit of putting poison in them.

On the 28th, the mayor and an alderman of Cahabón came to the fort because the Indians had fled and we lacked provisions. I made a church with two altars, where all of us said mass, and on the 30th, the Indians [in the fort] fled with the headman Yahcab. I celebrated Holy Week here and announced another indulgence; all confessed, received communion, and so did well for themselves. On the 31st of March, they left to open the road to the savannas. They were twelve soldiers with seventy-five archers. We went to look for the Lord President and Father Master Rivas, who had entered [the forest] from Ocosingo and Santa Eulalia.[31] It was the headman Tzac and other Indians that showed them the way to the right of the crags because the mules couldn't pass. This Tzac did good things, did not refuse us anything, and was very loving and the only Indian we found who supported us.

On the 2nd of April, two squads left to search the forest and they found forty-two houses and cornfields. The Indians fled, and we inferred from the number of cornfields and houses that there were many Mopans. All this time, we made many unsuccessful attempts to meet these rebellious, bad, deceitful, and savage Indians. On the 3rd, we wrote to the Lord President and Father Master Rivas, sending it by the hand of the headman of May, who promised to take the letter to Xocmo. He went from there to search for them. Perhaps he could find them. We found more than eighty houses in these forests with no more than about ten living in ten of them. Acquaintance with many showed us that they spoke another language. This nation had the entire coast of Manché up to Bacalar.[32] Father Friar Jose Delgado discovered them when he went from here to Yucatán.

On the 4th of April, eight soldiers and twenty-four archers left to search the forest, going to the right toward the seashore on the east. Within a short distance, they found four or five hamlets and old maize fields. Afterward, they found twelve tiny Indian hamlets whose inhabitants, like the Campin River, hurled themselves to the coast. In the afternoon, from the party that had gone ahead to open the road came a soldier and eight Indians. He said that the road was now open, that it wasn't bad, and two leagues within the savannas was a river. They had stopped here to make some straw huts and there was much deer. They had not discovered any signs of fire, nor [was there] news of the Lord President or Father Master Rivas.[33]

Declaration of Friar Cristóbal de Prada [1695?]

Having entered this forest on the 5th day of November, I spent three days with the Indians at the site of Tampamac.[34] The headman was Tomas Barrena and there was no more than a single house inhabited by five or six families. I ordered all the people assembled and, on the following day, counted some sixty Indians of all ages. They told me that some were absent, and on leaving on the road, I saw two other families.

After three days of travel, I found the hamlet of Domingo Canté depopulated for he had moved four leagues from here. It was evident from the census of the Reverend Father Friar Antonio Margil that there had been ninety-two persons.

Two days of travel brought me to another site called Tuilhá.[35] On seeing me, four Indians left a hut and told me I was still far from their town. Less than a day's travel brought me to Cancuén, to a settlement called

San Francisco de Tuve.[36] Here, I spent fifteen days teaching the Christian doctrine, for they were so ignorant that they didn't even know how to make a cross. I found others equally ignorant. I asked some why they had received holy baptism, and they responded that [it was] because they didn't want to die, nor have headaches or bruises on their skin.

A day's journey from here are three sites, each having 100 Indians. Ordering them assembled at each site, I spent five and more days teaching and baptizing some children, of which all told there were forty. I found two Indians and three old white-bearded pagans. . . . In the town of May there were three families, one being of eight pagans who had hidden from the Reverend Father Friar Antonio [Margil] at the site of Chocahau. I was here rather than in the others. . . . Five Indians helped [me] three leagues from here in San Miguel Manché. Some forty persons, officeholders and important persons, came to see me on different occasions. All of them had not come, for I knew there were forty houses.

Questioning those Indians that came three or four times, I discovered who are the most pagan. When I asked the number of Indians, they told me that I saw some 600, but I understand that certainly there are more of this Chol nation. Many of these who had fled the town of San Lucas had gone toward the coast of the ocean.

Another settlement, claims Fulano Vehin, an Indian interpreter of Cahabón, has some thirty houses in two separate locations a short distance from the town. I found on a path to one of them eight persons, and on another path, two people. Other paths went to Machuca, or from Chocahau to May. Another led me to five or six houses. Also, some of the muleteers that have entered these forests have seen otherwise unknown hamlets. Each day they saw new Indians. On these journeys, they discovered settlements with many Indians that I have not seen. Others, which I have counted, do not include all those scattered through these forests. From long experience, I have learned that the old fathers of this nation can have up to thirteen wives. There are always more than are shown, and always they say that it is the wife of the father, although one never sees the face of the father.

I have plenty of experience of their lying in this matter. Thus, some bring forth girls of three, four, or nine years and say that their fathers gave them.[37] This is not so. What they say in the matter of sacrament is certainly wrong for they seem to believe in baptism two or three times. One never sees others since while they all say that most families are small, all the experience that people have had with them says otherwise. When counted by Reverend Father Friar Antonio Margil, some came with wives different from those given in the censuses and others hid the children. All are the same liars. They can convince you that they do without or that they don't understand for they are very clever. Thus, I can't determine how many [there really are] because many of those counted by the censuses they hide, and those they didn't count appear; also because these people live without subjection to headmen.

They don't have someone to tell them what to do, nor to tell them to come together. I say that they don't have headmen for although there are some, and they name them, they don't pay them any heed and each one is independent. I have seen a little Indian lying down in a hammock being ordered by the headman to bring fire, and the overlord, who I deduced from the names between them, asked me to order him to help make his house. Beyond this, they confess that they don't do what the headmen say and they lack anything anyone would want to buy. . . . In short, unhappy and miserable, always starving, so that if the land was not well supplied with *corozos* and *pacayas,* they would all die of hunger for no Indians will harvest maize for another.[38]

Concerning their Christianity, I understand they have total disgust for the Holy Faith for these people flee from all subjugation. They incline neither to God nor the Devil since, despite all their idolatry, they will not do anything for even a stick or stone. Although they have dances on special days and many superstitions, they don't do anything either for the Devil or their own demon. Nor after a thousand miseries and hell every day would they do so without some investigation. Thus, asked if they want to go to the Devil or hell, they say that they don't want anything. Thus, they scoff and abominate without difficulty. What is certain is that they only worship their liberty dishonestly.

. . . For their conservation, it is necessary to bring them all together in one or two towns where a priest can live continuously to teach them. For this, to order them to make cornfields near the town and help the church, subjugation and fear are necessary. This is because I have seen them spend two or three days in the town and then go with their families to the cornfields. They can't do otherwise, since in the town they don't have anything to eat. Thus, they spend five or six days in coming and going. Two days after they arrive they ask for permission to leave, and thus, they are in constant movement and lack indoctrination. For them to remain in a town it is absolutely necessary that they have a cornfield and remain the only owner of the cornfield. The cornfields that they have, although two or three days away from what they call the town, are in reality not theirs but the field of the Ahau, which is the name they give to the town. Since each family lives in their cornfield, one can't take censuses of the towns because today they are in the land of Chocahau, tomorrow they go to Tuilhá, etc.

Concerning the Mopans, it happened that when I arrived in these forests, they told me that the Chols have contact with this nation; in brief, many of the headmen that I know belong to this nation. Taximchan, one of these headmen, has two zontles of people, which is 800 including soldiers, who live in the fort of the Mopan.[39] This year, I know that whatever path I take, I run into people. This tells me that this land is filled with people. Further proof is that in the town of Belén, of the valley of Urran, there are eighteen factions and settled sites of this Mopan nation.

Alonso Ixil, an Indian of Chocahau who knows the Mopan and Peten language as well as his own Chol, gave me the first notice of the number of people of Taximchan. Asking how he knows that there were 800 people of Taximchan, he responded that he knew because he grew up in the house of their headman. Thereupon, I understood the last lie and fiction of the Chols, showing how they all show much malice. For just hearing the name of Mopans they show great fear, and they say that they are their enemies, that they are thieves, and that they have much horror of them. It is false because there is much communication between them and they are very close to them. I discovered that they say this only so as not to be required to lead us to the Mopans, whose sites they know well. Especially those of Chocahau and the Indians of May all know the Mopan language, which would not be possible without having great communication with them. [But] not only the eldest but even the young children don't speak of it through fear of their parents.

As I said, if one doesn't seize them by their shoulders, they will go away. In this way, Christianity will vanish from the frontier and the ministers remain. Thus, I again express my feeling on the constancy of the Chols. I affirm to God, Lord Christ, that it is impossible that they remain in one place, without much desertion, without gathering them in one place or removing those to the town of Belén or wherever decided; this is more secure than remaining in the forest to corrupt the Mopans and Petenes by their great malice and depravity.[40] For as their minister I know that even if Chols changed into angels, they would in the end turn to witchcraft, heresy, and rebellion.

This is the statement written in his own hand by the Reverend Father Friar Cristóbal de Prada, from the site of Chacal as one can guess, and although not signed, the copy of this statement is a true copy.[41]

Very Illustrious Lord: Lord, I am providing here an account of the days since I arrived at this town of Cahabón, gathered the people, and made arrangements for the expedition to the forests of the Chol. Having received mail from it (sent by Matías Bolón, who I sent to explore) with news of having arrived at Tampamac, where the people of San Parada of the Chols live, and having discovered them and those of most towns gone, I made an investigation to trace the location of the Chols.[42] As had been previously resolved, I divided the expedition that I sent to the forests into three parts as this seemed the best way of exploring all of it.

The first part left for the forest on the 3rd of this month. It had 300 Indians from this town led by 4 sheriffs, and a head corporal to give the orders to all.[43] I ordered it to take the royal road to Tampamac and Santo Domingo Tuilhá.[44] I ordered that if in these sites they don't learn the location of the Chols, they should go to the other side of the Boloncot River, capturing the people of San Pablo Suncal, Chocahau, and other hamlets on the other side of the river, and that they should advise me of what they have seen and done.[45]

The second part, led by two Indian headmen who know the Chol language with 200 Indians of this town and adjacent San Agustin [Lanquin], went on the 5th day. These I ordered to go to the right on the royal road until they reach the Tiyú River, a location very attractive to the Chols. If having searched all without finding a trace, they should join the first part.

The third group, sent on the 6th day, had 150 Indians of both towns led by two experienced corporals. Their orders were to go wherever they wanted on the royal road and search all these forests. If they didn't find any trace of the Chols, they should also join the first part, with the head corporal giving the necessary orders.

These dispositions produced results, for the second part of the expedition that went to the Tiyú River found on the other side a trace of the Chols. Following this trace, and aided by Matías Bolón, they found those of San Parada. They captured the Chols, a total of ninety from the two towns of Tampamac and Santo Domingo Tuilhá, with their headman Domingo Canté.[46] These are Indians of much importance who govern all the Chols. Taken in a convoy by the 200 Indians who captured and fed them, it only took a day to move them. They rested here two days and then left with Father Friar Joseph Angel Senoyo for Cobán. He kept enough Indians to escort them to Belem.[47] The third part has met and joined the first, and both together passed to the other side of the Boloncon River. I am expecting a good catch of Chols.

Letter of Diego Pacheco, Cahabón, May 17, 1697

Very Illustrious Lord: . . . Domingo Canté advised that the Indians had fled their houses and cornfields because their companions from the towns of Suncal, May, and Chocahau, on the other side of the Boloncot River, told them that the Peten Indians intended to come to capture or kill them.[48] Since they were so few, because many of their people had died, and the enemy being close, they fled to the forest. The mayor of Tampamac knew that an Indian leader of the town had separated from them with forty persons, escaping to a site more hidden that they called the Saquija River.[49] The mayor . . . having been threatened with punishment for not telling the truth, Domingo Canté said from the beginning that what he said is so. Repeating it, he added that as the Indian leader, he himself had said good-bye to those going to the Saquija River and intended to join them the following summer. Domingo Canté assured me that he was certain and asked me to go take these people, for he wanted to lead them to that site (and he would leave here his wife and two sons) so they would not flee. For all these reasons, I resolved to quickly send eighty Indians of this town . . . and these people left.

Letter of Diego Pacheco, June 26, 1697

Very Illustrious Lord: In compliance with what Your Lordship has ordered of me, on the 1st of the current month . . . I have made a careful investigation and have established that the four nations of the Chol Indians closest [to Cobán] are those of the Poots, Uchins, Axmuls, and those in the forests of Lake Izabal near Amatique. The Indians of this town are in contact with them and they are numerous. All who are in the castle and warehouses of Lake Izabal confirm this, since they see every night the fires of the forest Indians.

Letter of Miguel Rodríguez Camilo, June 18, 1698

Don Gabriel Sanchez de Berrospe of the council of His Majesty, Lord: I have seen your orders of the 30th of May and since Tuesday, the 3rd of this June, I have undertaken the removal of the Matiques Indians.[50] For this conquest ordered by Your Lordship, I am preparing whatever is necessary for canoe or boat travel by water as well as for a march by land. . . .

Since the pilot Sebastian could take soundings in them after leaving

Amatique, knowledge of the waters where we were going wasn't so important.[51] From the mouth of the river of Amatique, it is by way of the ocean twelve leagues to the mouth of the Uschupan River and six leagues to that of the Canté; this other river is the Yaxal.[52] On the rivers are small hamlets and, in the interior, settlements of the Canantzins, Yacav, Chucullos, Titzaquins, Batenas, Mopans, and Axsacao. Each one is larger than Chiquimula.[53] They have governors and those that trade with those of the Peten and others inside this land who are both daring and cunning. Some of these towns have large numbers of people.

Those mentioned who are on the coast have trade with those of Bacalar. The interior lands bordering the Peten are well populated, as are the coasts bordering with Bacalar. The Indian pilot Sebastian and others who have had experience previously with the Bacales, who come in boats to this castle, mention seeing the Matiques in all the rivers.[54] Other river Indians, as evident in the papers on routes left to me by my predecessor Don Matías Munoz de Castro, smuggle goods and those of Bacalar . . . to this castle, bringing great amounts of cacao, achiote, and other things from these Indians.

Although it is true that these merchants don't contact any Indians other than those settled on the rivers and near the ocean, they have received news of many peoples and large settlements inland. They add also that they are fertile lands for crops and have a good climate. Lord, it can be that in returning to the Amatique, we can determine if this is true, although what I say is well known and it requires much preparation to prepare the boats. . . .

To achieve this conquest and remove the Indians, I will need to garrison their lands. Here, Lord, there is no funding for expeditions. Only if I can build boats for the enterprise are there any hopes of success. . . .

I have provided orders to the sergeant of this castle on the manner and circumstances appropriate for dealing with the people already removed: baptized Indians who total 114 men and women. The two Indian pilots will bring them from this castle to the land. In this, I suspect that nothing can succeed because of the uselessness of the Indians.[55] Those who I have for a garrison [at the castle San Felipe] are those who have retired from the infantry because of age or lack of stamina for a march.

Letter of Miguel Rodríguez Camilo, July 8, 1698

Lord Don Gabriel Sanchez de Berrospe of the Council of His Majesty: As in the account given on the 18th day of the past month, ten men, all volunteers from the Zacapa frontier, with the sergeant of this castle and two Indian pilots went down from Gualan to remove the Indian apostates in these forests.[56] On the 3rd day of this month of July, they returned to this castle, stating that they had discovered settlements on the alluvial plain of a river called La Ciénega twenty leagues distant from this castle.[57] They state that these settlements in the summer have abundant plantain groves, fresh sweet potatoes, and ollas and barbecues to smoke fish, plus many useless picked cornfields of the past year and many traces indicating many more people with the apostates. The rising waters of the river required them to return to the forest.

. . . The indications are of many, and fourteen leagues from these settlements I know of a large town, and all heard how easy it is to observe from this castle the land in the mountains called Gigimani.[58] Summer travel from this castle to the town of Cahabón, with smoke visible in the day and fire seen in the night, affirms that the region is well populated by Indians. Beginning on the 1st of February and extending until the 20th of May, one can see the same lights and smoke from the shores of Lake Izabal.

Letter of Francisco de Villela, December 8, 1698

Lord Commander Don Miguel Rodríguez Camilo, my very dear sir: . . . I heard that Your Mercy summoned Governor Don Simon Anton de la Luna, Captain and current Mayor Lorenzo Monterroso, and Alderman Lucas Berganza, who are the most important people of the town of San Pedro Amatique, to congratulate them on having removed thirty-six persons, small and large, twenty-one being male and fifteen females (there not being a list of children because they did not count them). Of them, only two were old men and three old women, most being boys of a good age taken on the Timax River.[59] The town only had two Indians, but they brought their wives, and among them they found my godfather Gregorio, and in all there were fourteen men and women. . . .

Alonso de la Cruz, the brother of my godfather, went forward with the others and captured on the 4th day of the current month thirty-six [Indians], among them three from the Yaxal River who had come to those of Timax fleeing from the Mopans, who had put to the sword all in the town of Yaxal. The Mopan took them away, leaving a boy to guard them. He said that it took little effort to escape. Only the three escaped, and among them was the badly cut up headman. Although still ill, he now came to ask me to write to Lord President Don Gabriel Sanchez de

Berrospe, requesting that he send soldiers to conquer and capture all the Mopans. . . .

This capture of thirty-six they say was the second raid; the first, made by the Yaxal River, captured ten persons. This town, they say, was so large that they only attacked four houses. . . . His Lordship, the President, deciding to continue the conquest, sent them sixteen souls with firearms and munitions to those who know how to use them, and provisions of bread or maize, meat or beans, since they were lacking in all and could but sparingly sustain the Indians. They also asked for four cutlasses for the military corporal, and axes, machetes, cloth, blouses, and petticoats for these Indians whom they have removed. . . . They are lost, and the wounds are very difficult for the Indians who escaped and those who fled. This is all the news and I say good-bye. May our Lord give Your Mercy many years.

Letter of Miguel Rodríguez Camilo and
Juan de Dios Dávila, January 5, 1699

In the castle of San Felipe on Lake Izabal, on the fifth day of January of the year 1699, I, Sergeant Major Don Miguel Rodríguez Camilo, commander of the castle and governor of the port of Santo Tomás de Castilla, made an interrogation of the headman and his companions. They stated that the population of the Matiques, three days by road from here, lives in a town of twenty houses without any far-off fields; furthermore, the settlement is three days by land from a large town and many hamlets of the Mopan nation. There are other settlements of the same nation on the coast of the ocean that border with this coast. These Mopans are those who kill people, and they seized this town of Chocahau . . . and the capital of those of the Paliac River.[60]

Three days by road from here are the large settlements of the Petenes. They retreated from their lands since the Spaniards were searching for them. Two days distant by land from the town is another settlement, called Testiaz, from whence within a day's travel is another large town called Queschan.[61] The Indians of Cahabón of the Verapaz have good relations and trade with another nation, called Xocmo, which pays them with achiote and cacao.

These hidden nations communicate less with the Mopans, Petenes, and Ahitzas, although in other times they say they frequently went there. Some settlements cut trails from one to another that only those who know the land can follow because they are afraid that the Spaniards will use them. Of these nations, the most outgoing and bold are the Mopans, and many of these are Petenes and Ahitzas.[62] The arms that these nations use against Spaniards are arrows and lances of flint. Those of Bacalar provide some of these nations with items of iron and other things in exchange for their harvests of achiote and cacao. This is what the headman and his companions, who were the leaders of the town of San Pedro Amatique, declared through interpreters, and affirmed and confirmed before me [Don Miguel Rodríguez Camilo], the governor. . . .

Don Miguel Rodríguez Camilo, commander of the castle and governor of the port of Santo Tomás de Castilla and the town of San Pedro Amatique for His Majesty, receiving the order of His Lordship Don Gabriel Sanchez de Berrospe, took steps to provide boats and other things to the Indians of the town of Amatique. Continuing the conquest, they sailed for two days to the mouth of the Yaxal River and went upstream nine days to where they would go by land.[63] Beginning their march at eight in the morning, they continued until four in the afternoon, when they discovered a settlement with four houses, where they captured ten male and female Indians. The next day, they passed another river, called the Timax, where there was a settlement of six houses, and in them they captured thirty-six Indians, large and small, including in this number the headman and two others of his lineage. These had moved here to escape death from the Mopans. Since they had not enough room in the boats, they left fourteen with the intention of returning for them.

Bringing their wives, they did what they could to attract two Indians who had fled from the settlement. These Indians explained that many of settlements of this part are of different nations because they are distrustful of what they themselves don't originate. They advised them that they could be in danger of their lives and should take all care in solving problems on the route of the expedition. So was sworn by Don Simon Anton de la Luna, governor of the town, and most of the leaders who held military positions or responsibilities involving the administration of justice. . . .

Don Miguel Rodríguez Camilo then settled the Matiques Indian men, women, and children taken from the forest at the site of Xocolo, which adjoins the field of this castle. He divided the lands with them, establishing first the church of Lord Saint Anthony by bringing his holy image from the town of Amatique, and then dressing him and giving the support provided by His Lordship the President for them.[64] He gave them to understand that the mayor [of Amatique] would govern them. The site has good lands for sowing, and being near the lake, is close to water good for fishing. The climate is temperate, and at the site the priest can be available all hours to offer his assistance and care for them. Certified and signed with the priest and chaplain of the castle, Juan de Dios Dávila.

Letter of Miguel Rodríguez Camilo, June 6, 1699

On the 4th of April 1699, Field Master Don Miguel Rodríguez Camilo, commander of the castle of San Felipe and His Majesty's governor of the port of Santo Tomás de Castilla, [was sent by] His Lordship Don Gabriel Sanchez de Berrospe . . . to the forest of the Chol to reduce the pagan Indians who live there. To do so, from the 1st day of May two apostolic preachers of the college of Santa Cruz de Caetano assisted me, these being Friar Antonio Bahamonde and Friar Pedro Campi, as well as 60 paid soldiers from the province of Zacapa, 59 Indian burden bearers from Chiquimula, and 8 Indian pilots from the town of San Pedro de Amatique. The new foundation of Saint Anthony of the Warehouses contributed 2 natives, who together with the others, made a total of 146 adventurers.

Since we would follow the previous route to the Timax River, Juan de Beraza, an Indian from the nation of Chocahau, would guide me to the port of Politan, where they know there are many towns. They are near two; one of them, Bolom of the Saques Indians near the ocean, has a great supply of maize and is the easiest way to enter the Mopan for roads from it go to all the nations.

On presenting this reasoning to the fathers, and concerning ease of support, they supported travel to the many settlements and people in them as indicated by the Indian. With no river to impede me, I expect to be able to surmount the worst difficulties. Knowing that my best guess in fulfilling the duties entrusted to me depends on a fate determined by my trust in God, our Lord, I said three masses on the 10th day, one to the Holy Spirit, one to Holy Mary, and one to him entrusted with the patronage of the town, Saint Anthony. I prayed to the glorious saint in the chapel of the castle and solemnly invoked the divine spirit to provide us with luck in following the route of the Indians.

At four in the afternoon, I gave the order to leave to a swift canoe and four boats. In the Golfete at eight in the night, a great storm with wind and rain fell on the ships, dividing one from the other.[65] The one that I and the fathers traveled on was large, but the steering qualities, on which the lives of my people depended, were very good so that we stayed with great accuracy on the route. I observed that thanks to foresight, there was a considerable amount of provisions. On the 16th day, arriving as before at the mouth of the Timax River, we went three leagues to the beach of Punta Gorda and some Indian hamlets.

According to the evidence discovered, more than sixty had been making salt on the trail three days into the forest. One league distant from us was the Uchupan River, where I conferred with the pilot.[66] He advised that, before following it, I obtain more information on the destination of the trail. On the 17th day, we went [north] to the port of Politan, twelve leagues away. Here, the pilot pointed out that there was no information on that river, and asked for permission to explore the beach and forest for clues, during which we met a man who had come to drink the water.

Going to him, I deceived the Indian regarding my intentions to sound him out on the matter. Consequently, I decided that on the 18th day we would return to the Uchupan River and sail the boats upstream. On the 19th, they were made secure. On the 20th, we began the march to the northwest through the flat forest. Subsequently, cutting our way through and after five leagues, in a narrow pass high on the banks of a ravine, at three in the afternoon, a soldier accidentally separated [from the rest of us] came across five pagan Indians.

Although he tried to seize them, one was as much as he could capture. So he brought me an eighteen year old, who gave the interpreters to understand that he had left that very morning from a settlement. With this notice, leaving everything, we promptly marched eight leagues to the northwest through a high forest partly broken by water from above into stones and bad passes. Our guide was lost, so we experienced an unpleasant night without shelter from the elements or any other comfort.

On the 21st at nine in the morning, I arrived at a settlement of nine houses placed on hills, some separated from the others because of the smoke made by burning the fields in preparation for maize plantings. The Indian said that the Indians who fled from their recently sown fields were of the nation of Yacal. Those who had escaped were the elders who maintained them. Questioning him again through the interpreters gave us to understand that all the nations to the north spoke of meeting with those of the west. It being felt that the Spaniards intended conquest, they had burned the houses and maize fields by the ocean and retreated to Mopan to make war.

I proposed to the Indian that he be an emissary to his companions so that they don't do something as monstrous as burning their houses and maize fields, that they return to their lands to care for their fields, and that he tell them that I come in peace. That I knew who would be their enemies and who were Christians. The Indian rebel resisted, saying to me that he wanted to die at the hands of the Spaniards and that none of the people of his nation would guide me. Because of the same hidden fear, the other Indians who assisted me being so afraid of the [A]matiques Indians, on the 22nd day I learned that these interpreters were telling the pagans that they really came for hunting and found it worthless to follow me.

In consideration of their rebellious nature and the disappearance of the [A]matiques, the soldiers stated that for the prosecution of the Indians they required more people for garrisons. I reprimanded them, saying that they should have less fear and needed to use more force. . . . Seeing that the soldiers were comforted, the [A]matiques maliciously that night all made their escape. . . .

Day 23, I marched through the forest on the road from the west. In a district two leagues long the guides became so lost that we found ourselves in the same place that we had begun that day. Again on the 24th day, in the march through the forest the road of the northwest doubled back on itself. Then after four leagues it crossed, using some bad passes, above water-filled stone ravines, going along the bank of a river from where, on the 25th day, the forest road from the northwest became swampy and difficult.

After four leagues, we came to an abandoned settlement of Indians of the Saques nation composed of three burned houses and burned maize fields, and another depopulated hamlet with large fields sown a month previously and much evidence that they still persisted in their vices. Following, we continued on a march of two more leagues on the same route, the trail going high above the bank of a ravine. From there on the 26th day, on the road to the northeast, the march went through swampy forest.

After five leagues appeared well-built houses that the Indians had destroyed; they even cleared the underbrush from around them and burned the maize. These hamlets were the work of the Saques nation, which had sown, perhaps a month before, many fields. On the 27th day, after going through the forest toward the northwest, we crossed a swamp as well as a league and a half of very bad terrain, scattering without being able to find the road. After four leagues, we came to a settlement of eleven houses abandoned by the Indians. There were traces of many people, some of whom had disappeared into the water, and many cornfields, planted earlier than those seen previously. Two more burned houses gave further examples of their bad practices.

On the 28th day, we marched through forest into much more mountainous and bad terrain above a river, going for four leagues high above the plain of a canyon. On the 29th, the march continued through forest, doubling back on itself on the road from the north northwest, going five leagues high above the plain of a canyon with the people well drenched and weak from the rains. On the 30th day, we continued to follow this road through the forest, which twisted and turned between hills and stones, crossing above water-filled ravines. After six leagues on a road cleverly constructed by the pagan Indians, we came across a settlement of two houses recently evacuated by Indians of the Saques nation, where I found a small amount of maize, manioc, and maize fields planted a few days previously. From there, on the 31st day, I continued the march on this high and twisted road with its large ravines in the bad terrain.

After two leagues, we came to another empty settlement of three houses and other hamlets. This one was the home of a little king called Yuncagui. There were large cornfields, planted earlier than the others, and a small supply of maize and other crops, which we divided among the people.

Close by, a number of bold Indians lying in ambush on the edge of a cornfield attacked a squadron of twelve men exploring the forest. . . . Here, they captured an Indian lady of eighteen years suckling a child of eight months with a boy of nine years. These and others were children of the little king. Finding that lady and boy, cunningly, some wanted to send them with an embassy to the father with some gifts. But it would be much better to save them from evil by catechizing them and sending them from their lands than not to do so. I had intended that she accompany the fathers, but the Indian excused herself with the rationale that as a woman she should not wander through the forests, nor go to any other settlements or leave their land. They should return to the care of their houses and field. This action would be good for those of their nation, since they could not maintain themselves for a long time in the forest with what they had taken from their houses, for they needed the fields and harvests of their sowings.

Leaving here on the first day of June, I marched on the road from the northwest. In little more than a league, we reached an abandoned Mopan settlement of up to forty-eight houses as well as many other destroyed hamlets, some having a little maize and other provisions from their plantings. There were large and fruitful fields of cotton, some going to seed, traces of many people, and various roads leading to other settlements. Given evidence of preparation for a great ambush, I have begun a wooden stockade to fortify this town, which is attested and sworn by the Indians of Bolom to be in a province of 8,000 Indians and takes eleven days to walk across.

Don Simon de la Luna, governor of the town of Amatique, came to this depopulated site with eight Indian leaders. They informed me of the flight without reason [of the Indians] and more of the great risk I was in because of the many pagan Indians who prepared against me, and how it pleased him to bring more soldiers to explore all parts of the forest. They had found by a hill an Indian who in flight died from lack of breath, and along with him, a small flask used for gunpowder, the trigger for a shotgun, ramrods for them, and pistols as well as a bell and pieces such as altar ornaments, and a half vase of glass, all being vestiges of the six friars of the Order of Lord Saint Francis whom they had killed with thirty-six Spaniards who helped them from the province of Campeche. . . . [67]

In consideration for having defeated on the ocean a large number of French and killed many of them, I had with me sufficient people, equipment, arms, munitions, and two small cannon.[68] Because the Indians lacked love for their houses and fields, they can go into the forests. Thus I have still not completed the most basic needs, namely, establishing a stronghold to control the natives.

Better to do this at the beginning of the winter because of the difficulty of obtaining help from the castle. For they block the way through the rivers and swamps, thus causing great expenses for His Majesty. Given the abundant supplies of maize and other fruits found in these settlements in the previous expedition, as sworn in the statements, and having examined the group plan of this town of Mopan, I will arrange to sail to it with fifty-nine Indian cargo bearers. . . .

I had to leave on the pier for lack of space since I brought so many people, beans, salt, and other things. Due to these circumstances I found myself short. Because of the mishaps, the Indians of the provinces of Zacapa and Chiquimula are reluctant to support the expedition.[69] Even though there were few supplies in the settlements it was not so difficult. I could discover or locate other sources that were more abundant. Thus, with the support of the measures of the king, my Lord, and the green maize already in the cornfields, I could continue the expedition.

Some rivers are so high that there is no way of crossing them in the forest with supplies without great danger to our lives. They are desperate because when recruited by the governor of Zacapa, as was well known, he did not tell them of the order of His Lordship, the Lord President, to go to the forest; nor to persist, as I had intended, in investigations for the entire winter. Thus they left unprepared, without cornfields sown, their women and children in their houses. It is this worry that concerns them. The other impossibility that leaves them woebegone is that most of the ill be permitted to return to their provinces and houses now that the summer is coming soon. To continue the prosecution of the pagans until they give their life is at the present all they can look forward to, and they lack strength for it.

Although our attempts to capture [the Indians] lacked the help of providence, given what we accomplished, we shouldn't stop now. I am sure that with greater effort to prosecute the pagan souls, God and the King will reward us. . . . It was the humidity of the forest that perverted the intent of the soldiers, [A]matiques Indians, bearers, and other people whom I found ill, exhausted, and with sores on their feet. These circumstances made it impossible for me to continue on the road that they had begun, to explore the forest toward the Ahitza of the Peten.

Considering the discouragements and impossibilities claimed by people, one should remember that they had helped with two payments and made great expenses above and beyond the material for His Majesty.[70] As the fathers beg that their strong faith be recognized in a sworn statement so that their sacrifices in my operations not be forgotten, so I do certify in the Mopan settlement on 6th day of said month of June of the year 1699 on this ordinary paper for not having any with a stamp.

Letter of Miguel Rodriguez Camilo and Pedro de Aldana y Vera, September 17, 1700

Don Pedro de Aldana y Vera, fifteen soldiers of the garrison, twenty-six Matiques Indians, and two guides from the same forest of the town of Lord Saint Anthony, were entrusted with an expedition to the forest of the Chol to reduce the pagan souls. I gave them all necessary supplies.

I intended them to go through the river of Timax for the reason that they would be following the same route given in my report of March 1699.[71] Having arrived at the town of Bolom, they continued to the Tipacha River, a distance of fourteen leagues from this town, where there were five houses.[72] Attacking it, he captured ten Indians: one male and the other [nine] women and children of the Sibalnaes nation. The Indian gave me information on twelve children, he being of the town of the Axehenes that had forty houses. He spoke of another nation, called Pehechi, with many people and said that the other road was to the town of Tesugum, the most important of the possessions of the Mopans. Being inclined to follow it, I met three Indian spies and captured two of them. There were settlements on the road where they captured the spies, along with a great number of Indians waiting in ambush with bows and arrows. . . .

The mayor of Amatique passed the ambush when going to the settlement, the first of Mopan, which was large and well populated with people, and he understood that it continued to the Tipu.[73] In the settlement, the Indians offered such resistance that it lasted into the night, and they laughed at the leader of the Matiques Indians.[74] Only a lack of gunpowder and munitions caused them to retreat. Always the Indians of Quiscollol followed them on the same road. . . . With great difficulty and high risk of losing lives from the retreat, they arrived at an arm of the Yaxal River. Thence they followed a trail toward another river, named Joxtum.[75] It was the site of a settlement of the Yaxcabes nation. Attacking, he captured thirty-two persons, more men, women, and children. From there, our spies sent word of another settlement of the abundant Chanes nation.

Our two spies also, when going to sell ocote wood, located another settlement of the Quischasqueles nation. It was impossible to pursue these pagan souls because of the circumstances requiring our retreat toward this castle with the profit of forty-six pagan souls, mostly older men, women, and children. This report I [Field Marshal Don Miguel Rodríguez Camilo] affirm, certify, and sign with Lieutenant Don Pedro de Aldana y Vera in said castle.

11

RAIDS OF THE MOSQUITO ZAMBO,

1704–1733

The Indians resettled in the "new town of Saint Anthony of the Warehouses" (San Antonio de las Bodegas), which had a Franciscan priest. It also had 111 Indians, females as well as males, from the age of ten years, of the newly converted Cholti and Mopangas obtained during the expedition of the previous year. This settlement, next to the castle of San Felipe, was intended to support and serve the garrison of that fort.

By August 30, 1702 (see Verapaz 1702), the priest was pointing out that in less than six years, more than 800 Indians removed from the forests and settled in or around Amatique had died because of "many plagues, abuse [and] grief." Neither Amatique nor San Antonio de las Bodegas would have an Indian population in twenty years, but this was not due to any of the aforementioned factors.

Xocolo also had a new occupation. Thanks to the efforts of Don Pedro Barona de Loayza, this settlement had 40 citizens or 100 inhabitants at the end of the seventeenth century. In this era, it was famous for its fine gun flints made out of local stone (Fuentes y Guzman 1933, 296).

There were appointments to the joint position of captain of the San Felipe fortress and mayor of Amatique-San Antonio well into the eighteenth century (Castellan 1725; Castellan 1753). Soon, the appointment of mayor was for a nonexistent town. In the census of October 1776, the inhabitants of San Felipe, numbering 122 people, were all either Spaniards or of mixed origin, and associated with the garrison of the fortress (Padron 1776). What happened to the indigenous population? Here are a few examples:

—In 1704, the Mosquito Zambos invaded the town of Amatique, capturing many Indians and killing others.

—In 1707, at San Antonio de Las Bodegas, the Mosquito Zambos captured the women.

—In 1708, the Mosquito Zambos penetrated the Peten, and a force of 30 Spanish soldiers and 400 Indian archers came to protect it against the attack.

—In 1717, 42 percent of the population of the town of Gualan, the first permanent settlement upriver from Lake Izabal, were refugees who had fled from Mosquito Zambo raids on the Caribbean coast (Feldman, Brown, and Garzon 1987).

—In 1722, the Mosquito Zambos attempted an invasion with a fleet of 30 pirogues crewed by 300 enemies commanded by some English.

—In 1730, the Mosquito Zambos, incited and armed by the English of Jamaica, carried off all the families of a town on the coast of Campeche; they also entered a town in Olancho province [Honduras] with more than 556 persons, most with firearms and some with bows and arrows. Having taken thirty-six prisoners, the Mosquito Zambos retired to the forests.[1]

In the end, the Mosquito Zambo raids—extending from Tabasco to Panama, filling the British colony of Jamaica with Mayan slaves, and sending refugees fleeing into the interior—were the plague that ended Mayan settlements on the Belize and Guatemalan coasts. Most of the eighteenth century would find the delta of the Motagua, and the coasts of Lake Izabal, an empty wilderness with only traces of abandoned settlements to mark the presence of the former inhabitants (Feldman 1991).

The Governor of Tabasco Informs Your Majesty:
Letter of Francisco Lopez Marchan, 1733

The governor of Tabasco informs Your Majesty about many Indians of the province of Yucatan stolen by the English and enslaved in Virginia and Jamaica. . . .

The governor of Tabasco, captured by a British ship of war while serving Your Majesty with his frigate in the Mercury squadron headed by Don Rodrigo de Torres, was carried to Virginia; to the port of Hampton at thirty-seven degrees [latitude]. In Virginia were some enslaved Indians of Campeche. One named Thomas Kem was in the house of Henry Urban.

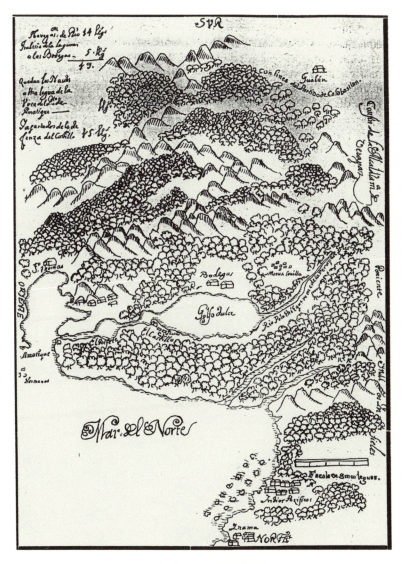

Figure 15. "The Indians resettled in the new town of
Saint Anthony of the Warehouses"
(Fuentes y Guzman 1933)

Being taken to Jamaica, I came across on the streets about fifteen
[Mayan slaves], among them a boy of about nine years. Seeing me, and
recognizing myself as a Spaniard, he began to cry. An Englishman vio-
lently took him away. In an inn, I spoke with two Indian women named
Rosa and Pascuala, natives of the town of San Juan Baptista Tenosique

of this province. Being hidden, I never saw them again. Passing by a field, I met another Indian woman who, as soon as she learned I was a Spaniard, went on her knees. Praying to our Father, she begged me to remove her from the miserable state in which she and her sister, who was six years old when sold, found themselves. For the Mosquitoes had sacked and carried off an entire town of the province of Campeche. On Jamaica there were an unlimited number of Indians sold to the plantations. . . .

Having arrived in Campeche, after great misfortunes and delays, I sent a report to our bishop of Yucatan so that he could forward it to Your Majesty, and not omitting my ardent zeal regarding a matter so grave, I have written this letter to Your Majesty. . . . The ships of the royal contract of Campeche with deceits steal many Indians: as verified with what befell the past fleets.[2] Thus, the merchant ship of Captain Montalvo took near Havana an English sloop that was carrying six Indians of Campeche, and [also verified by] those left there [in Jamaica].

It seemed important to me to inform Your Majesty of this so that Your Catholic and Royal person could take appropriate measures throughout all your dominions. . . . Villa de Tacotalpa de Tabasco, April 5, of 1733.

POSTSCRIPT AND FURTHER
READINGS, 1766–1823

The Spanish conquered the Ahitza and Mopan at the end of the seventeenth century. This is not the place to recount the history of the conquest of the Itza; for this one should read the work of Juan de Villagutierre Soto-Mayor (1983). Additional information on the eighteenth-century Mopan, after the Spanish conquest, may be found in the "Geographic Relation of the Peten," a 1765 document describing the people, commerce, and agriculture of San Luis in the middle of the eighteenth century.[1] The town of San Luis was most likely the descendant of that Mopan settlement north of Chocahau that caused so much grief for the Spaniards and Manche of Chocahau.

Manuscripts from the eighteenth century repeatedly refer to attempts to find the Xocmo.[2] Convinced that somewhere in the jungles of the Peten were these lost pagan people, Spaniards exerted much effort in searching for this mysterious community. Who were the Xocmo? Salazar identifies them as Yucatec speakers and puts them in the lands of the Acala. Expelled by the Chol Lacandon from the lowlands north of the Pasion River, they settled in the newly vacated lands of Acala.[3] Never conquered, lost and ultimately forgotten, what happened to the people of Xocmo? Perhaps they were the ancestors of the modern Lacandon. The Chol Lacandon had been removed from the lowlands at the end of the seventeenth century (Valenzuela 1979). The Yucatec-speaking Lacandon first appear in Chiapas in the eighteenth century (Hellmuth 1970). Could they have been Xocmo in search of a new homeland?

There are recent books on two other peripheral areas. Grant Jones, in *Maya Resistance to Spanish Rule* (1989), looks at the northern and central Belize coast, that portion speaking mostly Yucatec and under the influence of Bacalar and Merida in the colonial era. My own book,

Motagua Colonial (Feldman 1998), examines the cultures and peoples of the Motagua drainage region during the seventeenth and eighteenth centuries. This is the area that supplied the troops and burden bearers needed in the final removals of Chols from the southern Mayan lowlands. The Indians of this province of Chiquimula and Zacapa spoke closely related dialects of the same language used in the Manché.

In the manuscript of 1765 mentioned above there is a reference to the "old site of Manché." From the site of Campama, the old location of Santa Lucia Tzalac to San Luis of the Mopan, there were forty leagues of uninhabited lands (Santiago y Vetancurt et al. 1765). These Manché lands would not, of course, remain empty.

For those who want to learn what happened in these lowlands after the period covered in this book, I strongly recommend reading the *History of the Foundation of the Town of Chamiquin* (Feldman 1988). It discusses the resettlement of these lowlands in the eighteenth and nineteenth centuries by Pokomchi and Kekchi Maya of the Verapaz highlands. Another useful volume on the Kekchi lowland colonization in the twentieth century is *New Lands and Old Traditions* (Carter 1969). Of course, the Kekchi penetration into these lowlands antedated the removal of the Chol. As one Spanish friar noted, the Kekchi thought of it as their "Indies," and thus, an appropriate target for conquest, exploitation, and colonization. And today, much of the former Manché territory belongs to the so-called eastern dialect's area of Kekchi (see Freeze and Feldman 1975, 16).[4]

A study of the maps of the region locates seventeenth-century place-names still in use in the drainage of the Sarstun and the southeastern drainage of the Cancuén River. This implies contact with, and perhaps absorption of, Chol remnants by incoming Kekchi. Only in the drainage of the Moho and northwestern portions of the Cancuén are there no signs of earlier place-names. Here, the Spanish policy of subjugation and removal achieved its greatest success. Only here there was no one left to tell the incoming Kekchi colonizers the names of the rivers and hills of these lands.

APPENDIX 1. MANCHE AND

TOQUEGUA SURNAMES

This appendix is intended to serve as a convenient listing of surnames rather than an analytical study, but a few comments should be made. First, there is almost no overlap between the 142 Toquegua and 80 Manche names. Indeed, they have only one name in common. Yet both samples share an equal number of different names (six) with the distant Tixchel communities of the Candelaria River basin. Contact between Tixchel and the Manché area, through the Usumacintla River system, is mentioned by Salazar (chapter 2). But any connection between the isolated seventeenth-century Toqueguas in the delta of the Motagua River and Tixchel must date to pre-Hispanic times. Significantly, Itzamcanac, the pre-Hispanic capital of the inhabitants of Tixchel, had commercial contacts with those living in Nito, a community not far from the delta of the Motagua (see Scholes and Roys 1948).

Second, and hardly surprising given the constant contact between the two peoples, ten of the Manche surnames were shared with the inhabitants of Kekchi-speaking towns, most notably Cahabón and Cobán. Finally, the presence of numerous Nahua names (for instance, Chali, Chimal, Coatzun, Itzquin, Itzcoatl, Maquili, Suchicancaguat, and Tunali) among both the Manche and Toquegua reminds us again that neither region was isolated in pre-Hispanic times from the world beyond their lands.

Table 1   Seventeenth-Century Manche and Toquegua Chol Surnames

	Years and Towns/Peoples								
Names	1604A	1604B	1604C	1604D	1605	1620	1685	1695?	Other
Abincai					X				
Achavan					X				
Açiban					X				
Açibit					X				
Açicone					X				
Açiguan					X				
Acui					X				
Aguaçan					X				

Table 1   *Continued*

Names	Years and Towns/Peoples								
	1604A	1604B	1604C	1604D	1605	1620	1685	1695?	Other
Ahbin, Avin		X			X				Tixchel Abin
Ahcahcay							X		
Ahcanan		X							
Ahic		X							
Ahichih		X							
Ahixil						X			
Ahizcu			X						
Ahoc		X							
Ahquinem	X								
Ahtunalcu			X						
Ahzaguay			X						
Aitiquec					X				
Almonzo			X						
Aluma					X				
Amiztin					X				
Amus					X				
Asananbaren					X				
Atos					X				
Atrix					X				
Axoqui					X				
Axun					X				
Ayzcoqui					X				
Azthaan					X				
Batena							X		
Bol							X		See below[1]
Caçalla			X						
Caçiqui					X				
Can	X								Tipu[2]
Canaçin	X								
Cante								X	
Caun					X				
Cavatzin								X	
Cavil, Ahcavil		X	X						Tipu[3]
Cayun					X				
Cebrian			X	X					
Chacqan				X					
Chali	X								
Chaquic					X				
Chen, Chein									1695, Cobán

Table 1 *Continued*

Names				Years and Towns/Peoples					
	1604A	1604B	1604C	1604D	1605	1620	1685	1695?	Other
Chicayes							X		
Chimal					X				Tixchel
Chinamite					X				
Chinancan					X				
Chiquiz								X	
Choc	X								Carcha, Cobán
Choco									1653, Cobán
Chocoh Yancab							X		
Chuila					X				
Çiac					X				
Çian					X				
Çiancui					X				
Cibac[4]			X		X		X	X	Çipac at Tixchel[5]
Çiban					X				
Çicac					X				
Çican					X				
Çicun, Cicun					X				
Çiman					X				
Çinachac					X				
Çinan					X				
Çinati					X				
Çinqueman					X				
Çitigua					X				
Coatzun						X			
Cocahan								X	
Comiachic					X				
Cu									1620, Cobán[6]
Cuc	X								Tipu Kuk, Tixchel Akuk
Cuchan					X				
Cuchin					X				
Cucul, Σucul				X					1695, Cobán, Cahabón
Çulid					X				
Çunum	X								
Cuyuc					X				
Esquinan		X							
Guaçig					X				
Haeb		X							

Table 1   *Continued*

Names	| Years and Towns/Peoples								
	1604A	1604B	1604C	1604D	1605	1620	1685	1695?	Other
Hiloc					X				
Huchub				X					
Huizquin							X		
Huvb		X							
Icap					X				
Icay					X				
Ichacu					X				
Icui					X				
Ilxil									1677
Isto, Istu					X				
Itzquin	X								Yzquintz at Tixchel
Ix					X				
Ixachat					X				
Ixbol					X				Tixchel
Ixcacoc					X				
Ixcan					X				
Ixcata					X				
Ixcatec					X				
Ixcati					X				
Ixchama					X				Yschamali at Tixchel
Ixchavan					X				Tixchel
Ixchich	X								
Ixcubi					X				
Ixçucut					X				
Ixcuy					X				
Ixcuya					X				
Ixil							X		
Ixiquec					X				
Ixlamat					X				
Ixmacatin					X				
Ixmia					X				
Ixmux					X				
Ixnac					X				
Ixnia					X				
Ixon					X				
Ixpoc					X				
Ixpolic					X				

Table 1   *Continued*

	Years and Towns/Peoples								
Names	1604A	1604B	1604C	1604D	1605	1620	1685	1695?	Other
Ixtiliz					X				
Izbeque					X				
Izcapali					X				
Izcapay					X				
Izcoa, Izcoatl					X				
Izcuçan					X				
Izma					X				
Izmican					X				
Iznoche					X				
Izolo					X				
Izpan					X				
Iztan					X				
Iztin					X				
Iztoz					X				
Jibi					X				
Jigua					X				
Juanat					X				
Julua					X				
Lamat					X				Tixchel
Maquili					X				
Masacuate					X				
Masca					X				
Mascavan					X				
Mastin					X				
Matalun					X				
Matzin	X								1677, 1695
May								X	1695?, see below[7]
Maya					X				
Metan					X				
Mica					X				
Misit									1695, see below[8]
Mitan, Mixtan					X				
Mizquitan					X				
Moniqui					X				
Mulac, Muluc					X				
Nali					X				
Neb			X						
Nia					X				
Nicoat					X				

Table 1   *Continued*

Names	1604A	1604B	1604C	1604D	1605	1620	1685	1695?	Other
					Years and Towns/Peoples				
Oente					X				
Pach							X		
Palan					X				
Petz							X		1685
Pisote					X				
Pom	X	X	X	X					Cahabón
Pot									1695
Quahtan	X								
Quen					X				
Quimenche							X		
Quines							X		
Saput					X				
Suchicancaguat					X				
Sulba					X				
Tacahia			X						
Tayti					X				
Te			X						Cahabón
Tuanic					X				
Tunal, tunali	X				X				
Tuqueli					X				
Tuxte					X				
Tzac							X		
Tzaques							X		
Tzibalna									1653
Tzuncal								X	
Uchin									1695
Utun					X				
Vahtan	X								
Vehin								X	
Vizculu					X				
Xabam					X				
Xacata					X				
Xahau	X								
Xchacchan	X								
Xchah	X								
Xcheguen	X								
Xcismia					X				
Xcunun	X								
Xev					X				

Table 1   *Continued*

Names	1604A	1604B	1604C	1604D	1605	1620	1685	1695?	Other
				Years and Towns/Peoples					
Xican					X				
Xico					X				
Xiconac					X				
Xigun					X				
Xinalchan	X								
Xinan					X				
Xines					X				
Xoc					X				
Xoy									1653
Xtunal	X								
Xuactan		X							
Xuahtan	X								
Xuban					X				
Xuil					X				
Xuila					X				
Xuin					X				
Xuu	X								
Xuub	X								
Yaxali					X				
Yaxax									1620
Zaguay				X					

APPENDIX 2. MANCHÉ
POPULATION STATISTICS

Like Appendix 1, this is intended to serve as a convenient listing of data rather than an analytical study. One should note, however, that while just two of these compilations—1620 and 1676—have any claim to being a comprehensive survey, both are mere snapshots of a rapidly changing situation. If Antonio de Leon Pinelo (1986, 9–10) is to be believed, many more towns became subject to Spanish rule in the 1620s. Yet in the 1630s, with the temporary exception of San Lucas Tzalac (Gonzalez 1940), all this was swept away. Similarly, Gallego's 1676 count represents only a brief high point in Spanish influence shortly before the Indians again fled into the forests.

Who were the friars counting in their population surveys? Surely not tributaries, since none of these populations were paying taxes. Except where indicated, I am inclined to interpret these counts as including all adults, male and female, but not children before puberty. This seems to have been the practice elsewhere in the lowlands for censuses of nontributary but Spanish-controlled populations.

Table 2 Summary of Population Totals for Sixteenth- and Seventeenth-Century Manché Towns

Towns	Years					Location
	1574	1604	1605	1620	1676	
Ahixil, San Vicente		62	100?	40		
Amatzin, San Jacinto		95	100?	30	198	
Axoy, San Fernando					180	
Chiixtee, San Pablo		38	100?			Yaxha? Chixbox?
Chocahau, Asuncion			100?		150	
Cucul, San Felipe y Santiago		31	100+			Santiago Apóstol?
Manché, San Miguel		242	100+	50	242	
May, San Jose					300	
Noxoy, San Pedro				40	240	
Santiago, Apóstol					194	
Tzalac, San Lucas				26	190	
Tzibalna, Rosario					200	

Table 2   *Continued*

Towns	Years					Location
	1574	1604	1605	1620	1676	
Tzulben, San Lucas	60+					Same site as Tzalac
Uchin, San Sebastian					43	
Xicupin, Santa Maria				50		Same as Chocahau
Xocmo, San Francisco				200	185	
Yaxcoc, Santa Cruz				31		
Yaxha, San Pablo			100?	15		
Yol, Santo Domingo				100		
Totals	60+	468	700?	582	2,122	

APPENDIX 3. WORD LIST OF
CHOLCHI TERMS

There is only one known colonial dictionary of Cholchi.[1] This is an abstract of a manuscript traditionally ascribed to Friar Francisco Morán (1935). Therefore, a new word list of colonial Cholchi, no matter how brief, is of potential interest. For the convenience of linguists and interested others, what follows is a compilation of all the Cholchi terms defined by colonial authors that have appeared elsewhere in this volume or in the Poqom dictionary of Friar Viana (see Feldman n.d.).

bictehum: "amate bridge," hamlet (Ximénez 1695)
bolomtevitz: "nine hills," hills near ocean, east of Mopan (Ximénez 1695)
boloncot: "nine eagles," tributary of Cancuén River (Ximénez 1695)
buchiquin: "fenced ears," name of town northeast of Ahitza (Salazar 1620)
calic: "fields of chili," Carcha land near Xocmo (Salazar 1620)
chabac: "two zontles" or "eight hundred" (Gallego 1676)
chacvelen: "red pitch," name of pagan town (Salazar 1620)
choltí, cholchi: "language of the people of the hot lands" (P. Morán 1720)
cholvinac: "people of the hot lands, the Chols are thus called" (P. Morán 1720)
cholyak: "signifies land of this nation of the Chols" (P. Morán 1720)
conuntehila: "water of painted birds," Sacapulas River (Tovilla 1630)
cactun: "the egg," smooth-sided and sharp-pointed peak (Salazar 1620)
huh: "this is a reference to the bark of trees called huh, which they beat into a brown paper
    on which they paint; bark of trees called hun in their language, and they also called
    the paper hun; this tree hun is what we call the fig tree, a kind of ceiba, that in our
    Pokoman they name Cux" (P. Morán 1720, quoting Zúñiga of the early seventeenth
    century)
ixte: "chili wood," name of tree with dangerous sap (Ximénez 1695)
kanyum: "taken from the cholchi yum, which is land, and kan, which is yellow, yellow land;
    they thus call a canyon" (P. Morán 1720)
kolte: "beachcomber, canoeist, helmsman; is taken from Cholti and not heard in Ama-
    titlan" (P. Moran 1720)
niha: "water nose," river behind Xocoloc (Salazar 1620)
tanquinhá: "dry river," dry riverbed (Ximénez 1695)
tichahac: "lightning," name of stream (Ximénez 1695)
tinocacao: "large town," name of pagan town (Gallego 1676)

tuilhá: "smelly water," canyon (Ximénez 1695)

vayha: "zapoyol water," name of town northeast of Ahitza (Salazar 1620)

xeuluchan: "seats of snakes," name of a peak (Salazar 1620)

yaxhá: "blue water," river (Ximénez 1695)

zacchay: "white fish," stream (Ximénez 1695)

zachahlanté: "white pataxte," palos de María medicinal herb (Ximénez 1695)

zactum: "white stone," Sarstun River (Cano 1685)

zaczaclum: "white earth," site of Nohxoy (Ximénez 1695)

APPENDIX 4. BACKGROUND OF
THE AUTHORS

ALTAMIRANO Y VELASCO, FERNANDO DE [1654]: Count of Santiago de Calimaya. He was president and captain general of the Audiencia of Guatemala (1654–1657), and died in 1657.

CADENA, GUILLERMO [1574]: Dominican friar.

CANO, AGUSTÍN [1685]: Dominican friar. Born in Antequera, Spain, Agustín came to Guatemala as a small child. He entered the Dominican order in 1666 and was elected prior of the province at only age thirty-two (1683). He died in 1719.

DELGADO, JOSEPH [1677]: Dominican friar. Born in Zacapa, Guatemala, Delgado learned Chol there as a child.

EZQUERRA, JUAN [1605]: Dominican friar from the Spanish convent of Valladolid. Ezquerra arrived in Guatemala in 1593 and died in 1611.

FLORES, BARTOLOMÉ [1653, 1654]: Governor of the province of Verapaz.

GALLEGO, FRANCISCO [1676]: Dominican friar from the Spanish convent of Valladolid. Born in Benavente, Portugal, he was sent in 1656 as an agent of the Guatemalan province to Rome. After returning, he administered Escuintla, became prior of the province, and corresponded with the ruler of the Ah Itza. Gallego died in 1682.

GALLEGO, LUCAS [1574]: Dominican friar from the Spanish convent of Salamanca. He arrived in Guatemala in 1559, was prior of Cobán in 1572, and died in 1601.

LOPEZ MARCHAN, FRANCISCO [1733]: Governor of Tabasco.

MORÁN, FRANCISCO [1636]: Dominican friar. Morán was born in 1592 in León, Spain. He arrived in Guatemala in 1618 from the Spanish convent of Valladolid, was prior of the province, and died in 1664.

NUNEZ, ANTONIO [1606]: Notary public of the province of Verapaz.

OCHOA, JUAN [1653, 1654]: Dominican friar. Born in Vitoria Vizcaya, Spain, Ochoa arrived in Guatemala in 1625 from the Spanish convent of Salamanca. He was parish priest of Cahabón and Lanquin for twenty-four years, wrote in Cacchi (Kekchi), and died in 1655.

PACHECO, DIEGO [1697]: Spanish governor of the Verapaz.

PAEZ DE GRAJEDA, ALONSO [1655]: Public scribe of Guazacapan.

PRADA, CRISTÓBAL DE: Dominican friar. Born in Seville, Spain, Prada became a Dominican in 1677. He arrived in Guatemala in 1687 from the Seville convent and died in 1696.

RIBERA, FERNANDO [1655]: Parish priest of Gueymango.

RODRIGUEZ CAMILO, MIGUEL [1698–1700]: Sergeant major and commander of the Castle of San Felipe, and governor of the port of Santo Tomás de Castilla.

SALAZAR, GABRIEL [1620]: Dominican friar. Salazar, from the convent of Atocha in the province of Castile, was fluent in the Quiche, Cakchiquel, Poqom, Tzeltal, Tzotzil, Kekchi, and forest Chol languages as well as Spanish and Latin. He taught music to the Indians and was known as the first apostle of the Manché. He died in 1649.

TOVILLA, MARTIN [1630, 1635]: Spanish governor of the Verapaz, he died in 1640.

VIANA, FRANCISCO [1574]: Dominican friar. Viana, from the Spanish convent of Salamanca, arrived in Guatemala in 1556. He became famous posthumously for his dictionary of Poqom. He died in 1608 at the age, approximately, of eighty.

VILLELA, FRANCISCO DE [1698]: Subordinate of Miguel Rodríguez Camilo. He held the college degree of bachelor.

XIMÉNEZ, FRANCISCO [1695]: Dominican friar. Born in 1666 in Ecija, the location of his "home" convent, he arrived in Guatemala in 1688. After serving in various localities, Ximénez became parish priest of Chichicastenango from 1701 to 1704. During this period, he discovered the Popol Vuh, and began work on his grammar and dictionary of Cakchiquel, Quiche, and Tzutujil. From 1704 to 1714, he served as parish priest in the town of Rabinal. In 1715, he was the parish priest for Santo Domingo Xenocoj, and during this time, wrote most of the *Historia de la Provincia de San Vicente y Chiapa de Guatemala*. From 1718 to 1720, Ximénez was parish priest of Candelaria in Guatemala. He wrote his *Historia Natural del Reino de Guatemala* around 1722, and died in 1730.

NOTES

⊕

Preface

1   Because the intended audience is wider than those specialists familiar with the terminology of the Spanish colonial legal system, I have translated wherever possible any technical terms into English. Thus, unless noted to the contrary, *alcalde mayor* is always *governor, cacique* is *headman,* and *audiencia* is *tribunal.* The "lost shores" of the title of this volume, as the reader will soon discover, were frequently riverine shores; routes of trade, avenues for attack or retreat, the numerous streams and rivers of these lowlands often provided the best way of entering these unknown lands.

1   Beginnings, 1574–1606

"Report of the Province of the Verapaz" is based on the Spanish text published as Viana, Gallego, and Cadena (1955). The original manuscript of the "Letter of Friar Juan Ezquerra" is in AGI Guatemala 181; the translation here is based both on a photocopy of that document and a transcription published in Saint-Lu (1968, 506–9). The "Hair Usually Worn Long" piece is excerpted from "Testimony by the Friars of Santo Domingo of the town of Cobán" as translated from the original manuscript in AGI Guatemala 174.

1   One league is equivalent to 20,000 feet, or 3.8 miles in modern Spain.
2   Tucuru, or "Tururub" in the Spanish text, is also known as the Panima River. Cahabón, or Cahbón in the Spanish text, is also known as the Cobán River; it joins the Polochic River downstream.
3   This is referred to as Golfo Dulce in Spanish colonial texts.
4   The Nito River today is the Golfete and Dulce Rivers, which connect the Lago de Izabal with the ocean. The area of Cabo de Higueras is Amatique Bay. Cape Higueras was, according to López de Velasco (1971, 159) at 16° latitude, putting it just south of Punta Gorda and the Moho River in southern Belize. It probably is the modern Punta Manabique. Nito was an important trading center, somewhere near modern Livingston, when Cortés came through the area in the 1520s. The settlement had already vanished when this report was written. In the first half of the sixteenth century, the province of Higueras included all of northwestern Honduras, from a line drawn from Comayagua to San Pedro Sula going west to the modern Guatemalan frontier (Chamberlain 1953).

5   Tayasal, today Flores in Lake Peten, was the fortified islet.

6   The Acala region is identified by Friar Alonso Escobar (in Feldman 1988, 38) as the "mountains of Chisec."

7   Guatemala here means the highlands around the town of Antigua. The South Sea region refers to the Pacific coastal plain of Guatemala.

8   Viana, Gallego, and Cadena (1955) use Tzentzonatl for the Sonsonate, a town and colonial province in the southwestern portion of El Salvador.

9   Liquidambar, the sap of the gum tree (*Liquidambar styraciflua* L.), was sent to Spain to be used as an ingredient in the incense burned in the censers of the Roman Catholic churches. It was particularly common in the forests surrounding the town of Rabinal (Ximénez 1967, 244–45).

10   This was a root "gathered from a wild, uncultivated, scattered plant in swampy, difficult terrain" (MacLeod 1973, 66).

11   In the sixteenth century, the towns of Cahabón, Tucuru, Tamahú, San Cristóbal, and Cobán sent Indians to gather sarsaparilla root in the lowlands (Casa de Ayante 1567).

12   Mechuacán was a certain kind of white root used in medicine as a purgative (see Diccionario 1992).

13   These are howler monkeys (*Alouatta talliata* as cited in Leopold 1959, 329).

14   The published Spanish text uses the word *azañuelo*. This is a mistake for *anzuelo*, or hook. A hook was used to catch the tail feathers, forcing a bird to sacrifice its feathers to gain freedom (Feldman 1985, 90).

15   Tamahú, in the Spanish text, is called Tamahún.

16   Cuculin was in or near southern Belize.

17   Chiquimula refers to the modern-day Chiquimula de la Sierra.

18   Patastle or *theobroma bicolor*, often spelled as *pataxte* in the colonial documents, was an inferior yet more hardy kind of cacao. On the Pacific coast, it served as a shade tree for the more delicate *T. cacao* (McBryde 1947, 148).

19   One real was worth thirty-four maravedis (Polzer, Barnes, and Naylor 1977, 38). In other words, the Indians were getting sixty-eight maravedis on the south coast per day for work that was paying ten maravedis per day in Verapaz.

20   Jochomit may be a variant of *Tochomitl*, or rabbit hair, in Nahua (Molina 1944, 148). Oaxaca was a major source of the red dye cochineal.

21   There were four reals to a toston.

22   Increase in tribute resulted from few taxpayers and new, royal taxes. Tax assessments were based on total number of taxpayers in a town; hence few taxpayers meant those left had to pay more (or at least until the next census).

23   Kekchi and Poqom were the two languages that everyone understood. Possible candidates for the other five languages are Nahua, Quiche, the Alaguilac language of Acasaguastlan, the Cholan language of the San Marcos section of Cobán, and the dialect of Kekchi spoken in Cahabón and Lanquin. See Feldman (1986) for a survey of the native languages of colonial Guatemala.

24   This was a Cholan Mayan language closely related to others in southern Belize and the lowlands north of the Verapaz. Names of places and things from this region, as given in colonial dictionaries of the Poqom language, are often in a Cholan language.

25   Newly resettled people were exempted, in 1566, from paying tribute. People from the town of San Marcos in the forests were resettled in Cobán in 1596 (Feldman 1992,

24, 53). See Gabriel Salazar, in chapter 2 of this volume, for details on how the Indians of San Marcos, or Acala (they are the same place), were brought to Cobán.

26   Dependencies is a translation of the term *visitas*. These are communities subject to supervision and inspection from someone stationed in the Cobán.

27   The weight the small bell was derived from the text's use of a quintal, which is equivalent to 100 libras or 101.5 pounds.

28   Most Indian towns in Guatemala were under the supervision of encomenderos: Spaniards who received all the municipal head tax in return for seeing to the welfare of the inhabitants. The Verapaz was one of the few areas not subject to this regime but directly under the control of the colonial government.

29   These towns were originally in what is today southern Belize. See Feldman (1992, 27) for further details on the history of their people.

30   The indicated map, or diagram, is missing.

31   Associated with Friar Ezquerra's letter is a "Book of Those Baptized of the Manché." With a final date of February 24, 1605, it has lists of those baptized from the towns of San Felipe de Cucul (February 22, 1604), San Miguel Manché (1604), San Vicente Ahixil, San Pablo Chiixtee, and San Jacinto de Matzin. Friar Salvador Cipriano is mentioned in this book, along with Ezquerra (prior of the convent of Saint Dominic of Cobán), as one of the two friars baptizing Indians in the town of San Felipe Cucul in February 1604 (Montes 1604).

32   See Feldman (1998) for a description of the discovery and an analysis of the culture of the Toqueguas. These Indians lived in the delta of the Motagua River and, from their surnames, were Cholan speakers with a distinct trace of Nahua influence. Those removed from their lands were quickly assimilated into the population of the town of Amatique.

33   In another letter of the same date, and in the same file, Friar Ezquerra (AGI Guatemala 181) states that there were some fifty apostate Indians, some having "many children who were born after they had fled."

34   These other reports have not been located in the archives.

2   *Geography of the Lowlands: Gabriel Salazar, 1620*

A highly abridged and slightly modified version containing these two texts is published in Ximénez (1930, 211–17). The published version, which has a 1636 date, lacks most of the ethnographic details and candid comments that make these 1620 texts so interesting. I have transcribed and translated the documents here from the original manuscript in AGI Guatemala 67. Prepared at different times during a two-year period, and never really edited into a single paper by Salazar himself, these pieces exhibit various inconsistencies. In the first text, for example, Salazar writes that the current year is 1620 and, just one paragraph later, says it is 1619.

1   In this context, "old Christians" refers to highland Guatemala Indians converted in the 1540s. The conversion of the Manche Indians didn't really begin until the seventeenth century. Tzulben was called San Lucas Zulben in 1574 (see Viana, Gallego, and Cadena's work in chapter 1 of this volume).

2   Niha is a tributary of the Sarstun River or one of the streams—such as the Seja, Ciénaga, or Chocón Machaca—that drains into the channel connecting Lake Izabal with the ocean.

3   Chiyu is a tributary of the Sarstun River, close to what is now the town of Chahal.

Hechonoche would be the part of that river known today as the Sarstun. Some claim that Tzoite, or Soite, is located near what is today Stann Creek in Belize (Jones 1989, xv). This passage could be interpreted to mean that a town named Tzoite sat at the mouth of the Sarstun River.

4   "It is proper to weep for Martin and to rejoice for Martin," as translated by Robert Trisco of the Catholic University of America.

5   This seems very far to go. There were other towns with Spanish goods much closer to Xocmo. As indicated below, there was also the possibility of buying goods from travelers. Perhaps another town is meant here.

6   Sapper (1985) and Ezquerra (see chapter 1) spells this town's name Matzin.

7   Ahitzachi is composed of the name of the Ahitza people ("the Itza") and Chi "language"—in other words, the "language of the Itza." This would have been a dialect of Yucatec Maya.

8   Mojarras are a type of fish with a spiny dorsal fin like perch or tuna.

9   Francisco Morán (1935) defines Icbolay as "a kind of snake." In other Chol dictionaries, I found ik'bolay defined as "jaguar, tiger." In the Motul dictionary, bolay is "a generic name for all wild animals who kill." The first element, ic, refers to the color black (comments of Marelike Sattler). Tuhalha means "water of Sacapulas." It is called the river of Sacapulas because the origin of a major tributary is close to this highland town.

Since this is the first textual mention of this subject, this is an appropriate time to review Salazar's treatment of the Usumacintla River and its major tributaries (see maps). Icbolay, spelled here as Ycbolay and elsewhere in the text as Ixbolay or Izbolac, is the Usumacintla after the Tuhalha or Chixoy is joined by the Lacantún and Pasion to form a single river. The Icbolay is today the name of a tributary of the Chixoy that has its headwaters between Cobán and Chisec. The river of the Lacandon of Salazar, the Çacacha, is the Lacantún. The Yaxcaba, a one-day journey downstream from Yol on the right bank of the Cancuén, may be the El Subin River. Its drainage belonged to the people of Xocmo before Lacandon raids forced them to flee. The river of Manché, the Pasion, in the seventeenth century had the name of Cancuén (the name still appears on modern maps for part of its drainage). At least part of the river of San Marcos, the Rio Ixaccha near the site of San Marcos and further upstream called the Çactohom or Çactocom, was occupied by the people of Xocmo not long after the inhabitants of San Marcos were sent to Cobán. This may be the modern Icbolay, noted above, that enters the Usumacintla from the Alta Verapaz near the Salinas de Nueve Cerros south of the Rio Cancuén. This river, which still has a tributary known as the Soctela, drains the area beyond Cobán between the Lacandon and Manché territory. The Laguna de Términos, where the Usumacintla enters the Gulf of Mexico, is still on modern maps.

10 The salt hill refers to the salt deposits (Salinas de Nueve Cerros) in the Alta Verapaz. In 1564 a Dominican missionary brought a number of Lacandons to the frontier at Ocosingo. "Sometime between 1595 and 1603 San Jacinto Ocosingo, until then a dependency of Ciudad Real, became the capital of a new 'vicaría de los Cendales,' with eight Tzeltal pueblos as visitas" (Gerhard 1979, 156).

11 The Σ, the Greek sigma symbol, stands for the Spanish Tresillo. It has the phonetic value of /k'/ (Mareike Sattler, personal communication). Given the context of this use, $\Sigma\alpha$ probably refers to the Itza.

12 Achacan is spelled here as Acchacan.

13 Tzibistun is the road from the town of Tipu to the island of the Itza. Two leagues west of Tipu, it crosses the Mopan River (Jones 1989, 141–42).

14 This was Tayasal, the capital of the Itza on an island in Lake Peten Itza.

15 Ahitzachi means those who speak the language of the Itza, who speak their dialect of Yucatec Maya. Ah Mopan would be the town with the different language (Mopan Maya).

16 Bacalar was a Spanish fortress and settlement in what is now southern Quintana Roo, Mexico.

17 This refers to the expedition of Cortés, who visited the island in 1526. Villagutierre Soto-Mayor (1983, 40–42, 63–77) provides another version, written eighty years after the destruction of the image of the horse, whose details (Villagutierre Soto-Mayor speaks of a horse made from stone) vary at times from this account recorded two years after the visit of these friars in 1618 to the island of the Itza.

18 The Rio Yaxal is the Moho River of the Toledo district of Belize (Sapper 1985); see Feldman (1992) for sixteenth-century references to the town of Yaxal.

19 Cuculem is listed later on as an unconquered Yucatec-speaking town. Perhaps the author is confusing the name with Caccolon, which became the Christian town of Cactan (Zacatan in Jones 1989), located on the coast not far from the Belize River.

20 This is Chanpotoná in the Spanish text. In other words, these towns are between what are now the Mexican states of Campeche and Quintana Roo. Xibun was a Yucatec-speaking town somewhere upstream on the Sibun River in Belize. There is a Campin in southern Belize. Çactam is the town called Zacatan between the New and Upper Belize Rivers in Belize (Jones 1989, 288–89).

21 Xibun is Xibum in the Spanish text.

22 Teacher, in the Spanish text, is fiscal. As can be seen above in previous reports, the Dominicans appointed Indians, called fiscals, to teach the principles of the Christian religion.

23 This sentence identifies Tzoite as a Chol-speaking town.

24 Perhaps this is the Poqom-speaking town of Santa Cruz in the Verapaz highlands.

25 Today, the Rio Chixoy.

26 The Çacacha is today's Rio Lacantún; for further information, see footnote 9 and Vos (1988, 493).

27 Icbolay, or Ixbolay in the Spanish text, is today the Usumacintla River. The Cancuén is the river known today as the Rio de la Pasion. Streams enter it from the north, of which at least one begins close to Lake Peten Itza.

28 Tixchel was in what is now the Mexican state of Campeche; see Scholes and Roys (1948) for the location of the towns of Tixchel. The Indians of Tixchel spoke the closely related (to Manché) Mayan Chontal language.

29 Buchiquin is correctly translated as "seven ears," from *vuc* (seven) and *chiquin* (ears) (Mareike Sattler, personal communication). Zapoyol is the red Zapote fruit tree (see Feldman 1985, 45).

30 As noted elsewhere, the Ah Mopan spoke their own language, one close to both Yucatec and Chol. Given the presence of Chol place-names and related dialects at Tixchel and in the Rio Candelaria Basin (Scholes and Roys 1948), it would not be surprising to find Chol speakers in this zone. Indeed, the statement that they are administered in two languages (Yucatec and that of the Chol) implies this.

31 Spelled elsewhere as Buchiquin.

32 Underlined in the original.

33 From 1611 to 1626, Gomera was president of the tribunal (MacLeod 1973, 391).

34 There is no map associated with this manuscript.

35 On modern maps, the Sibun River is just south of Belize City.

36 A town named Chinam was just north of present-day Santa Rita Corozal.

37 Don Pablo Paxbolon, "last of the Acalan chieftains," is mentioned in a document dated September 25, 1614, but the reference suggests that he did not have long to live (Scholes and Roys 1948, 299).

38 Carey refers to tortoise or large marine snail shells, which in the Antilles is often the mollusk *Strombus gigas*.

39 Friar Salazar, a Dominican, is implying (as he did with the story of the destruction of the Itza's pottery horse), that the Franciscans, who were missionaries among the Yucatec Maya, were not very competent. This is a reference to the "vaguely defined area called La Montaña or Las Montañas (in what is now the Mexican state of Campeche) where several mission stations were founded in 1604–1606" (Gerhard 1979, 122).

40 This may be the Laguna de los Cruces. It did provide an outlet for the water of the Rio Usumacintla system (including that of the Lacandon), but the Rio San Pedro y San Pablo was much more important.

41 Achiote (*Bixa orellana*), from the Nahua *achiyotetl*, was used as a food coloring (Ximénez 1967, 27; Feldman 1985, 46). It is "a small tree with red berries from which dye is made for coloring fabrics and foods [and still is used in margarine]. The Maya used it for painting pottery, and later Indians put it in their chocolate" (Villagutierre Soto-Mayor 1983, 106).

42 Mexicana is Nahua, a common trade language in Central America (where there are also enclaves of native speakers).

43 According to Robert Trisco, this title would translate as *Theology of the Indians*. This manuscript, of Viana, is lost.

44 But the reader should note (see below) that it was the Lacandon, and not the Itza, who played a role in these and subsequent events.

45 Artifacts of this type have been discovered in archaeological investigations. One, not yet described in a publication, was found by Feldman at the late Postclassic site of Beleh (Chinautla Viejo), several kilometers north of Guatemala City.

46 Villagutierre Soto-Mayor (1983, 49) dates the death of Friar Vico as occurring in the year 1555. Tovilla (1960, 126) states that the first Spanish governor of the province of Verapaz was installed in the year 1558. Either the year of the death is wrong or the Salazar text is in error here.

47 One day's journey downstream from Yol, on the right bank of the Cancuén, is the El Subin River.

48 They may have moved to the Rio Icbolay, which enters the Chixoy upstream from the Rio Pasion. It drains the area behind the town of Carcha.

49 The only river that appears to meet these criteria is San Pedro Martir, which enters the Usumacintla but not the Pasion (or Cancuén), in the Mexican state of Tabasco. It doesn't directly drain Lake Peten Itza yet does start very close to it.

50 Tuhalha is Tuhal in the Spanish text.

51 The implication of an all-water route to Lake Peten Itza from the Cancuén is more wishful thinking than reality, although a route that involves hiking between relatively close yet unconnected streams and lakes was certainly possible. As Tovilla (1960)

would discover in his tracking of an Itza raiding party, even in the rainy season, this was not a route that could be done only by canoe; see chapter 5 herein for a translation of the Tovilla account.

52 Chiapa is another highland province in what is now the Mexican state of Chiapas. The name comes from the town of Chiapa de Corzo.

53 The Tzibistun route goes far north of what is usually considered Manché territory.

54 Tuhalha, again, is Tuhal in the Spanish text here and elsewhere on this page. This comment is, here, on the left margin of the original manuscript page and in another hand.

55 Elsewhere in the text (see below), Çactohom is spelled Çactocom.

56 A pike's worth is equivalent to 12¾ feet.

57 The "even larger river" is the Lacantun, or Çacacha, coming from the west.

58 Çactohom, or Çactocom, in the Spanish text, is today's Rio Icbolay. Downstream it is the Ixaccha. The Ixbolay, or Icbolac in the Spanish text, is called the Rio Usumacintla today.

59 The salt deposits are upstream on the Rio Tuhalha, or Chixoy, before it joins with the Lacantun and other rivers to form the Icbolay.

60 Perhaps the lake mentioned here is Laguna Lachuá.

61 The Spanish text lists copal and liquidambar, both tree resins.

62 The bay of Amatique was also known as the bay of Santo Tomás. The Amatique of Salazar was close, or identical, to modern Puerto Barrios.

63 The day of San Francisco is January 24. This comment is in reference to the rainy season that occurs about that time of year.

64 The Spanish text mentions *coyoles* and *palmitos*. These are edible or fruit-bearing palm trees.

65 The Spanish text uses "lakes of Bacalar" here.

66 This adds up to twenty-eight, not thirty.

67 Today, the Acalan River is known as the Candelaria River.

68 The two mouths of the San Pedro y San Pablo River, one of which was known as the Grijalva River and the other being the San Pedro y San Pablo were the main outlets for the "river of Sacapulas" in that era.

69 Hence, the modern name of Chixoy, which Salazar derives from the Poqom-speaking inhabitants of San Cristóbal [Cahcoh] Verapaz.

70 The Mercedarians, a mendicant religious order (equivalent to the Dominicans or Franciscans), served as the priests for the Indian towns of what are now the Guatemalan departments of San Marcos and Huehuetenango.

71 This incident probably took place in Santa Eulalia or Ixtatan, towns that report other instances of contact with the Lacandon (see Tovilla in chapter 4).

72 The Xocmoxilba is the Icbolay River; see the related footnotes elsewhere in this chapter. Yaxcabilha is spelled elsewhere as Yaxcaba, but either version translates as the "water of the Yaxcab." This is the Lacantún River.

73 Verapaz lost its bishopric in 1608 (Feldman 1988, 14).

74 Elsewhere, this is called the Ixaccha River as well as the river of San Marcos. Perhaps the Bonolhacha is Laguna Lachoá.

75 The closest stream to Cobán, of those that go to the Usumacintla, is the Setzac.

76 In the Spanish text, the Spanish speaker is referred to as a Ládino.

3   Across the Ocean Sea: Martin Tovilla, 1630

This translation of Tovilla (1960) derives mostly from the Spanish text edited by Frances Scholes and Eleanor Adams. I also had the opportunity to consult the original manuscript in the Biblioteca Publica of Toledo, Spain. There is a more recent Spanish edition of Tovilla (1985), but lacking the commentary of Scholes and Adams, I found it less useful. Those portions of Tovilla translated here all reflect events known to him from either his own experience or immediate contact with individuals who had firsthand knowledge of them. For this reason, I have omitted chapters copied by Tovilla from other published works, such as *The General History of the Western Indies of Friar Antonio Remesal*. I have also not retained Tovilla's original chapter order, but the reader can reconstruct this from the original chapter and book numbers provided here.

The Tovilla manuscript was written in the 1630s, but the surviving copy is more recent. It has a cover sheet with a 1733 date and a note that it was then in Guatemala, yet at least some of the margin annotations (which are not by Tovilla) date from the 1680s. The editors of the Scholes and Adams edition thought that these margin notes might be attributed to the seventeenth-century Guatemalan historian Fuentes y Guzman. So, to summarize, the original manuscript was written by Tovilla. The surviving copy also dates from the seventeenth century and someone other than Tovilla added comments in the margin in the 1680s. Finally, the cover sheet of the document has an early-eighteenth-century date.

This copy, the manuscript in the Public Library of Toledo, Spain, was originally in the private library of Francisco Antonio de Lorenzana y Butrón, who was named archbishop of Toledo in 1772 after having held the same job in Mexico City. Thus, one can date its arrival in Spain to the eighteenth century.

1   Tovilla uses the spelling Ajiçaes for the Ah Itza Indians.
2   The fleet departed from Cadiz on July 28, 1630 (Chaunu and Chaunu 1956, 186).
3   The fleet was originally anchored to the south, and it took the entire day to leave the bay and assemble in the Atlantic just west of Cadiz. Las Puercas was northeast of Cadiz. According to Serrano Mangas (1992, 131), there were shipwrecks near Las Puercas in 1556, 1623, and 1657.
4   Cadiz is thirty-six degrees, thirty minutes latitude. Thirty-seven degrees is north of Cadiz and on the Spanish coast, between the mouth of the Guadalquivir River and the city of Huelva.
5   An Almiranta was the ship that served as headquarters for the second in command of a fleet—in this instance, also the ship going to Honduras.
6   The Mares Gulf, the sea between the Spanish mainland and Canary Islands, got its name because of the loss in winter storms of boats filled with mares, or alternatively, because with the great storms and high seas that ships faced, going through it was like riding a wild horse (Escalante de Mendoza 1985, 72).
7   According to Chaunu and Chaunu (1956, 186), the eight warships separated from the rest of the fleet on August 5, 1630, in the harbor of La Palma, leaving eighteen vessels.
8   Underlined in the published Spanish text.
9   The Capitana, the headquarters of the fleet commander, may have been the Nuestra Senora de Juncal, which at 700 tons was the largest ship of the fleet. This was the Capitana of the return voyage of the fleet in 1631, a journey that saw the Juncal lost in a hurricane off the coast of Yucatan, and many of the ships stranded on the coasts of

what are today the Mexican states of Veracruz, Tabasco, and Campeche. The captain general of the 1630 fleet, Miguel de Echazarreta, died shortly before the fleet of 1631 left Veracruz. The San Jose, a 600-ton ship originating in Vizcaya, was carrying a cargo of 300 quintals of Mercury and had an intended destination of Nueva Espana (Chaunu and Chaunu 1956, 194).

10 According to Chaunu and Chaunu (1956, 188–89), this vessel was the Nuestra Senora del Rosario, weighing 150 tons.

11 An astrolabe is a metal instrument used in the seventeenth century to determine the latitude from the positions of the pole and the stars.

12 Under the name of La Désirade, this islet still is administered from Guadalupe Island in the Caribbean. Désirade is about sixteen degrees and nineteen minutes, and Guadalupe sixteen degrees and fifteen minutes.

13 "We Praise You God" is a hymn sung as the first prayer of the day and on occasions of joy.

14 Marie-Galante, administered today from Guadalupe Island, is about fifteen degrees and fifty-six minutes.

15 The Natividad y San Francisco, according to Chaunu and Chaunu (1956, 188), was a ship of Viscayan origin. It had a tonnage of 450 and a destination of New Spain.

16 This name, spelled in the text both as Matalino and Mataleno, perhaps derives from *matar,* "to kill," and *montesino,* "bred in the mountains," or *montecillo,* "of the hills," with a meaning of "death mountains."

17 Icarus, according to Greek legend, flew too close to the sun and, his wings disintegrating, fell into the ocean.

18 La Beata and Altovela are tiny islands off the southern tip of Hispanola. The Tiburón Peninsula is on the southwest corner of what is now Haiti.

19 A letter from General Echazarreta (Chaunu and Chaunu 1956, 194) confirms this. In other words, the ships would be following the southern coast of Cuba to the Yucatán Peninsula. Cape Catoche, spelled Cotoche in the Spanish text, is off the northeast corner of the Yucatán Peninsula. Cozumel Island is a short distance south of it. The Isle of Pines is south of Cuba and east of Cabo Catoche.

20 Chaunu and Chaunu (1956, 194) state that the ships of Honduras and Havana separated from the fleet on September 18. The Spanish text spells Echazarreta as Chacarreta.

21 *Botijas* is the term used for jars in the text. These were probably earthenware jars, each containing about 12.67 gallons of water. They were massive, thick-walled containers, and derived in shape from the Roman amphor (for further details, see Lister and Lister 1976, under *tinaja*).

22 Lagartos is a site on the northern coast of the Yucatán Peninsula. Cape San Anton is the most western point on the island of Cuba. The "island where they lost some galleons" most likely was Swan Island in the Gulf of Honduras.

23 Actually, the Indians that the author met at Guadalupe were the Carib Indians of cannibal fame. The hostile Jicaque controlled lands immediately to the east of Trujillo.

24 The remainder of the fleet—that portion under the general going to New Spain—arrived in Vera Cruz on October 5 (Chaunu and Chaunu 1956, 194).

25 *Pedreros* is the term used in the Spanish text for small cannon.

26 Cazabe is manioc root flour and the bread made from it. The root itself is bitter and must be processed to be edible.

27 Culverins were 4,800-pound pieces shooting an 18-pound projectile with an effective range of 1,700 yards and a maximum range of 6,700 yards. Swivel guns, or pedreros, weighed 3,000 pounds and used a 30-pound projectile with an effective range of 500 yards and a maximum range of 2,500 yards. Culverins were designed to fire accurately and at long range. Pedreros were intended to fire relatively heavy projectiles for shorter ranges. For a discussion of the armaments and provisioning of Spanish fleets of this era, see Serrano Mangas (1989).

28 Harquebuses are matchlock guns that require a burning fuse to fire.

29 The Spanish text used the word tortillas for the cakes described here. As Tovilla found out, and any traveler learns today, the tortilla of Spain is quite different from that served in Central America.

30 Xocolo is Socolo in the Spanish text.

31 Here, and except as noted elsewhere in Tovilla, Xocolo is spelled Jocolo in the Spanish text.

32 The Golfete is a lake between the Dulce or Nito River and Lake Izabal.

33 Since a cubit (codo in the Spanish text) is equivalent to 16.5 inches, the boat was 412.5 inches (34.4 feet) long by 132 inches (11 feet) wide.

34 Ayate comes from the Nahua word ayatl, which refers to a thin cotton blanket or shawl worn like a cloak with the ends tied in a knot to hold it in place. Here, Tovilla compares the ayate to the prayer shawls used in synagogues.

35 In Spain, and yes in Guatemala, one still finds today the use of triumphal arches that are specially erected on festive occasions. It is actually a continuation of a practice that goes back to Roman times. People march under them, as part of their ceremonial duties. These days these arches are flimsy structures, intended for ceremonial purposes, and are quickly disassembled after the event.

4 Borderlands: Martín Tovilla, 1635

See unnumbered note at the beginning of the notes for chapter 3.

1 The master sexton in the Spanish text is referred to as a teopantaca, which comes from the Nahua teopaneque, "the owners, or those who have charge of the church" (Molina 1944, 101).

2 Tatoques, or native rulers, comes from the Nahua term for rulers (literally, "those who speak" for the community).

3 The Spanish justice would normally be the Spanish governor of the province. The review, or residencia, was a formal, public legal proceeding that took place at the end of a term of office, when individuals were encouraged to come forth and bring charges concerning abuse of office. Many records of residencias exist in the Hispanic archives, particularly for governors of provinces and members of royal courts.

4 Notary public archives, common in Hispanic lands, are often quite extensive, going back several centuries. In Guatemala, however, the only known repositories of this type to extend back to the sixteenth century are for Antigua and Guatemala City. Currently, the volumes for the colonial period are in the Archivo General de Centro America, and many are as yet uncataloged.

5 The use of jueces de milpas, or agricultural supervisors appointed by local officials, was common in the sixteenth and seventeenth centuries. "These Spanish overseers were supposed to inspect the fields to see that the Indians were clearing, planting, weeding, and harvesting them adequately. The system never seems to have worked, and one of

the two basic rationales for it was an absurdity: this was that Indians were lazy, and were simply not working hard enough. . . . The crown repeatedly banned the appointment and the activities of jueces de milpas . . . because royal officials understood the second reason why Creoles wanted to legalize the institution. It would create another stratum of offices, paid . . . by the Indian communities" (MacLeod 1973, 210).

6   Cofradia fields, to support the activities of individuals celebrating church-related holidays, were common by the eighteenth century, and are frequently mentioned in the volumes recording inspections of church property and activities made by the Guatemalan bishops (such as those of Cortés y Larraz) kept in the Archivo Episcopal General in Guatemala City.

7   One can distill all these sweets into alcohol.

8   Firelocks were tubes with projectiles packed on top of an explosive charge and fired by applying a flame to a touchhole (Newton 1990, 8).

9   Two hundred ducats was equivalent to 275 pesos or 550 tostons.

10   The Spanish text uses the term *pascua del año* rather than Christmas, pascua meaning any church festival that lasts for three days, usually either Easter or Christmas.

11   A not very successful law since this dance is still being held today in the Indian towns of Guatemala.

12   Ximénez (1985, 551) calls trumpets *tun* and notes the presence of a dance of that name.

13   These taxes are called *alcabalas* in the Spanish text.

14   One fanega is equivalent to 2.58 bushels.

15   A dedo is .690 inches, and a vara is 32.99 inches (Polzer, Barnes, and Naylor 1977, 39). Remesal was a seventeeth-century historian well known to colonial writers. His 1620 *Historia General de Las Indias Occidentales* has been republished several times in the twentieth century.

16   Purification celebrates the presentation of Jesus at the temple forty days after his birth, Annunciation marks the angel's salutation to the blessed Virgin, and Assumption recalls the ascent of the Holy Virgin to heaven.

17   The text uses the term *témporas,* which are three days (a Wednesday, Thursday, and Friday) in each quarter of the year considered fast days.

18   In the margin it is noted this practice was ended "because it is indecent to cause women to go half naked, with the face exposed."

19   A festival held in honor of the birth of Baltasar Carlos, a son of Philip IV who was born in 1629.

20   A note in the margin indicates "written without reference to tradition."

21   Margarita, an island off the coast of Venezuela, was famous for its pearl fisheries.

22   The omitted text comes from the published works of Remesal. The reference is to the words of the widow of Pedro Alvarado, the conqueror of Guatemala.

23   See my chapter 5, "Coming of the Soldiers," for further details.

24   Tovilla spells Cubulco as Copulco.

25   A clarion is a wooden musical instrument similar to a clarinet.

26   Encomiendas were a stipend, given in lieu of taxes to the crown, to an individual who performed some service for the King. Generally, they were supposed to be awarded to conquistadores and their children for a period not to exceed three "lives" (that is, the father, son, and grandson). The recipient, the encomendero, was supposed to support the local church and provide other services to the community out of the stipend he or she received from them.

27 Next to "three leagues" is written in the margin in another hand, "4 good."

28 Allen notes that "the wild pigs with a scent gland on the back are Peccaries of which two species live in tropical America, the smaller, the Collared Peccary (*Pecari angulatus yucatanensis*) and the larger, White lipped Peccary (*Tayassu pecari subsp.*)" (Landa 1941, 204).

29 Tovilla uses the Spanish term *cunera*, which means foundling or maker of cradles, for this town, but its actual name is Cunen.

30 Ah Itza is Ajiça in the Spanish text.

31 The following is in the margin: "River of Sacapulas, its name Tuhaluiachim, which is the town of the baths of Tuh; and from Tepet the town, and thus the Indians call the town Tuhal."

32 It is written in the margin: "The kings of the Quiche are the same as those of Utatlán."

33 Noted in the margin: "Today, it is very little but marvelous."

34 Written in the margin: "As in other wards of the kingdom."

35 Noted in the margin: "Between the river and the mountains, it is on the southern side."

36 For further information on colonial salt production in Guatemala and the organization of Sacapulas, see Andrews (1983) and Hill (1987).

37 In the margin near "large baskets" is: "Packed very tightly." The earthenware jars are called *tinajónes* in the Spanish text. Tinajas were amphora-shaped, large jars capable of holding about 12.67 gallons of liquid. Tinajón is the augmentative form. This implies that the jars cited here had greater than standard capacity (Lister and Lister 1976, 85–86).

38 Someone notes in the margin that "today sugar is made in this manner."

39 Written in the margin is: "Today, nothing like this is added, and it is very active and strong." These words were illegible in the photograph of this page of Tovilla's manuscript used by Scholes and Adams (Tovilla 1960). I obtained them by examining the manuscript of the Biblioteca Publica of Toledo.

40 Only ten towns, of which eight were in the province of Sacapulas, are mentioned here. These are: Sacapulas, Santa Cruz del Quiche, San Pedro Jocopilas, Ilotenango, Santo Tomás del Quiche, Zaqualpa, Cunen, and Chajul.

41 In the margin next to San Pedro Jocopilas is noted: "There are many people here." Ilotenango is spelled by Tovilla as Holotenango.

42 Jaguars are *tigres* in the Spanish text, here and elsewhere below.

43 Near Cakchiquels in the margin the "king of Guatemala" is written.

44 As noted in the margin, it was a "stone of sacrifice."

45 The "other twenty-four" are referred to as "his officers" in the margin.

46 Someone wrote in the margin: "Quetzaltenango."

47 Someone noted in the margin: "D. Pedro de Alvarado was the soldier, the one who hurt and killed him."

48 Speaking about Tovilla, someone states in the margin: "He has seen few histories."

49 Next to Zacualpa of the Holy Spirit, "Tzaculapa" is written in the margin.

50 Ahixil is spelled Agisil in the Tovilla text.

51 Noxoy is spelled Nosoi in the Tovilla text.

52 "Neck" in the Spanish text.

53 In the margin it says: "They were disarmed while hearing mass and tied to the roof beams of the church, and they [the Indians] removed their living hearts. From Father

Friar Juan Enríquez, Franciscan, they removed it by breaking [open] the breast above the chasuble." See Scholes and Adams (1991) for further details on this expedition.

54 The next chapter, "Coming of the Soldiers," gives further details on this miracle.

55 See Salazar, chapter 2 herein, on the death of Domingo de Vico.

56 Next to Chajul, someone clarifies in the margin: "Not Chaul but Σhaxul." The present-day name is Chajul. The use of the symbol "Σ," found in a script prepared by the friars for the transcription of Indian languages, suggests that a friar made this remark.

57 Between lines here, someone wrote "anabal."

58 Cagbalan is spelled Caguatan in the Spanish text. The Toledo Biblioteca Publica manuscript has an additional comment on this leaf (f. 86), which does not appear in the Scholes and Adams (1960) version. This is a margin note referring to 50 individuals in each of the 300 houses, making a total of 15,000 Indians.

59 Aquischan is perhaps identical to the town known as Achacan in the Salazar text (chapter 2). In the Tovilla text, Xocmo is spelled Sogmo and Noquichan is spelled Noquischan.

60 Someone adds in the margin: "More was found about the status of the Ah Itza, confirming what was discovered in the current campaign of this summer of 1691 toward the Peten."

5 Coming of the Soldiers: Martin Tovilla, 1635

See unnumbered note at the beginning of the notes for chapter 3.

1 For Salazar's views, see Vos (1988, 125) and elsewhere in this volume.

2 As someone writes of Conuntehila between the lines: "It is that of Sacapulas."

3 The chapter ends with this sentence: "And thus we leave it in this state, returning to our inspection, from which this had been a long, but important, digression."

4 The five languages used were Kekchi, Pokonchi, Cholti, Mexicano (Nahua), and Quiche. The term for province used here is *alcaldía mayor*. Tovilla's jurisdiction included part of the modern department of Izabal, and all of El Quiche, Alta, and Baja Verapaz departments.

5 According to Francisco Viana (cf. Feldman n.d.), Salama or Tzalam Ha comes from the Quiche word meaning "on the banks of the river."

6 Golfo Dulce would be the area around Lago de Izabal and the lower portion of the Polochic River.

7 In the margin near "a grant to build his house," someone notes: "The Dominican fathers now long for what in the beginning they scorned."

8 One fanega is equivalent to 2.58 bushels.

9 Here and elsewhere in the Spanish text, Cahabón is spelled Chagbon.

10 Alcaraz is in the province of Albacete, part of present-day Castilla-La Mancha.

11 This sentence begins by repeating the titles from the previous paragraph.

12 Promoted is translated from *escudos de ventaja*, literally "shields of advantage."

13 These comments are in reference to the campaign of 1580 when Philip II sent an army to occupy Portugal, which he inherited after the death of the last king of the old dynasty. There was some fighting on the outskirts of Lisbon, and the city itself surrendered at the end of August of that year.

14 Probably 1505 or 1515 is meant here since Emperor Maximilian was already dead by 1525.

15 Baza is a town in the province of Granada. The campaign to conquer it took place in 1489.

16 They arrived on Easter Sunday.

17 Between the lines near "the blessed apostles" is written: "Felipe y Santiago quiere decir." Actually, May 1 is the day of four saints: Felipe, Jacobo, José, and Santiago (De Platt 1978, 72).

18 In the Tovilla text, the town name is spelled Jasa.

19 Quilted cotton armor was common in pre-Hispanic central Mexico. Hassig (1988, 88) states that it was from one and a half to two fingers thick.

20 In the Spanish text, Yaxha is spelled Ayasa.

21 Other authors (see below) call this river the Yaxal. Today, it is known as the Moho.

22 Alcaraz is a town in the southwest corner of the province of Albacete of Castile-La Mancha.

23 The word *tiquitines* is derived from the Nahua *tequitin,* meaning "those who pay tribute."

24 Several possible instruments could have been used for torture here. For a detailed discussion of instruments of torture in Europe during this period, see Held (1983).

25 The spears are *ianzones* in the Spanish text.

26 See Jones (1989, 178–87) for a detailed description of this massacre of a Spanish expeditionary force advancing on the Ah Itza from Yucatán in 1622. The Spaniards had only posted one guard, who was easily overcome, and they were attacked and killed while attending church services.

27 The word used in the Spanish text is *tahalíes,* which were belts "of some leather that goes from the right shoulder to the left side of the waist where it supports a sword" (*Diccionario* 1991, 863).

28 Piñol is a drink made from toasted maize flour and water.

29 The word used in the Spanish text is *cizalla* ["metal cutters"], but *cisma* ["discord"] makes more sense. This might be an error of the scribe who copied the Tovilla manuscript.

30 In the margin of the page, someone adds: "Comments about what the Spaniards say are necessary."

31 Emphasis in the original. Someone notes in the margin: "Proof how necessary are the Spaniards in similar conquests, which are prevented in these Verapaz highlands by the agreement with Bishop Casaus."

32 Noquichan is spelled Noquischan in the Spanish text. Regarding Çapeten, there is a Lake Zacpeten just east of Lake Peten Itza; perhaps this town was associated with it.

33 The towns of Yaxha, Noxoy, and Ahixil are listed as Yasa, Nosoi, and Aguil in the Tovilla text.

34 That is approximately 16.5 inches long.

35 "This is all," someone states in the margin.

36 As someone notes in the margin, "This expedition, due to the orders of the tribunal, remains incomplete."

37 In the margin, someone writes: "Mopán, which is now conquered, was then of apostates."

38 In the Tovilla text, Noxoy, Ahixil, and Yaxha are spelled Noqxoi, Agisil, and Yasa here.

39 In 1634, San Lucas Tzalaj, with thirty married families, remained "after the universal fleeing" as the only Manché Chol town under Spanish rule (Gonzalez 1940, 175–77).

6 The Lies of Friar Morán, 1636

This report, written by Friar Francisco Morán to Friar Nicholas Ricardí in 1636, is in the America section, vol. 259: 174–80, of the Propaganda Fide Archive, Rome, Italy.

1 In 1640, both Catalonia and Portugal declared their independence from Spain. There were also plots to do the same in Aragon and Andalucia. It would take many years of war to reconquer Catalonia. Despite efforts that would bankrupt the Spanish state, Portugal never again submitted to Spanish rule.

2 Provincial is used in the Spanish text to mean head of a province of a monastic order.

3 This completely ignores the role of Friar Salazar and his account given above. Indeed, the towns were already reduced (that is, under Dominican control) before the arrival of Morán.

4 Ciudad Real is today's San Cristóbal Las Casas in the Mexican state of Chiapas.

5 In the Spanish text, Tayasal is spelled Taiza, and Ahitzas are referred to as Tayzas, here and elsewhere in Morán.

6 Salazar—who as noted in a previous chapter, actually interviewed participants in this event—identifies the Acala and not the Ahitza as the ones who killed Friar Vico and his companions.

7 Salazar had already visited and described these lands several years earlier.

8 In the Spanish text, the Icbolay River, today's Usumacintla, is spelled Ibolay. The Tuhalha is a tributary known today as the Chixoy River.

9 These were the Acala, who were resettled at Cobán after killing Friar Vico.

10 Antonio de Hervias was the third bishop, and Juan Fernandez Rosillo the last, until the twentieth century.

11 Morán is comparing the capital of the Ahitza, Tayasal, to the Protestant Calvinist Geneva, Switzerland, which in this period had the reputation of being the center of fanatic resistance against Catholicism.

12 This is precisely what Governor Tovilla, with the aid of Friar Morán, attempted to do.

13 Propaganda Fide, otherwise known as the Congregation of Propaganda, was an office established by Pope Gregory XV (1621–1623) for the purpose of directing and encouraging Catholic missions throughout the world (Ogg 1972, 383). Since in Spanish America missionary activity was (by agreement with the Pope) under the direct supervision of the royal government, while it could influence royal government decisions, Propaganda Fide would be unlikely to provide direct support.

7 Between Two Worlds, 1653–1654

All of the information given in this chapter, except as otherwise cited, comes from the Archives of the Indies, Audiencia de Guatemala section, manuscript bundle 19 (usually cited as AGI Guatemala 19). The author of each cited letter or document, of this bundle, is given in the text.

1 Some of them returned afterward to Cobán (Ximénez 1930, 451–52).

2 As lands of San Marcos were the lands of the Acala, Friar Ochoa is referring here to the Acala Indians who were originally settled in the Verapaz after the death of Friar Vico and were taken back to the lowlands by Friar Morán. They evidently stayed in the lowlands after the expulsion of the Spaniards.

3 Los Esclavos is today a town in the Guatemalan department of Santa Rosa.

4 Officials, in the Spanish text, are referred to as *alcaldes y tatloque,* or "mayors and rulers."

5 These letters are not given here.

6 Velasco is in error here: these Indians were not Lacandon Chols but Acala Chol who had been living among the Manche Chol. The towns listed here were all in the province of Guazacapan.

7 Of these towns, only Tepeaco and Guanagazapa were immediate neighbors of Atiquipaque and in the same province of Guazacapan. The others were on the route to the city of Guatemala (Antigua today) or the valley of Guatemala. Either direction would have led back to the lowland homeland of these Chol Indians.

8 School, in the Spanish text, is incorrectly spelled *esquila.*

9 For the kitchen, the text uses the term *tetunte,* a Guatemalan word for the burned clay found in the fireplace of the kitchen (Armas 1982, 206).

10 The Spanish text uses the term *almahigo* for the grains in the cacao fruit pod, which after being harvested, are ground up in the preparation of chocolate.

11 The Villa de Trinidad is today Sonsonate El Salvador, and its port is Acajutla. These were the closest Pacific ports at that time to Guatemala City.

12 The Tlascaltecas of Ciudad Vieja were Nahua-speaking Indians whose ancestors were brought by the Spaniards from central Mexico in the sixteenth century. They no longer exist as a separate group.

13 This petition was a request for compensation for the money expended by the priest. The petition was approved, and the money was ordered to be paid to the priest, by the office of the captain general.

8 *The Rediscovery of the Manché Chol, 1676*

A copy of the printed text (Gallego 1676) for this chapter was discovered in the Archivo General de Indias. Originally inserted into AGI Guatemala 25, it is currently in the part of AGI reserved for early printed works.

A portion of Gallego (1676) was translated into English as part of Villagutierre Soto-Mayor (1983, 99–107). But Villagutierre Soto-Mayor comes from Valenzuela (1979) and not directly from the Gallego document. The differences between the Villagutierre Soto-Mayor version and the earlier texts are almost certainly transciption errors, and therefore, one should rely on Gallego (1676) rather than any subsequent versions of his text.

1 "This city" is today known as Antigua.

2 As is also noted elsewhere in the text, the mission of Friars Gallego and Delgado was in response to a Chol request for Spanish priests. This follows a pattern begun in the last century, where the Chol are portrayed as repeatedly asking for Spanish missionaries.

3 The castle, or *castillo,* in this document is the castle of San Felipe on what is today Lake Izabal. When this manuscript was written, it was administered separately from the Verapaz and its priest was not a Dominican friar.

4 The text adds "today it is worth three." A zontle was a unit of measurement for cacao (and sometimes people). There were 20 zontles to a xiquipile and 3 xiquipiles to a carga. There are 400 cacao seeds (or people) to a zontle.

5 Given the punishments that a Spanish governor could apply during an inspection

(see Tovilla in chapter 4), one could argue that the comments of the Christian Indians were not defamation but accurate description.

6 Jocotenango is a small Cakchiquel Maya town close to Antigua.

7 The Villagutierre Soto-Mayor (1983) text incorrectly appears to refer here to the region of Manché rather than the town of San Miguel in the Manché.

8 The northwest is the correct direction. Ximénez (1930, 451–52) says that Gallego resettled the Ahxoyes at Atiquipaque.

9 A tepezcuinte is a paca (*Agouti paca*).

10 For snails, the text uses the term *jute*, which commonly refers to freshwater snails, either of the Pomacea or Pachychilus genera. These are often found at Mayan archaeological sites and are still eaten, raw, today. The reference to "little palms" is to edible sprouts of small, palmlike plants.

11 Pozol is a drink made out of maize.

12 This is hard to believe. Perhaps Gallego and Delgado arrived during a season when trees were not providing any fruit.

13 Peña (1684) gives the figure of "4,800 souls, great and small, men and women" reduced and catechized by Friar Delgado in just the three towns of Santiago, Rosario, and San Lucas. Of course, this may have been two or three years after Gallego's count.

14 Peña (1684) tells us how three of these towns (Santiago, Rosario, and San Lucas) were abandoned by their inhabitants not long after their "conquest." Francisco Gallego ordered sixteen of the Indian children sent to Antigua in order to indoctrinate them in the Christian religion. So "the Indian Choles, having seen this and deeply moved by the order, took their children, depopulated the said three towns, and returned to their forests" (Peña 1684). The total given by Gallego in the text (2,346 souls) is greater than in the total obtained by adding up the number for each town (2,122 souls). This may reflect counts made at different times.

15 Factum is actually Zactun (see Villagutierre Soto-Mayor 1983, 106 n. 419). The area around Lake Izabal shifted between the jurisdiction of Dominicans, Mercedarians, Franciscans, and secular priests. As can be implied from the writings of Salazar, there was no love lost between the Dominicans and Franciscans. And the secular priests, who often enough felt that the friars occupied posts that could be filled by them, would have gladly seen the friars expelled from all their parishes.

16 Pages 17 to 22 of the original text present the arguments of Friar Gallego for a peaceful conquest of the Manché, mention the incident in which Friar Vico lost his life, and provide detail on an attempted conquest of the Lacandon by Diego Ordoñez de Villaquiran, governor of Chiapa, at the request of Friar Francisco Morán. Since these pages are not relevant to the Manché, or are better described elsewhere in other primary sources, they have not been translated here (see Leon Pinelo 1986).

9 The Itinerary of Friar Joseph Delgado, 1677

There are several versions of Friar Joseph Delgado's accounts and a number of English translations (Bunting 1932; Stone 1932; Thompson 1988). I have relied on Delgado (1677), Valenzuela (1979), and Ximénez (1930). Variant spellings are given in brackets. The original manuscripts are said to be in the National Library, Paris, France (Thompson 1988). For the identification of the localities in the Belize portion of these accounts, I have relied primarily on Thompson (1988). The manuscript is divided into two portions: the itinerary from Cahabón to the Manché and from the Manché to Bacalar. Both date from 1677. For descriptions of twentieth-century Indian commercial travel in part of this area, see Hammond (1978).

1 In order to provide a more accurate translation, the organization of this English text differs from that of the Spanish.

2 "And Martin Petz [an Indian] said that those of Xocmo are very brave and feared by the Ahitzas and Ah Mopans" (Ximénez 1930).

3 "And Martín Petz said that from the town of Chocahau, which was previously in the Manché, the Ahitzas were not far, and the Ah Mopans came to trade with those of Chocahau and the Indians of Agustín Coatzun" (Ximénez 1930).

4 Peña (1684), who participated in the expeditions of Gallego and Delgado, gives the following itinerary: "From the town of Cahabón to that of San Lucas, which is one of those that has been reduced, there is twenty-two or twenty-four leagues. Between them are some nine small rivers. It is a bad road for it is all hills and swamps. From the town of San Lucas to that of Nuestra Señora [Rosario] it is two leagues, but between them is a large river that one must cross with a canoe. From Rosario to Santiago Apóstol there are five leagues with some small lakes between them and bad roads. From Santiago to San Miguel Manché is five or six leagues with some small streams between them. For going to these sites, the weather is bad because it rains continuously in this province. The months of March, April, and May are the best time to come to them. I advise that it is quite inconvenient to obtain the help of the Indians of the Verapaz because they badly counsel the Chols."

5 According to Delgado's text, the Yaxal is "known outside the forest as the Sacapulas River" (Delgado 1677). Apparently, Delgado thinks that this river is part of the Usumacintla River system. Thompson (1988) identifies it with the modern Moho River of Belize.

6 The Thompson (1988, 36) text adds: "At Juan Petz's home, the Yaxal River is called Puzilha because in times past, there was a town there called Santa Catarina Puzilha."

7 Thompson (1988, 39) identifies this language as Mopan.

8 Schwartz (1990, 16) provides a description of this savanna: "The great plains begin some 12 km south of Flores and continue up to the Subín River. . . . La Libertad is at the heart of the plains and some 30 km from Flores."

9 Given elsewhere in the manuscript as the town of "Octzutz [Yoctzuitz], whose headman is Tziquen."

10 But Delgado notes elsewhere that he was refused permission to go to Tipu (see Thompson 1988, 40): "As they did not permit entry either to me or those of Bacalar, we returned by way of another settlement until we arrived at the Tezach River."

11 The headman was called Pot.

12 The Paliac River is the Rio Grande, according to Sapper (1985) and Thompson (1988).

13 This is the Sittee River, according to Thompson (1988) and Stone (1932).

14 According to Thompson (1988), Sapper (1985), and Stone (1932), the Texach is the Mullins River, the Tahach is the Manatee River, and the Xibun is the Sibun River. Norman Hammond (personal communication) notes that the Balix River probably refers to Haulover Creek in the center of what is now Belize City, and the Tipu River is today the Belize River proper just up the coast.

15 He notes elsewhere that they were captured because "being at the Tezach River,

we wished to wade across, but we could not because it was so great. We set off from there for the sea, a distance of eight leagues. We reached the sea very late, and that night, we lit a fire to warm ourselves and dry out our clothes, and that was our ruin, for a league upstream there was an island populated by some English pirates. [So] because it was raining, they captured us" (Thompson 1988, 40–41). Thompson observes that "Delgado and his companions were taken to Cocina, present-day St. George's Caye, where the famous—or infamous—Bartholomew Sharpe" ordered their release.

10   Collection and Removal, 1865–1700

Friar Agustin Cano's excerpted account is from chapter 45 of Ximénez (1930, 458–63). The piece by Friar Francisco Ximénez, a low-ranking participant in this 1695 expedition, has been translated from Ximénez (1931, 15–23). Friar Cristóbal de Prada's declaration is in AGI Guatemala 153. The letter from Diego Pacheco is in AGI Guatemala 344, 1047–48v. Diego Pacheco's letter of May 17, 1697, is in AGI Guatemala 344, 1049–50; and his letter of June 26, 1697, is in AGI Guatemala 344, 1062–63. Miguel Rodríguez Camilo's letter of June 18, 1698, is in AGI Guatemala 344, 854–59v; and his letter of July 8, 1698, is in AGI Guatemala 344, 859–61v. Francisco de Villela's letter is in AGI Guatemala 344, 861–63v. The joint letter from Miguel Rodríguez Camilo and Juan de Dios Dávila is in AGI Guatemala 344, 873–74v. The June 6, 1699 letter from Miguel Rodríguez Camilo is in AGI Guatemala 344, 950–66v. Finally, the joint letter from Miguel Rodríguez Camilo and Pedro de Aldana y Vera is excerpted from a report, titled "On the Reduction of the Indian Barbarians Removed from Part of the [Province of] Golfo Dulce and Settled in the New Town of Holy Saint Anthony of the Warehouses by His Lordship, the Lord Don Gabriel Sanchez de Berrospe of the Council of His Majesty, President of the Royal Court, Governor and Captain General of this Kingdom, [in the] Year 1701" (Sanchéz de Berrospe 1701), in AGCA, A1.12–333–07017, 14–15v.

1   As late as the 1840s, legends persisted of wild Indians whose drums in the time of their grandfathers could be heard in Cahabón. The Indians of that era also believed that "Lacandon" Indians changed into birds in order to spy on the town (Morales Hidalgo 1983, 66, 68). These stories could be interpreted as implying that in the eighteenth century, a few Manche Chols still survived in the hinterlands of Cahabón. If so, by the end of that century, they were certainly gone, probably absorbed by the incoming Kekchi settlers.

2   AGCA manuscript A2.1–169–9, 7, refers to a Chol descendant, "removed from the forest of the Chol," still living in the town of Santa Cruz del Chol in 1792 and claiming tribute exemption because of a promise made to his ancestors in 1685.

3   According to Friar Alonso de Escobar in Feldman 1988, 39.

4   Much of this appears in Feldman 1991.

5   In 1717, only 33 percent of the inhabitants of Gualan were *not* refugees from the lowlands (see Feldman, Brown, and Garzon 1987, 417).

6   This is the term that the Dominicans used to refer to members of their order.

7   A scapular is the sleeveless outer garment of a friar's habit that falls over the shoulder and down the front and back, usually almost to the feet, and may include a cowl.

8   The Guadalquivir River runs past Seville in Spain. Today, the Maytol is known as the Chahal River and the Tiyú as the Chiyu. They eventually join other rivers to form the

Sarstun, the Zactum of the seventeenth century, which today defines the Belize/Guatemala border.

9 The Toisón reference is to the symbol of the Order of the Golden Fleece, a knightly order founded by Philip the Good of Burgundy, whose head is the king of Spain.

10 As noted elsewhere, the president wanted the expedition to leave Cahabón on February 28, at the same time as expeditions entering the lowlands from elsewhere in the highlands.

11 This and the following information comes from chapter 58, "All Entered the Forest and What Happened," in Ximénez (1931).

12 As noted above, the Zactum is the Sarstun River.

13 Today, this is the Bolonco River, a tributary of the Cancuén River.

14 A volcano near Antigua, then the capital of Guatemala.

15 The Spanish text is "*de los nombres de los tomar muchos el nombre.*"

16 The resin of this tree (*Croton stipulaceus* H.B.K.), called "dragon's blood," was obtained from forests near the town of Guanagazapa in what is now the Escuintla department (see Mariano Ximénez 1936 and Feldman 1985, 80).

17 This would be a fern, since the doradilla is a fern.

18 Cacchi is the Kekchi language of Cobán.

19 As suggested by an eighteenth-century dictionary (*Diccionario* 1780), this is some type of tree resin perhaps, balsam (*Myroxilon balsamus*) or something similar.

20 This stream is a tributary of the Bolonco River.

21 In the Spanish text, the "little bean of Nicaragua" is "*la habilla de Nicaragua.*"

22 Spelled as Tezacum in the Spanish text.

23 *Gallos de la tierra*, in the Spanish text.

24 These fish, in Spanish, are called *mojarras*.

25 The Spanish text has the insert here: "This is not so since they are different from those they call Lacandones, as will be seen." Salazar did point out earlier that the Xocmo spoke the same Yucatec language as the Ahitza.

26 Tzac may be the same headman whose name was spelled previously as Tzuc.

27 That is, those who interviewed them didn't realize they were not speaking in Chol.

28 In the Spanish text, Taximchan is spelled Tacinchan.

29 Today, Urran is in the Guatemalan department of Baja Verapaz; the town of El Chol is in this valley.

30 Teosinte is a wild, grasslike relative of maize used for forage.

31 Ocosingo is in today's Chiapas, and Santa Eulalia is in the modern-day department of Huehuetenango. These were the jumping-off points for the other two expeditions that entered the lowlands at the same time as that of Cahabón.

32 This sentence is unclear. Other authors indicate that those on the Manché coast, today the Toledo district of Belize, spoke a Cholan language close to that of the Manche. Mopan speakers may have entered part of this territory by the end of the seventeenth century.

33 After this, the expedition continued toward Lake Peten Itza and outside the area of the Chols.

34 Campamac in the Spanish text.

35 Tuilac in the Spanish text. The Tuija is a tributary of Cancuén River.

36 In Ximénez (earlier in this same chapter), this is the place called San Francisco Zaczaclum. It is downstream from the Tuija.

37 The practice of old men marrying several young girls was common among the

Toquegua Maya, another Chol group, who lived at the mouth of the Motagua River at the beginning of the seventeenth century (see Feldman 1998).

38 Corozos (*Orbignya cohune* or *tuch* in Cholti) and pacayas (Chamaedorea sp.) are palm trees whose fruit, or flower in the case of the pacaya, was eaten. In 1765, it was noted that when harvests of maize were bad, the inhabitants of the Peten lived on "plantains, manioc, sweet potatos, and macales," and searched the forests for "ramón, mameyes, and zapotes" (Santiago y Vetancurt 1765, 78v). *Macal* is a root crop, the *ramón* a nut, and *mamey* and *zapotes* fruit trees.

39 Taximchan is spelled Tasinchan in the Spanish text.

40 By the Petenes, Prada is here referring to the Tahitza.

41 Friar Prada, who participated in the same expedition as Ximénez, would achieve an unusual distinction. He went on to the Ahitza of Lake Peten, where he became one of the last Europeans offered in sacrifice, by removal of his heart with a flint knife, on a temple pyramid (see Ximénez 1931).

42 The Spanish text uses the spelling Campamaca for Tampamac. This is the same location as the Tampamac of Ximénez (earlier in this same chapter).

43 The word used in the Spanish text for sheriffs is alcaldes.

44 The Spanish text uses the spelling Tuijal. This is the same location as the Tuilha of Ximénez (earlier in this same chapter).

45 The Boloncot is the Bolonco River in the Spanish text.

46 According to a letter from Diego Pacheco in the same document, dated May 17, 1697, they arrived in the town of Cahabón on May 13: "Their count was ninety-two persons, forty-eight males and forty-four females, all Mopan, in which were included forty-two children of both sexes, of which they baptized seven still feeding from the breast."

47 Today's Santa Cruz del Chol in the department of Baja Verapaz.

48 According to a letter in the same manuscript from Pedro Pereira, dated June 11, 1697: "Near Mopan on the western side of a large river called Surtun is Alonso Tuncal, headman of the town of San Pablo Tuncal, with some of his hamlets, and on another adjacent river to that called Canquén was Matías May, headman of San Joseph May, with the people of his town. And on this same river fled Francisco Canté with some people." As well, the Boloncot River is spelled Boloncon in the Spanish text.

49 Tampamac is spelled Campaniaca in the Spanish text.

50 This appears to mean all coastal Indians from Amatique north to the Bacalar province.

51 As Camilo notes in an earlier section of this manuscript (not included here), this information comes from "an Indian called Sebastian del Monte, a native of these parts who has come to and married in the said town of Amatique."

52 From the context, one must assume that the Uschupan is another name for the Sarstun River. The Yaxal River is the present-day Moho River.

53 This was Chiquimula de la Sierra, then the administrative center for much of southeast Guatemala and today the capital of the Guatemalan department of the same name.

54 The Bacales probably refers to those Indians who travel on boats from Bacalar, in what today is Quintana Roo, Mexico, to Castile San Felipe.

55 Camilo remarks elsewhere in the document that Indians settled in the mainland have a tendency to flee into the interior, thereby avoiding Spanish control.

56 The area between Gualan and Castile San Felipe was not under direct Spanish

control. The frontier of Zacapa province was somewhere close to the archaeological site of Quirigua. Gualan was the closest town to this frontier.

57 La Ciénega, which means "the swamp," is probably the delta of the Motagua River. For a description of Indians who were removed from this region at the beginning of the seventeenth century, see Feldman (1998).

58 Today, this is known as the Sierra de Santa Cruz.

59 The Timax, or Temash, River flows into the ocean from Belize immediately north of the Sarstun River.

60 In the Spanish text, Chocahau is Chocuyo and Paliac, which lies north of the Yaxal River, is Paliaca.

61 Probably, Noquixchan is meant here.

62 This is an apparent reference to the political control over the Mopans said to be exerted by the Ahitza. The Ahitza and Petenes are the same people. The difference is between those who inhabited the island of Tayasal and those who lived on the shores of the lake containing that island.

63 This makes no sense since the Yaxal River is north of the Timax. Probably, the Sarstun River is meant here.

64 The "holy image" was a manikin whose clothing was provided by the sergeant major.

65 The Golfete is the channel that joins the Lago de Izabal with the ocean.

66 The Uchupan is probably the stream called, by Delgado (see previous chapter), the Yechupan. It was one league north of the mouth of the Yaxal (present-day Moho) River.

67 The shotgun, in the Spanish text, is an *escopeta*.

68 Pedreros in the Spanish text.

69 The text notes elsewhere: "Mostly they were given a ration of beans and salt. And wanting to be provided with maize . . . all the squadrons jointly resisted, not accepting it, saying that it would not sustain them and was evil, and they moved unanimously that they would sicken from the said sustenance."

70 These two payments are presumably the biannual tribute payments due from every Indian commoner (for example, they paid their taxes before going on the expedition).

71 The Timax is called the Timais in the Spanish text.

72 Bolom is spelled Bolon in the Spanish text. The Tipacha is the Texach River of Delgado's expedition, which was farther north than the other expeditions of Camilo.

73 A Yucatec-speaking town in northern Belize.

74 That is, the mayor of Amatique.

75 Probably, Zactun or Sarstun River is meant here.

11 Raids of the Mosquito Zambo, 1704–1733

Francisco Lopez Marchan's letter is in AGI Guatemala 302 (Lopez Marchan 1733).

1 Except as noted, data cited here on the Mosquito Zambo raids comes from Duardo (1704), Pereira (1708), and Lozada y Quiroga (1712).

2 British ships sailing under contract to the Spanish port of Campeche.

Postscript and Further Readings, 1766–1823

1 Santiago y Vetancurt et al. 1765. Each different section, for the various towns, has its own author.

2 The manuscript of 1765 (Santiago y Vetancurt et al. 1765), although it doesn't mention the Xocmo by name, has many references to unsuccessful searches for "barbarians" in mid-eighteenth-century Peten. In 1754, AGCA, A1.12.11–185–3799, does speak of Xocmo as a place where some families of the Peten town of Santa Ana had fled and "never had been removed" (37). It was identified as "a large settlement of barbarian Indians called Xocmoes . . . in the forest between [San Luis of the province of Peten Itza] and that of Cahabón of the Verapaz" (47).

3 See Salazar in chapter 2 of this volume.

4 The 1847 report of the priest from Cahabón and Lanquin remarks the presence of migrants from Cahabón in many of these lands (see Morales Hidalgo 1983).

Appendix 1   *Manché and Toquegua Surnames*

The sources for the table in appendix 1 are: the "Libro de los Bautizados del Manche" (Montes 1604) for those of 1604 (Matzin = A, Chiixtee = B, San Miguel Manche = C, and Cucul = D). The "Autos sobre la Reducion de los Indios infieles llamados Tequeguas comarcanos al dicho Puerto de Amatique as cited in Feldman (1998) for 1605; 1620 (Salazar), 1653 (Ochoa et al.), 1677 (Delgado), 1685 (Cano), 1695 (Ximénez), and 1695? (Prada) manuscripts translated elsewhere in this volume. Coban (1816, A3.16–954–17780), Carcha (1816, A3.16–953–17776), and Cahabón (1821, A1.44–3021–29117) are all early-nineteenth-century census documents in the Archivo General de Centro America. Tipu names come from the 1655 census published by Scholes and Thompson (1977). Tixchel names come from the 1612–1615 list published by Scholes and Roys (1948).

1 Surname used in both the ward of San Marcos and the main ward of Coban, and at Tixchel.

2 Surname found in Uecum in the Chiapas lowlands in 1697 (Vos 1988, 286).

3 Surname found in Dolores de Los Lacandones in 1697 (Vos 1988).

4 Variant spellings of this surname are Çibaac and Zibac.

5 Also Tzibac or Zibac in 1685.

6 Used also in Petenacte (1712) in the Chiapas lowlands (see Vos 1988).

7 Also, Cahabón and Tixchel.

8 At both Tipu and Cahabón, the form used is Mis.

Appendix 2   *Manché Population Statistics*

The sources for the table in appendix 2 are as follows: 1574 is from Viana, Gallego, and Cadena (1955); 1604 is from "Libro de los Bautizados del Manché," in AGI Guatemala 181 (it is only for baptized individuals and, therefore, counts only part of the total population); 1605 is from Ezquerra, and thus approximate, since the author was counting houses and not people; 1620 is from Salazar; 1676 is from Gallego. The text of all these sources, except the 1604 document, appears elsewhere in this volume.

Appendix 3   *Word List of Cholchi Terms*

1 The published literature and some colonial manuscripts use the term "Choltí" (Feldman 1986). But being that a contemporary whose work is published here (Salazar)

calls it "Cholchi," it seems appropriate to use this term as the name for the language of the Manché Chol. I would like to take this opportunity to thank Mareike Sattler for her invaluable advice in preparing a transcription of the Cholchi terms used in the Salazar manuscript of 1620.

Appendix 4 Background of the Authors

Appendix 4 is compiled from: Ximénez (1930, 1931, 1993), Ciudad Suárez (1996), Villagutierre Soto-Mayor (1983), and the manuscripts translated in this volume. Bracketed dates are the dates of those documents of these authors that were translated for this work. When, as is sometimes the case, they are the only dates for the author, they indicate when the author "flourished." Birth and/or death dates are not available for many of these individuals.

WORKS CITED

AGI: Archivo General de Indias, Seville, Spain

AGCA: Archivo General de Centro America, Guatemala City, Guatemala.

Andrews, Anthony P. 1983. *Maya Salt Production and Trade*. Tucson: University of Arizona Press.

Armas, Daniel. 1982. *Diccionario de la Expresión Popular Guatemalteca*. Guatemala City: Editorial Piedra Santa.

Autos Sobre la Reducion de los Indios Infieles. 1610. In Probanza for Friars Salvador Cipriano and Alejo Montes. AGI Guatemala 174.

Bunting, Ethel-Jane. 1932. From Cahabón to Bacalar in 1677. *Maya Society Quarterly*.

Carter, William E. 1969. *New Lands and Old Traditions: Kekchi Cultivators in the Guatemalan Lowlands*. Gainesville: University of Florida Press.

Casa de Ayante y Gamboa, Pedro. 1567. Residencia que era de Alonso de Paz, Alcalde Mayor que fue de la Provincia de Verapaz, tomada por Pedro Casa de Ayante y Gamboa, Alcalde Mayor de la misma provincia. AGI Justicia 313.

Castellan and Alcalde Named for Castillo de San Felipe and the Town of Amatique. 1725. AGCA A1.39, legajo 4604, 260v.

Castellan Named for Castillo de San Felipe and Alcalde Mayor for the towns of Amatique and San Antonio. 1753. AGCA A1.39, legajo 1752, 219.

Chamberlain, Robert S. 1948. *Conquest and Colonization of Yucatan*. Washington, D.C.: Carnegie Institution of Washington.

——. 1953. *Conquest and Colonization of Honduras*. Washington, D.C.: Carnegie Institution of Washington.

Chaunu, Huguette, and Pierre Chaunu. 1956. *Le Trafic de 1621 a 1650*. Vol. 5 of *Seville et l'Atlantique, 1504–1650*. Paris: Librairie Armand Colin.

Ciudad Suárez, Maria Milagros. 1996. *Los Dominicos: Un Grupo de Poder en Chiapas y Guatemala*. Vols. 16–17. Seville, Spain: Escuela de Estudios Hispano-Americanos de Sevilla.

Cortés y Larraz, Pedro. 1958. *Descripción Geografico-Moral de la Diocesis de Goathemala (1768–1770)*. 2 vols. Guatemala City: Biblioteca "Goathemala."

De Platt, Lyman. 1978. *Una Guia Genealogico-Historica de Latinoamerica*. Ramona, Calif.: Acoma Books.

Delgado, Joseph. 1677. Memoria de Los Parajes y Rios desde el Pueblo de Cahbon. AGI Guatemala 152, 140v–45.

Diccionario de la Lengua Castellana, reducido a un tomo para su más fácil uso: Facsímil de la primera edición. 1991 [1780]. Madrid: Real Academia Española.

Diccionario de la Lengua Española: Vigésima primera edición. 1992. Madrid: Real Academia Española.

Duardo, Geronimo. 1704. Testimonio de los autos . . . sobre las noticias participadas por el castellano del Castillo del Golfo Dulce de haver ymbadido el enemigo que se compone de Yndios Sambos . . . 26 de Septiembre. AGI Guatemala 299, 690–912v.

Escalante de Mendoza, Juan de. 1985 [1575]. *Itinerario de Navegacion de los Mares y Tierras Occidentales: Transcripcion Completa del Texto, según la copia manuscrita de Martín Fernández Navarrete, realizada en 1791, y publicado en 1985.* Madrid: Museo Naval.

Ezquerra, Juan. 1604. Letter. AGI Guatemala 181.

Feldman, Lawrence H. 1985. *A Tumpline Economy: Production and Distribution Systems in Sixteenth-Century Eastern Guatemala.* Culver City, Calif.: Labyrinthos Press.

———. 1986. Colonial Language of the Gobierno of Guatemala: A Review of the Primary Sources. *Journal of Mayan Linguistics* 5, no. 2:1–15.

———. 1991. Review of *Maya Resistance to Spanish Rule: Time and History on a Colonial Frontier,* by Grant D. Jones. *Journal of Field Archaeology* 18:121–23.

———. 1992. *Indian Payment in Kind: The Sixteenth-Century Encomiendas of Guatemala.* Culver City, Calif.: Labyrinthos Press.

———. 1998. *Motagua Colonial: Conquest and Colonization in the Motagua River Valley of Guatemala.* Raleigh, N.C.: Boson Books [online at www.cmonline.com].

———. n.d. *A Dictionary of Poqom Maya in the Colonial Era.* Expected publication by Labyrinthos Press in 2000.

———, trans. 1988. *History of the Foundation of the Town of Chamiquin by Father Friar Francisco Aguilar, O.P.* Culver City, Calif.: Labyrinthos Press.

Feldman, Lawrence H., Robert E. Brown, and Susan Garzon. 1987. Alien Spouses in Eighteenth-Century Guatemala: Implications for Language Change and Distribution. *Anthropological Linguistics* 29, no. 4: 409–24.

Freeze, Ray A., and Lawrence H. Feldman. 1975. *A Fragment of an Early K'ekchi' Vocabulary with Comments on the Cultural Content.* Department of Anthropology, Columbia: University of Missouri.

Fuentes y Guzman, Don Francisco Antonio de. 1933. *Recordacion Florida discurso historical y demostracion natural, material, militar y politica del Reyno de Guatemala: Biblioteca "Goathemala"* 7. Vol. 2. Guatemala City: Sociedad de Geografia e Historia de Guatemala.

Gallego, Francisco. 1676. Memorial Que Contiene las Materias y Progressos del Chol, y Manché. Pamphlet. Guatemala: Joseph de Pineda Ibarra.

Galves Corral, Bartholome, et al. 1707. Informe de Junta de Guerra, 7 de Octubre. AGI Guatemala 299, 1023.

Gerhard, Peter. 1979. *The Southeast Frontier of New Spain.* Princeton, N.J.: Princeton University Press.

Gonzalez, Lucas. 1940. Informa de las Reducciones del Manché. Archivo General del Gobierno (Guatemala), Boletin 5, no. 3:175–77.

Hammond, Norman. 1978. Cacao and Cobaneros: An Overland Trade Route between the Maya Highlands and Lowlands. In *Mesoamerican Communication Routes and Cultural Contacts,* edited by Thomas A. Lee Jr. and Carlos Navarrete. New World Archaeological Foundation Paper 40, Brigham Young University, Provo, Utah.

Hassig, Ross. 1988. *Aztec Warfare, Imperial Expansion, and Political Control.* Norman: University of Oklahoma Press.

Held, Robert. 1983. *Inquisition, Inquisición: A Bilingual Guide to the Exhibition of Torture Instruments from the Middle Ages to the Industrial Era.* Presented in various European cities in 1983–1992. Florence, Italy.

Hellmuth, Nicholas M. 1970. The Yucateco Lacandon of San José de Gracias Real, Chiapas, 1786–180?. Pt. 2 of Progress Report and Notes in Research on Ethnohistory of the Sixteenth to Nineteenth Century Southern Lowland Maya. Guatemala City: Foundation for Latin American Anthropological Research. Mimeographed.

Hill, Robert M., II, and John Monaghan. 1987. *Continuities in Highland Maya Social Organization: Ethnohistory in Sacapulas, Guatemala.* Philadelphia: University of Pennsylvania Press.

Jones, Grant D. 1989. *Maya Resistance to Spanish Rule: Time and History on a Colonial Frontier.* Albuquerque: University of New Mexico Press.

Landa, Diego. 1941 [1566]. *Landa's Relación de las cosas de Yucatan.* Edited by Alfred M. Tozzer. Peabody Museum Papers, no. 18, Peabody Museum, Harvard University, Cambridge, Massachusetts.

Laylaya, Diego. 1718. Testimonio del Gobernador de Costa Rica. AGI Guatemala 303.

Leon Pinelo, Antonio de. 1986 [1638]. *Report Made in the Royal Council of the Indies.* Culver City, Calif.: Labyrinthos Press.

Leopold, A. Starker. 1959. *Wildlife of Mexico: The Game Birds and Mammals.* Berkeley: University of California Press.

Lister, Florence C., and Robert H. Lister. 1976. *A Descriptive Dictionary for 4,500 Years of Spanish-Tradition Ceramics [Thirteenth through Eighteenth Centuries].* Special publication no. 1, Society for Historical Archaeology.

Lopez Marchan, Francisco. 1733. Informe del Alcalde Mayor de Tabasco sobre Yndios de la Provincia de Yucatan y esta esclavonuados en la Virginia y Jamaica, 5 de Abril. AGI Guatemala 302.

López Velasco, Juan. 1971 [1574]. *Descripción Universal de las Indias.* Madrid: Ediciones Atlas.

Lozada y Quiroga, Juan. 1712. Testimonio . . . [sobre la] entrada el enemigo Zambo en el pueblo de San Antonio de las Bodegas del Golfo Dulce. AGI Guatemala 299, 1010–143.

MacLeod, Murdo J. 1973. *Spanish Central America: A Socioeconomic History, 1520–1720.* Berkeley: University of California Press.

McBryde, F. Webster. 1947. *Cultural and Historical Geography of Southwest Guatemala.* Washington, D.C.: Carnegie Institution of Washington.

Miles, S. W. 1957. The Sixteenth-Century Pokom-Maya: A Documentary Analysis of Social Structure and Archaeological Setting. *American Philosophical Society: Transactions* 47, no. 4: 733–81.

Molina, Alonso. 1944. *Vocabulario en Lengua Castellano y Mexicana.* 1571. Reprint, Madrid: Ediciones Cultura Hispanica.

Montes, Alejo de. 1604. Libro de los Bautizados del Manche. AGI Guatemala 181.

Morales Hidalgo, Italo. 1983. Los pueblos indigenas de Cahabón y Lanquín en el departamento de Verapaz, Año de 1847: Informe del Cura de Cahabón y Lanquin, al Sr. D. M. Yrungaray, Corregidor del departamento. *Academia de Geografia e Historia de Guatemala* 57:55–79.

Morán, Francisco. 1935. *Arte y Diccionario en Lengua Cholti: A Manuscript Copied from the Libro Grande of Friar Francisco [Pedro] Moran of about 1625.* Baltimore, Md.: Maya Society.

Morán, Pedro. 1720. Bocabulario de solo los nombres de la lengua Pokoman. Library of Congress, Washington, D.C. Photographic copy by William Gates.

Newton, Michael. 1990. *Armed and Dangerous: A Writer's Guide to Weapons.* Cincinnati, Ohio: Writer's Digest Books.

Ogg, David. 1972. *Europe in the Seventeenth Century.* New York: Collier Books.

Padron que encierra esta real fortaleza del Castillo de San Felipe del Golfo Dulce de Honduras, 18 de Octobre. 1776. AGCA A3.29, expediente 28130, legajo 1749, 215.

Peña, Andres de La. 1684. 22 Octubre: Peticion. AGI Guatemala 158.

Pereira, Pedro. 1708. Testimonio de los Autos . . . sobre la entrada del Sambo en los pueblos de Peten . . . , 25 de Septiembre. AGI Guatemala 299, 13–75.

Polzer, Charles William, Thomas C. Barnes, and Thomas H. Naylor. 1977. *The Documentary Relations of the Southwest: Project Manual.* Tucson: Arizona State Museum, University of Arizona.

Recinos, Adrian, and Delía Goetz, trans. 1953. *The Annals of the Cakchiquels.* Norman: University of Oklahoma Press.

Saint-Lu, André. 1968. *La Vera Paz: Esprit Évangélique et Colonisation.* Paris: Centre de Recherches Hispaniques.

Sanchez de Berrospe, Gabriel. 1701. Autos fechos sobre la Reduccion de los Indios Barbaros . . . fundados en el Pueblo Nuevo del San Antonio de las Bodegas. AGCA A1.12, expediente 7017, legajo 333.

Santiago y Vetancurt, Manuel, et al. 1765. Relacion Geografica y Descriptive del Peten. AGI Guatemala 859.

Sapper, Karl. 1985 [1936]. The Verapaz in the Sixteenth and Seventeenth Centuries: A Contribution to the Historical Geography of Ethnography of Northeastern Guatemala. Occasional paper 13, Institute of Archaeology, University of California, Los Angeles.

Scholes, Frances V., and Eleanor B. Adams, eds. 1991. *Documents Relating to the Mirones Expedition to the Interior of Yucatan, 1621–1624.* Culver City, Calif.: Labyrinthos Press.

Scholes, Frances V., and Ralph Roys. 1948. *The Maya Chontal Indians of Acalan-Tixchel.* Washington, D.C.: Carnegie Institution of Washington.

Scholes, Frances V., and J. Eric Thompson. 1977. The Francisco Pérez Probanza of 1654–1656 and the Matricula of Tipu (Belize). In *Anthropology and History in Yucatán,* edited by Grant D. Jones. Austin: University of Texas Press.

Schwartz, Norman. 1990. *Forest Society: A Social History of Peten, Guatemala.* Philadelphia: University of Pennsylvania Press.

Serrano Mangas, Fernando. 1989. *Armadas y Flotas de la Plato, 1620–1648 (Silver Fleets and Squadrons, 1620–1648).* Madrid: V Centenario del Descubrimiento de America.

——. 1992. *Naufragios y Rescates en El Tráfico Indiano durante el Siglo XVII (Shipwrecks and Salvage in the Traffic with the Indies during the Seventeenth Century).* Madrid: Colección Encuentros, Sociedad Estatal Quinto Centenario.

Stone, Doris Zemurray. 1932. Some Spanish Entradas, 1524–1695. Middle American Papers 14, Middle American Research Series, Tulane University of Louisiana, New Orleans.

Thompson, J. Eric S. 1988. *The Maya of Belize: Historical Chapters since Columbus*. 1974. Reprint, Belize: Cubola Productions.

Tovilla, Capitán don Martin Alfonso. 1960 [1635]. *Relación Histórica Descriptiva de las Provincias de la Verapaz y de la del Manché*. Frances V. Scholes and Eleanor B. Adams, paleographers and editors. Guatemala City: Editorial Universitaria.

———. 1985 [1635]. *Relación Histórica Descriptiva de los Provincias de la Verapaz y de la del Manché del Reino de Guatemala*. In Villagutierre Soto Mayor (1985), 593–779.

———. 1985. *Relación Histórica Descriptiva de los Provincias de la Verapaz y de la del Manché del Reino de Guatemala*. In Villagutierre Soto Mayor (1985), 593–779.

Valenzuela, Nicolás. 1979 [1695]. *Conquista del Lacandón y Conquista del Chol: Bibliotheca Ibero-America*. 2 vols. Berlin: Colloquium Verlag.

Vellerino de Villalobos, Baltasar. 1984 [1592]. *Luz de Navegantes donde se hallaran las derrotas y señas de las partes maritimas de las Indias: Islas y Tierra Firme del Mar Océano*. Madrid: Museo Naval de Madrid–Universidad de Salamanca.

Verapaz, Golfo Dulce. 1702. AGCA A1.4, expediente 15361, legajo 2151.

Viana, Francisco, Lucas Gallego, and Guillermo Cadena. 1955 [1574]. Relación de la Provincia de la Verapaz: Hecha por los religiosos de Santo Domingo de Coban. *Sociedad de Geografía e Historia de Guatemala: Añales* 28:18–31.

Villagutierre Soto Mayor, Juan de. 1983 [1701]. *History of the Conquest of the Province of the Itza*. Culver City, Calif.: Labyrinthos Press.

———. 1985. *Historia de la Conquista de Itzá*. Edited by Jesús María García Añoveros. Madrid: Cronicas de America 13.

Vos, Jan de. 1988. *La Paz de Dios y del Rey: La conquista de la Selva Lacandona, 1525–1821*. Mexico D.F.: Fondo de Cultura Económica.

Ximénez, Francisco. 1930 [1719]. *Historia de la Provincia de San Vicente de Chiapa y Guatemala de La Orden de Predicadores*. Vol. 2. Guatemala City: Sociedad Geografia e Historia de Guatemala.

———. 1931 [1719]. *Historia de la Provincia de San Vicente de Chiapa y Guatemala de La Orden de Predicadores*. Vol. 3. Guatemala City: Sociedad Geografia e Historia de Guatemala.

———. 1967 [1722]. *Historia Natural de Reino de Guatemala*. Guatemala City: Pineda Ibarra.

———. 1985 [1701–]. *Arte de las Tres Lenguas Kaqchikel, K'iche' y Tz'utujil*. Guatemala City: Academia de Geografia e Historia de Guatemala.

Ximénez, Mariano. 1936 [1765]. Esquintla. *Archivo General de Gobierno: Buletín* 3:309–14.

INDEX

Achiote: from Cahabon and Lanquin, 97; Verapaz fair of, 177
Ahixil (San Vicente), 19, 26
Ah Itza, 130, 156; ceramic horse of, 28; conquest of, 2
Ah Yol, 12
Ah Manche, 12
Amatique, 217
Anax, 184
Axoyes, 176–77

Bachih, 36
Batena, 183
Belize, 19, 182; and Mosquito Zambo raids on, 218
Beycuha, 179
Bictehum, 194
Bol, 182

Çactun [Zactun], 23–24
Cadena, Guillermo, 234
Cagbalan, 114
Cahabón, 5, 10, 171, 182, 198
Cales, Pablo de, 133–34
Campeche, 218
Campin, 30, 179, 186
Canary Islands, 56
Cancanha, 194
Cano, Agustín, 234
Canquen River, 182
Cantelac, 183–84
Captain general: head of colonial government, xix; subordinates of, xix

Carcha, 9
Cerro Tituz, 182
Chajul, 113–14
Chamelco, 9
Chibui, 179
Chichicastenango, 107–8
Chixbox, 19
Chocahau, 19, 150, 182
Choco, Domingo, 160
Choco, Juan, 160
Choco, Pedro: and Gaspar Xoy, 161; instruction of natives, 159
Chojom, Domingo, 164
Chol, 168, 202, 203; number of baptized, 178; towns of, 32
Cholchi: list of terms, 232–33
Coban, 8
Conconha, 183
Conuntehila, 117
Copper axes: used in pagan times, 52–53
Cucul, 19
Cucul, Augustin, 190–91; devil image on body, 190–91
Culamay, 179
Culuacan, 114
Cunen, 103
Cupulco, 102

Delgado, Joseph, 234
Dominican: Chol language of study, xxi; Manche protectorate, xxi

Ezquerra, Juan, 234

San Felipe, 18
San Jacinto, 175, 198
San Jacinto Matzin, 182
San Juan Atiquipaque, 165
San Lucas, 171, 182, 190
San Lucas Tzalac, 22
San Miguel Tucuru, 13
San Pablo, 14, 23
San Pedro y San Pablo, 175, 194
Santa Cruz Cahahoncillo, 13
Santa Cruz del Quiche, 105–7
Santa Maria Tactic, 12
Santiago, 66, 171, 172, 194
Santo Domingo Yol, 25, 127
Santo Tomás de Castilla: port of, 77
Saques, 213
Soyte, 186

Tahach, 186
Tampamac, 192, 193, 200
Taximchan, 203
Techtutz, 184
Texach, 186
Temax, 179
Timax, 207, 215
Timilahau, 184
Timuchuch, 192
Tinocacao, 179
Tipachché, 192, 193
Tipata, 179
Tite, 179
Tixayah, 184
Tixchel: house of governor Don Pablo
    Paxbolon, 34–35
Tiyu, 172, 204
Tochomit, 7
Toqueguas, 19
Toro de Acuña: Verapaz capital, 131–33
Tovilla, Friar Andres de la, 162
Tovilla, Martin, 235
"Town of mulattoes," 182
Triana, Friar Alonso de, 162
Trujillo, 73, 75
Tuhalha, 31, 44, 155
Tute, 179
Tuve, San Francisco de, 201
Tzequischan, 179

Tzetum, 179
Tzibac, 179, 182
Tzibalna, Sebastian, 164
Tzibalna: settlement, 179
Tzisibin, 179
Tzoite, 34
Tzucah, 179

Uchapan, 179
Uinal, 18, 111

Vacan, 179
Vain, 186
Verapaz: diminution of population of, 15
Viana, Francisco, 235
Villega, Francisco de, 235
Virginia: enslaved Indians at, 218
Volcanic eruption: in 1617, 99

Xibun, 186
Xicupin, 26
Ximénez, Francisco, 235
Xocmo, xxiii, 134, 182; search for, 221
Xocolo (San Mateo), 14, 23, 24, 81, 217
Xoy, Agustin, 160

Yacal nation, 211
Yaxal, 207
Yaxapeten, 179
Yaxcaba, 40
Yaxcabes nation, 216
Yaxha, 19, 175, 182
Yaxtihal, 179
Yaxtxal, 179
Yechupan, 186
Yocab, 184
Yucatec towns, 32

Zactun river, 188–89, 190
Zacualpa, 108
Zapeten, 144
Zaczaclum: formerly called San Pedro y
    San Pablo Noxoy, 194
Zaqui, 185
Ziguana, 144
Zimin, 186
Zulben (San Lucas), 11; settled Zulben, 12

Lawrence H. Feldman, an independent scholar, is the author and translator of many books, including the following: *Mountains of Fire, Lands That Shake: Earthquakes and Volcanic Eruptions in the Historic Past of Central America (1505–1899)* (Labyrinthos, 1993); *Indian Payment in Kind: The Sixteenth-Century Encomiendas of Guatemala* (Labyrinthos, 1992); *Anglo-Americans in Spanish Archives: Lists of Anglo-American Settlers in the Spanish Colonies of America: A Finding Aid* (Genealogical Pub., 1991); *A Tumpline Economy: Production and Distribution Systems in Sixteenth-Century Eastern Guatemala* (Labyrinthos, 1985); *War against Epidemics in Colonial Guatemala, 1519–1821* (Boson Books, 1999); *Motagua Colonial: Conquest and Colonization in the Motagua River Valley of Guatemala* (Boson Books, 1998); and *The Last Days of British Saint Augustine: A Spanish Census for an English Colony* (Genealogical Pub., 1998). He also translated, edited, and provided a new introduction to *History of the Foundation of the Town of Chamiquin Verapaz by Francisco Aguilar* (Labyrinthos, 1988).

Library of Congress Cataloging-in-Publication Data
Lost shores, forgotten peoples: Spanish explorations of the South East
Mayan lowlands / Lawrence H. Feldman, ed. and translator.
p. cm. — (Latin America in traduccion/en traducao)
Includes bibliographical references and index.
ISBN 0-8223-2630-2 (cloth : alk. paper) — ISBN 0-8223-2624-6 (pbk. : alk. paper)
1. Chol Indians—History—Sources. 2. Chol Indians—Government relations.
3. Chol Indians—Social life and customs. 4. Mayas—First contact with Europeans.
5. Spain—Colonies—America—History—Sources. I. Feldman, Lawrence H. II. Series.
F1221.C57 .L67 2000   972.81004'97415—dc21   00-029397